INTERNATIONAL AND CC
EDUCATION

MW00784204

International and Comparative Education offers detailed and wide-ranging illustrations of the ways in which comparison can illuminate our understanding of contemporary education systems by exploring issues in relation to specific educational sectors, from early-years and primary schooling, through to further, adult and higher education.

Key areas and debates examined include:

- Alternative education provision
- Early-years pedagogy and training
- Spiritual, moral, social and cultural development in primary schooling
- Work-related learning in secondary schools
- The world of private tutoring
- Economic austerity and further education
- Apprenticeships and vocational education
- Adult education and training
- Higher education in a globalised world
- Teacher training and international rankings

Drawing on these wide-ranging themes across a number of national contexts to provoke critical thinking and reflection, each chapter includes discussion points and further reading, providing a valuable resource for all Education Studies students.

Brendan Bartram is Senior Lecturer in Education Studies at the University of Wolverhampton, UK.

THE ROUTLEDGE EDUCATION STUDIES SERIES

Series Editor: Stephen Ward, Bath Spa University, UK

The **Routledge Education Studies Series** aims to support advanced level study on Education Studies and related degrees by offering in-depth introductions from which students can begin to extend their research and writing in years 2 and 3 of their course. Titles in the series cover a range of classic and up-and-coming topics, developing understanding of key issues through detailed discussion and consideration of conflicting ideas and supporting evidence. With an emphasis on developing critical thinking, allowing students to think for themselves and beyond their own experiences, the titles in the series offer historical, global and comparative perspectives on core issues in education.

INTERNATIONAL AND COMPARATIVE EDUCATION

Contemporary Issues and Debates

Edited by
Brendan Bartram

Routledge
Taylor & Francis Group

LONDON AND NEW YORK

First published 2018
by Routledge
2 Park Square, Milton Park, Abingdon, Oxon OX14 4RN

and by Routledge
711 Third Avenue, New York, NY 10017

Routledge is an imprint of the Taylor & Francis Group, an informa business

© 2018 selection and editorial matter, Brendan Bartram; individual chapters, the contributors

The right of Brendan Bartram to be identified as the author of the editorial material, and of the authors for their individual chapters, has been asserted in accordance with sections 77 and 78 of the Copyright, Designs and Patents Act 1988.

All rights reserved. No part of this book may be reprinted or reproduced or utilised in any form or by any electronic, mechanical, or other means, now known or hereafter invented, including photocopying and recording, or in any information storage or retrieval system, without permission in writing from the publishers.

Trademark notice: Product or corporate names may be trademarks or registered trademarks, and are used only for identification and explanation without intent to infringe.

British Library Cataloguing-in-Publication Data
A catalogue record for this book is available from the British Library

Library of Congress Cataloging-in-Publication Data
A catalog record for this book has been requested

ISBN: 978-1-138-68157-6 (hbk)
ISBN: 978-1-138-68158-3 (pbk)
ISBN: 978-1-315-56309-1 (ebk)

Typeset in News Gothic
by codeMantra

Contents

Figures and tables

Figures

Tables

Contributors

Professor Patrick Ainley, previously Professor of Training and Education, University of Greenwich, School of Education and Training, now Visiting Scholar at the Business Faculty and Visiting Fellow at New College, University of Oxford. His books include: *The Betrayal of a Generation: How Education is Failing Young People*, Policy Press 2016; with Martin Allen – *Lost Generation? New Strategies for Youth and Education*, Continuum 2010 and *Education Make You Fick, Innit?*, Tufnell Press 2007; *Learning Policy, Towards the Certified Society*, Macmillan 1999; *Apprenticeship: Towards a New Paradigm of Learning*, (edited with Helen Rainbird) Kogan Page 1999; *The Business of Learning, Further Education in the 1990s* (with Bill Bailey), Cassell 1997; *Degrees of Difference, Higher Education in the 1990s*, Lawrence and Wishart 1994; *Class and Skill*, Cassell 1993; *Training for the Future, The Rise and Fall of the Manpower Services Commission* (with Mark Corney), Cassell 1990; *From School to YTS*, Open University Press 1988.

Dr Brendan Bartram is Senior Lecturer in Education Studies at the University of Wolverhampton. He was awarded a National Teaching Fellowship by the Higher Education Academy in 2012. His research and publications cover a wide range of issues that reflect the eclectic nature of Education Studies. Focusing primarily on comparative issues in secondary education and the student experience in Higher Education, Brendan's research has explored staff-student interactions and university student mobility, support and motivation. His book – *Attitudes to Modern Language Learning – Insights from Comparative Education* – examining language learning in the UK, USA, Australia, Germany and the Netherlands, was re-issued in paperback in May 2012. He has presented on the above themes at a number of national and international conferences. Brendan is a member of the British Education Studies Association (BESA) and was honorary secretary of British Association of International and Comparative Education (BAICE).

Dr Richard Budd is a Lecturer in Education Studies at Liverpool Hope University. His chief research interests revolve around sociology and higher education, with a focus on social justice, social theory and policy analysis, often with an international comparative perspective. He started his career in construction in Germany before studying Psychology and Management at what is now Leeds Trinity University. He then conducted international education policy research for government agencies in the UK and New Zealand. This was followed by a sabbatical period teaching English in Japan and conducting freelance research, before engaging in postgraduate studies – a Master's at the University of Oxford and a Ph.D. at the University of Bristol. His doctorate explored how students in Germany and England understand, experience and negotiate their university contexts. He is currently investigating doctoral funding policies in the UK social sciences, and the relationship between social inequality, mathematics attainment and university entry.

David Burghes has been Professor of Mathematics Education at the University of Plymouth since 2005. He was previously Professor of Education at the University of Exeter, where he founded the Centre for Innovation in Mathematics Teaching (CIMT). The Centre was set up to provide help and support to mathematics teachers around the world through research, development, evaluation and dissemination of good practice in mathematics teaching and learning. He has directed three international longitudinal comparative projects concerned with making recommendations for enhancing the teaching and learning of primary and secondary mathematics and the teacher training of mathematics teachers. He is passionate about enhancing mathematics teaching for all pupils and students, whatever their ability, and sees mathematics as a lively, relevant and interesting topic to study at all levels.

Roy Y. Chan is Ph.D. candidate in Education Policy Studies at Indiana University Bloomington. Roy holds a Master of Arts (M.A.) degree in Higher Education Administration from Boston College and a Master of Education (M.Ed.) degree in Comparative Higher Education from The University of Hong Kong. His research interests have focused on the globalisation and internationalisation of higher education, and the role of philanthropy and fundraising in shaping education policy in East Asia and the Pacific. Roy has published research articles in *Studies in Higher Education*, *International Journal of Chinese Education*, and *Journal of Education Policy, Planning and Administration*. He is coauthor of the book *Higher Education: A Worldwide Inventory of Research Centers, Academic Programs, Journals and Publications*, 2014, and is the coeditor of *The Future of Accessibility in Higher Education*, 2017. Roy is an active member of ASHE, CIES, NASPA, and NAFSA. Roy can be reached by e-mail at rychan@indiana.edu

Patrick Delaney is Master's degree candidate in Curriculum & Instruction at the University of West Florida. Currently Patrick serves as an English language instructor at the Beijing International Bilingual Academy in Shunyi District, Beijing, China, and was previously English instructor at Tsinghua University. Between 2008 and 2016, Patrick served as a private tutor for children, high school students and college students across Beijing and Qingdao. He holds a B.A. in English from Georgia State University. Patrick is originally from Atlanta, GA, and has two sons, Tommy and Timmy. Patrick can be reached at pd14@students.uwf.edu

Sarah Elsey is Senior Lecturer at the University of Wales, Trinity St. David. In her previous appointment at the University of Wolverhampton, she led on PSHE/SMSC across all Primary routes, with shared responsibility for teaching English and Professional Studies to student teachers following both the B.Ed. and PGCE routes. Before that, Sarah taught in a number of primary schools and at an International School in Indonesia. She is currently studying for her Professional Doctorate and has a particular interest in the current practice of PSHE/SMSC in primary schools and its impact on children's social and emotional development. Through her work in schools, she is working to raise the profile of SMSC to support children's development in becoming resilient learners.

Professor John Field is Emeritus Professor at the University of Stirling, where he currently serves as the School of Education's Director of Research. He has a long-standing background, interest and involvement in lifelong learning. Recent publications include edited collections on Mental Capital and Wellbeing and Researching Transitions in Lifelong Learning. In 2013 he completed a book on British work camp systems before 1939, published by Manchester University Press. He is also editor of the new Sage Handbook on Aging, Work and Society. Externally, he has served as a Visiting Professor at Birkbeck College, University of London. Currently he chairs the Advisory Board for the ESRC Research Centre on Learning and Life Chances in Knowledge Economies and Societies (LLAKES), University of London. He also served as a commissioner of the National Commission of Inquiry on the Future of Lifelong Learning.

Dr Hei-Hang Hayes Tang is Assistant Professor of Education Policy and Leadership at The Education University of Hong Kong. As a sociologist, Dr. Tang is interested in the fields of education policy, academic profession and youth studies. He is committed to create new knowledge in application for better education governance in the age of citizen activism, and for enhanced alignment between education and the world of work/professions in East Asia entrepreneurial societies. Currently his research interests have focused on youth entrepreneurship and Hong Kong research-intensive universities, as well as Hong Kong Post-90s generation's political participation and national identification. Dr. Tang holds a Ph.D. in Sociology of Higher Education, an M.Phil. in Sociology, and a B.S. in Political Sciences from The University of Hong Kong. Hayes can be reached by e-mail at hhhtang@eduhk.hk

Dr Mike Lambert is a writer on education and educational research (http://wlv.academia.edu/MikeLambert). Previously, he taught in a variety of schools, with particular interest in the education of students with special educational needs and disabilities, and worked internationally for voluntary organizations in this field. Subsequently, he was Principal Lecturer in Education at the University of Wolverhampton; his doctorate focused on pedagogy for gifted students.

Dr Matt O'Leary is a Reader in Education at Birmingham City University in Birmingham. He has worked as a teacher, teacher educator, head of department and educational researcher in colleges, schools and universities in England, Mexico and Spain. His main research interests focus on the impact of education policy on practice, particularly in the Further Education (FE) sector, as well as teacher learning and teacher assessment. He is well known internationally for his work on classroom observation, which has been instrumental in challenging engrained orthodoxies and influencing policy makers and national debates. He is the author of *Classroom Observation: A Guide to the Effective Observation of Teaching and Learning* (2014) and author and editor of the recent book *Reclaiming Lesson Observation: Supporting Excellence in Teacher Learning* (2016), both of which are published by Routledge.

Dr Justin Rami is Director of the Further Education and Training Research Centre (FETRC) and a Lecturer and Researcher in the School of Education Studies at Dublin City University in Dublin, Ireland. His research expertise is focused predominantly in the FET area. At undergraduate level, he teaches on modules such as: teaching and learning methodologies, advanced teaching strategies, curriculum implementation and assessment, feedback, microteaching,

teaching preparation and developing a research perspective. He also delivers lectures and workshops on academic writing and using critical voices in academic writing. At postgraduate level, he teaches in the area of organisational behaviour and organisational communications.

Dr Tunde Rozsahegyi is Senior Lecturer in Education and Subject Leader for Special Educational Needs, Disability and Inclusion Studies at the University of Wolverhampton. Previously, she trained and worked as a 'conductor', specialist educator of children and adults with disabilities through Conductive Education, at the Pető Institute in Budapest, Hungary, then played a key role in establishing the National Institute for Conductive Education in Birmingham, England. Tunde has a strong interest in early education and support for children with special educational needs and disabilities; her doctorate examined developmental needs of young children with cerebral palsy.

Dr Sean Starr is a Senior Lecturer in Education at the University of Wolverhampton. As part of his role he supports teacher education, ranging from beginning teachers to working with executive leadership. He has worked in education over the last 20 years as a senior leader, middle manager and teacher in secondary schools. He has also been a school improvement advisor, before joining the University of Wolverhampton. His research interests include educational policy, leadership and school improvement/effectiveness. He has also presented at both national and international conferences.

Dr Paul Wiseman began his career as a geography teacher. After completing his MA (Ed), he became a research officer for Sandwell Health Authority where he had responsibility for evaluating the impact of all early years' initiatives, including the newly introduced Sure Start programmes. In 2001, he was appointed as a Senior Lecturer at the University of Wolverhampton where he continued his research interests with early intervention programmes. He was subsequently appointed senior research fellow at the University of Birmingham where he worked on the National Evaluation of the Children's Fund (NECF-the largest social science research project undertaken in the UK). Following the completion of this project, he worked for Telford and Wrekin Council before moving to Sandwell MBC where he was strategic lead for school-based extended and wrap-around services, and key contact to the DfE via the TDA. During this time, he completed his doctorate on work-place behaviour within children's services in 2014. In 2011, he returned to the University of Wolverhampton as Senior Lecturer in Education Studies.

Series editor's preface

Stephen Ward

Education Studies has become a popular and exciting undergraduate subject in some 50 universities in the UK. It began in the early 2000s, mainly in the post-1992 universities that had been centres of teacher training, but, gaining academic credibility, the subject is being taken up by post-1992 and Russell Group institutions. In 2004, Routledge published one of the first texts for undergraduates, Education Studies: A Student's Guide (Ward, 2004), now in its third edition. It comprises a series of chapters introducing key topics in Education Studies. While teacher education and training are largely determined by government diktat, there is continuing discussion among academics about the aims and curriculum for Education Studies, and the three editions of this book have contributed to the thinking and development of the subject.

Education Studies is concerned with understanding how people develop and learn throughout their lives, the nature of knowledge and critical engagement with ways of knowing. It demands an intellectually rigorous analysis of educational processes and their cultural, social, political and historical contexts. In a time of rapid change across the planet, education is about how we both make and manage such change. Education Studies thus includes perspectives on international education, economic relationships, globalisation, ecological issues and human rights. It also deals with beliefs, values and principles in education and the way that they change over time.

It is important to understand that Education Studies is not teacher training or teacher education. Its theoretical framework in psychology, sociology, history and philosophy is derived from teacher education, and undergraduates in the subject may well go on to become teachers after a PGCE or school-based training. However, Education Studies should be regarded as a subject with a variety of career outcomes, or indeed, none: it can be taken as the academic and critical study of education in itself. At the same time, while the theoretical elements of teacher training are continually reduced in PGCE courses and school-based training, undergraduate Education Studies provides a critical analysis for future teachers who, in a rapidly changing world, need so much more than training to deliver a government-defined curriculum.

Intended for second and third year undergraduates and masters students, this book is the fourth in a series of Routledge publications which builds on the introductory guide and looks in depth at a current priority in education. Probably the strongest and most distinctive feature of Education Studies is its potential to apply critique to policy and practice: that we should not take the status quo or government policy for granted. One of the strongest ways of subjecting policy to critical analysis is to make international comparisons. There is always a tendency for us to take for granted current practice and the assumptions behind it. Understanding the way educational processes can work differently in contrasting contexts wakes us up to the wide range of exciting possibilities that exist for both educators and policy-makers. For those who are – or plan to be – teachers, an international and comparative perspective is essential to free them from the trap of taken-for-granted assumptions.

The book offers comparative examples across the whole range of educational topics and phases. There are surprising differences across countries, but it is also interesting to note similarities and those features that are assuming international acceptance. Activities interspersed throughout raise such questions and enable us to reflect on our own understanding and assumptions.

Stephen Ward, Bath Spa University

Note: The academic network for tutors and students in Education Studies is the British Education Studies Association (BESA). It has an annual conference that shares academic practice and research in Education Studies and to which students are welcome. There are two e-journals, one designated for students and early researchers: www.educationstudies.org.uk.

Reference

Ward, S. (2004) *Education Studies: A Student's Guide*. London: Routledge.

Abbreviations

The following abbreviations are used in the text:

ACARA	Australian Curriculum, Assessment and Reporting Authority
AE	Alternative education
AHS	allgemeinbildende höhere Schule
ALHELO	Assessment of Learning Outcomes in Higher Education
AoC	Association of Colleges
APEC	Asia-Pacific Economic Cooperation
BIS	(Department for) Business Innovation and Skills
CHERI	Centre for Higher Education Research and Information
CPD	Continuing professional development
CTC	City technology college
DES	Department of Education and Skills (Ireland)
DfE	Department for Education
DfEE	Department for Education and Employment
DfES	Department for Education and Skills
DFG	Deutsche Forschungsgemeinschaft
EBD	emotional and behavioural difficulties
EEF	Education Endowment Foundation
EFA	Education for All
EHEA	European Higher Education Area
EI	Economic Insight
EMF	European Monetary Fund
ESF	European Social Fund
ESRI	Economic and Social Research Institute
ETBI	Education and Training Boards Ireland
EU	European Union
EYFS	Early Years Foundation Stage
EYPS	Early Years Professional Status
FE	Further Education
FEE	Foundation for Environmental Education
FEFC	Further Education Funding Council
FET	Further Education and Training

GCSE	General Certificate of Secondary Education
GDP	Gross domestic product
GRE	Graduate Record Examinations (USA)
HC414	House of Commons Committee of Public Accounts
HE	Higher Education
HEFCE	Higher Education Funding Council for England
HKDSE	Hong Kong Diploma of Secondary Education
IEA	International Association for the Evaluation of Educational Achievement
IIEP	International Institute for Educational Planning
IMF	International Monetary Fund
IoE	Institute of Education
JRF	Joseph Rowntree Foundation
LCVP	Leaving Certificate Vocational Programme
MOOC	Massive Open Online Courses
NAPLAN	National Assessment Programme in Literacy and Numeracy (Australia)
NCEE	National College Entrance Examination (Hong Kong)
NCETM	National Centre for Excellence in the Teaching of Mathematics
NFER	National Federation for Educational Research
NMS	Neue Mittelschule
NUIG	National University of Ireland Galway
OECD	Organisation for Economic Cooperation and Development
Ofsted	Office for Standards in Education
PIAAC	Programme for the International Assessment of Adult Competencies
PISA	Programme for International Student Assessment
PLC	Post Leaving Certificate
PRU	Pupil Referral Unit
PSHE	Personal, Social and Health Education
PST	Private supplementary tutoring
REF	Research Excellence Framework
SAT	Standard Assessment Test (or Task)
SEAL	Social, Emotional Aspects of Learning
SMSC	Spiritual, moral, social and cultural education
SOLAS	An tSeirbhís Oideachais Leanúnaigh agus Scileanna
STEM	Science, Technology, Engineering and Mathematics
TIMSS	Trends in International Mathematics and Science Study
TOEFL	Test of English as a Foreign Language
TUI	Teachers' Union of Ireland
UCU	University and College Union
UNESCO	United Nations Educational, Scientific and Cultural Organisation
UTC	University Technical College
VET	Vocational Education and Training
VHS	Volkshochschulen (German)
WEA	Workers' Educational Association
WPO	Wet Primair Onderwijs
WTO	World Trade Organisation

1 Comparative and international education

Brendan Bartram

Introduction

In our attempts to understand the diverse and changing nature of all aspects of education, various theoretical perspectives are routinely enlisted. Concepts and theories from sociology, psychology, history, philosophy and politics are individually, and sometimes collectively, applied to educational phenomena in order to produce nuanced and sophisticated accounts. In one respect, comparative education is just another tool that can be employed to deepen our understanding of educational matters. However, given its ability to fuse multiple theoretical perspectives with contextual and sociocultural factors, comparative education is, of course, an important discipline in its own right (hence, its long history as a field of enquiry) and one that is particularly suited to the sizeable challenge of exploring and understanding the educational questions that Cowen (2005:179) refers to below:

> How do societies relate to (that is, affect, shape, influence, frame, penetrate or determine) educational systems and their components, such as teacher education provision, types of schools, administrative structures, universities, examination systems and so on? The problem is a tricky one because clearly, history, economics, social stratification patterns, politics and religious belief systems are all potentially forces that define the 'nature' of societies, and in ways that are not crystal clear, extend into the institutional patterns of educational systems...and curriculum practices.

It is also a particularly diverse and multidisciplinary area of enquiry, bringing together many different fields of interest and styles of investigation. The exact parameters of the field are subject to much debate, and as Cowen (2009:1289) argues, 'what we call comparative education, in its growth, in its shape-shifting, is itself part of international, political, economic, cultural and educational relations'. Debate similarly surrounds the distinction between the two related areas of comparative and international education. 'Comparativists' may be more concerned with such matters as the processes of policy borrowing (Phillips and Ochs, 2004); the uses and abuses of educational rankings and league tables and the potentially endless number of educational issues relating to sectors, institutions, curricula, learners and teachers. Phillips and Schweisfurth (2008) suggest that 'international education' tends to encompass an equally diverse collection of issues, such as global citizenship education, international schools, globalisation studies, education and development studies.

The motives behind educational comparisons are, if anything, as diverse and debated as the discussions about the nature of the earlier-mentioned twin fields. For some, endeavours are driven by intrinsic scholarly interest, as Lauwerys and Tayar (1973:xii) comment:

> Comparative education is not, in essence, normative: it does not prescribe rules for the good conduct of schools and teaching. It does not aim at laying down what should be done. It does not offer views as to what education ought to be like. It attempts only to understand what is being done and why.

Intrinsic motives like these, however, are not without potential utilitarian benefits, even if these were only restricted to advancing our understanding of aspects of our own system. In this respect, Sadler's words from 1900 are still as valid as they were over 100 years ago:

> The practical value of studying, in a right spirit and with scholarly accuracy, the working of foreign systems of education is that it will result in our being better fitted to study and to understand our own.
>
> *(Sadler, 1900, in Higginson, 1979:50)*

Phillips and Schweisfurth (2008:16–17) attempt to provide a composite list of the wide-ranging aims of the comparative study of education, among which they include such factors as follows:

- Illustrating alternative educational approaches;
- Producing benchmarks for evaluating the performance of education systems;
- Highlighting the pitfalls and positive outcomes associated with courses of educational action and policy;
- Providing a basis for informing educational reforms.

Recent years have, of course, seen a significant expansion of interest in such motives, and the diverse drivers behind these interests are partly responsible for the comparative shape-shifting that Cowen refers to earlier. On the one hand, interest in the field has developed as a result of changes in modern life – in a world characterised by increasing mobility, migration, travel and pervasive technology, many of us are able to experience aspects of other education systems directly and indirectly. Such changing conditions have themselves, in part, created new and greater demands for establishing equivalences and comparability, while politicians the world over, along with supra-regional authorities and entities like the OECD and the EU, have only further intensified new appetites for comparative rankings and educational transfer in a global climate increasingly inclined to see education as an economic instrument. Crossley identifies how such political interest has 'for the wider general public its most visible manifestation in … the shape of cross-national studies of educational achievement, and the widespread influence of related league tables' (Crossley, 2006:7). The challenges and dangers involved in achieving some of the aims mentioned earlier are discussed in this book, with several chapters highlighting the need for a sharp and critically developed awareness of the contextual factors that influence the workings of education.

The aims of this book

This book brings together a collection of studies and accounts from all sectors of education. As different as the individual sectors and subjects they cover, they all engage with aspects of the earlier debates and topics, while reflecting and illustrating the diversity of comparative study. As such, the book aims to provide higher-level undergraduate students (already equipped with some understanding of these issues) with detailed and wide-ranging illustrations of the ways in which comparison can illuminate our understanding of contemporary education systems by exploring issues in relation to specific educational sectors, from early years and primary schooling through to further adult and higher education. Using these levels as an organising framework, each chapter illustrates key issues and principles in comparative education in an attempt to offer students the examples and case studies of topics they may wish to select and explore in their own assignments and education projects. As such, the book is a useful resource and stimulus for students whose interests are more aligned to particular educational levels and sectors.

Integrating contributions from experienced academics and teachers, and with Education Studies students strongly in mind, each chapter includes discussion activities, case studies and suggestions on further reading and topics which students may wish to delve deeper into.

An overview of the chapters

Paul Wiseman begins the book with an examination of 'alternative education provision' – an area often marginalised in educational accounts and research. This chapter therefore attempts to readdress this and explores the provision available in the USA, Canada and the UK for those children and young people who opt out of or are denied access to formal education. Definitions of and philosophies on 'alternative education' are considered, before moving on to an examination of case studies relating to such diverse aspects as home-schooling provision and global networks offering alternative educational visions.

Turning to the start of the formal system, Rozsahegyi and Lambert invite readers to examine and reflect on the contrasting societal values underpinning the professional training for educators of very young children in England and Hungary. They explore the pedagogical values underlying these systems and compare England's emphasis on personal responsibility for one's own efforts and Hungary's more collective beliefs. A further contrast is drawn between England's pragmatic view of early provision as a preparatory version of cognitively based school education and Hungary's separate notion of 'upbringing' (nevelés), seeking children's readiness for school at age six or seven, but not imitating school itself. In relation to provision and practice, the authors argue that England pursues ideals of variety and choice: state, private and voluntary, and localised systems by which families gain access to it, while Hungary traditionally maintains free, state facilities as part of long-standing national social policy. In curriculum terms, England prioritises young children's individual or group 'play' activity, often minimally structured, while Hungary emphasises collective responsibility; knowledge of social and natural worlds and stimulation of energy, interest and healthy development.

Sarah Elsey moves on to primary school in the next chapter, exploring practice and policies on spiritual, moral, social and cultural development in the Netherlands and Britain. In England, Wales and Northern Ireland, the provision of Personal, Social and Health Education is interwoven within other areas of learning in line with the new Ofsted framework for schools. In the Netherlands, opportunities to develop primary aged children's learning and understanding of these key issues are housed in 'social and environmental studies'. Comparing these two forms of provision highlights the principles of two different systems that share the same goal – to develop and strengthen children's resilience and well-being. Case studies illustrate the varied ways in which UK and Dutch practitioners endeavour to provide children with tools and strategies to cope with everyday conflicts and unfamiliar situations inside and outside of school environments, enabling them to manage their responses to issues and dilemmas.

In the following chapter, Sean Starr compares English and Austrian secondary schools. He examines their contrasting organisational structures and curricula and focuses in particular on the varied ways in which both systems attempt to prepare pupils for the transition from compulsory schooling to work. The chapter reviews recent policy attempts to improve this important dimension of educational responsibility in the English context and compares current innovations with practices in Austria, where, for more than 40 years now, the secondary education system has been characterised by great educational diversity and vocational commitment.

In a sideways step from the compulsory secondary sector, Chan, Tang and Delaney examine private tutoring – something of a global phenomenon in the twenty-first century and one of the fastest growing 'edu-industries' in many developed countries. Their chapter focuses on the case of Mainland China and examines the expansion and prevalence of 'shadow education' and its implications for high-stakes testing and college test preparation. Specifically, the chapter reviews the effects of shadow education activities on family expenditure and family income inequalities with a view to improving our understanding of college inequality, social stratification and educational mobility in Mainland China. Special attention addresses the extent of private supplementary tutoring that is delivered by pre-professionals in tutoring centres and cram schools that often specialize in high-stakes test preparation by teachers, postgraduate students and parents. The chapter raises a number of concerns about the social stratification effects and inequity of private tutoring.

In the next chapter, O'Leary and Rami discuss how economic austerity measures have left an indelible mark on the further education (FE) landscape in England and Ireland in recent years. The financial meltdown of 2008 triggered the most far-reaching recession in almost a century, sending shockwaves across the globe. 'Greedy bankers' and stock market brokers are often apportioned the blame for the crisis, yet to date it is public sector workers who have suffered most from the subsequent fallout, with millions losing their jobs and many more forced to accept pay cuts and pay freezes. Their chapter explores how austerity has affected those working in FE in England and Ireland and considers what this reveals about the standing of this sector in both countries.

Ainley explores the nature of apprenticeship learning in the next chapter. He reviews the history of education and training to find the origins of academic and vocational learning as they developed in secondary schooling and tertiary further and higher education in England. The changing meanings of these terms are traced across the first and second industrial revolutions to the present global boom in tertiary-level learning. Ainley argues that this prolonged preparation is undercut by the latest applications of new technology in many countries and the chapter concludes by asking what prevocational general preparation would best prepare people for the variety of employments they are likely to undertake during their lifetimes in technology-based Internet societies.

Field moves to an examination of adult education in the next contribution – a broad concept, which is defined and operationalised very differently in different national contexts. Indeed, it seems highly likely that national systems for adult education vary more than any other part of the education and training system. Yet, in spite of these national variations, adult education has increasingly moved centre stage in international discussions of policies for education and training, and it has become a frequent focus for international benchmarking exercises. Field provides an overview of different adult education systems and summarises some of the main types of approach in different countries. There is an obvious difference between the priorities, institutions and practices typical of the global South and those that characterise the older industrial nations, as well as the emerging systems of the newly industrialising countries; within these groupings, the chapter explores the ways in which these systems both reflect and shape national and regional cultures. The chapter also discusses the role of international organisations like the EU, OECD and UNESCO in exchanging knowledge and ideas about the role of adult education, all of which conduct benchmarking exercises and promote policy transfer, but with very different sets of members. Field concludes that while national differences remain strong, the combined effects of globalisation, technological change and intergovernmental policy developments mean that there is a marked shift towards (a) the weakening of national influences on adult education and (b) increasing heterogeneity of provision reflecting factors other than national differences.

In Chapter 10, Burghes considers the impact that international comparisons have had on education policy in Western countries, with a focus on mathematics in teacher education. In particular, he considers the success of taking strategies from mathematically high-performing countries and implementing them in the UK and elsewhere. He notes the impact of PISA and TIMSS on policy in many countries, including the UK, alongside current interest in the strategies for teaching and learning mathematics in Shanghai and Finland; methods observed in Japan have similarly had considerable influence in many Western countries through their use of 'lesson study' for both continuing professional development and specifically for mathematics, where their open problem-solving approach is used to develop the mathematical thinking of learners. The chapter looks at some of the cultural issues that are raised when attempting to implement strategies that have worked well in one country and in another country, where the environment and ethos might be rather different, and concludes by considering the validity and reliability of some of the tests that have been used for comparisons.

Before considering what overall conclusions might be distilled from these wide-ranging contributions, Budd brings us to an examination of higher education in a globalised world, characterised by a compression of space, time and meaning. He discusses how people, resources and information – and, thus, ideas – are being shared more quickly and widely than ever before. Some see this as leading to a convergence in the ways things are done and understood. At one level, we can see this in higher education, as university sectors all over the world are undergoing significant changes in the same direction – more and more people are going to university and entering the labour market as graduates; there are reductions in public funding for higher education and rankings or 'league tables' are now pervasive, encouraging competition and responsiveness to 'the market'. These trends have been well documented, and the story of swelling, more privately funded, competitive university sectors is a widely recognised one. However, Budd argues it would be a mistake to assume that everything is becoming the same, and a closer look at the detail shows that distinctive national flavours are still very much present. Germany and England offer interesting examples through which to explore this topic, as the broad brushstrokes paint a familiar picture but with striking differences within them. This chapter takes an overview of the global and then regional dimensions in higher education before examining the national and local levels in these two countries, identifying in the process not only a number of similarities but also some fundamental contrasts in how developments observed globally actually play out 'on the ground' in different countries.

Individual/group task

- What do you see as the main aims of comparative and international education? Do you consider some of these aims to be more important than others?
- In what ways might political interest in educational comparisons be problematic?
- In what ways might we question the use(-fulness) of international rankings of educational performance?
- As you read the book, critically consider what it reveals about current trends, developments and challenges in education, and the extent to which these reflect converging or diverging educational preoccupations.

Conclusion

Comparative education is, as revealed, a diverse field of enquiry that aims to help us understand how a broad range of factors operate to influence educational phenomena in different contexts. The twin fields of comparative and international education are constantly evolving, and it was noted that global interest in comparative education is increasingly driven by political and economic motives. This interest will no doubt continue to expand as the growing influence of international and supra-regional entities like the EU create new impetuses, platforms and technologies for educational comparisons.

References

Cowen, R. (2005) Extreme political systems, deductive rationalities and comparative education: education as politics. In D. Halpin and P. Walsh (Eds.) *Educational Commonplaces*. London: Institute of Education.
Cowen, R. (2009) Then and now: unit ideas in comparative education. In R. Cowen and A. Kazamias (Eds.), *International Handbook of Comparative Education*. New York: Springer.
Crossley, M. (2006) *Bridging Cultures and Traditions: Perspectives from Comparative and International Research in Education*. Bristol: University of Bristol.
Lauwerys, J.A. and Tayar, G. (1973) *Education at Home and Abroad*. London: Routledge and Kegan Paul.
Phillips, D. and Ochs, K. (2004) Researching policy borrowing: some methodological challenges in comparative education. *British Educational Research Journal*, 30(6), 773–784.
Phillips, D. and Schweisfurth, M. (2008) *Comparative and International Education: An Introduction to Theory, Method and Practice*. London: Bloomsbury.
Sadler, M. (1900) How far can we learn anything of practical value from the study of foreign systems of education? In J.H. Higginson (Ed.) (1979) *Selections from Michael Sadler*. Liverpool: Dejall and Meyorre.

2 Alternative education provision – international perspectives

Paul Wiseman

Introduction

The introduction of mass state-funded education was a hugely significant historical event in the UK, and indeed across the globe, as it served to empower large sections of society that had previously been disenfranchised. However, state education is not always depicted as a force for 'public good' as it can also be seen to reproduce social inequalities by acting as 'a vehicle for oppression' (Francis and Mills, 2012:251). These differing outcomes are a result of the functions that state education can take, whether it is providing knowledge and creativity for its own sake or simply meeting the demands of the economy. The debate regarding this appropriation of education within the Organization for Economic Cooperation and Development (OECD), a group of 34 countries, is seen by Francis and Mills (2012) as now being revitalised following two decades that have focussed upon school standards and effectiveness, with children in England being seen to be the most tested in the world.

Individual/group task

- What is your understanding of 'alternative education (AE)'?
- How would you define it?
- How is it different from mainstream education?

Sliwka and Yee (2015) believe that AE has played a significant role in this shift in focus and state that

> Schools in public systems across the OECD are increasingly broadening their philosophy of teaching to create settings for learning which aim at the integration of learners' cognitive, metacognitive and social-emotional development. To some extent, this shift has been driven by providers of alternative education which are gaining in popularity among parents, to create more holistic approaches to education and focus on student potential for growth.
>
> *(2015:175)*

Yet what is meant by 'AE'?

McGregor and Mills (2012) believe that there is no agreed-upon definition due to the breadth and variety of programmes on offer globally, but Hayes believes that AE can be seen 'to disrupt and challenge default grammars of schooling which prioritise surveillance, control and disciplinary practice over pedagogical ones' (2012:649) while Sliwka sees it as

> An approach to teaching and learning other than state-provided mainstream education, usually in the form of public or private schools with a special, often innovative, curriculum and a flexible programme of study which is based to a large extent on the individual student's interests and needs.
>
> *(2008:1)*

This link to innovation is shared by Barr, who states that 'at their best alternative schools have functioned as an exciting laboratory where unique and often daring experiments are conducted and evaluated' (1981:571). However, the picture is not always as rosy as this with Barr also acknowledging that 'at their worst alternative schools represent some of the most unfortunate tendencies toward social tracking, political manipulation and educational hucksterism' (ibid).

AE, however, is not, as the name would suggest, available for all pupils, with McGregor and Mills (2012) claiming that the majority of those who attend have often had traumatic experiences at mainstream schools and as a result are seen by Hayes (2012) to have been transformed from pupils into 'non-citizens'. Baroutsis *et al.* (2016) relate this sense of 'disconnectedness' to Freire's (1993) notion of a 'culture of silence' within schools whereby the voice of the child is ignored. Clive Harber (2004), in his book 'Schooling as Violence', also portrays a similarly bleak portrayal of mainstream education, believing that an institutionalisation of violence takes place that harms pupils and ultimately the society within which they live.

Historical perspective

The history of AE is seen by Miller (2007) as being a colourful story of social reformers, religious believers and romantics. As a result of this exotic mix, the landscape is fragmented, including both global networks and individualised provision. Despite this complexity, Levin believes that 'the philosophical roots of AE derive from two related but conflicting educational traditions' (2006:1): 'progressive' and 'libertarian'. The progressive movement is predominantly associated with John Dewey, who highlighted the need to match teaching and curriculum to the stages of development of the child together with a gradual integration into society through planned experiential learning opportunities (ibid). The libertarian tradition asserts the rights of parents and children to make their own educational and life choices. A.S. Neil in the UK and John Holt in the USA can be seen as pioneers of this philosophy, believing that it is essential to 'uphold the individual freedom and innate goodness of the child against institutional and social conformity and the corrupting influences of modern society' (Levin, 2006:1). Although these traditions share similar features, they also have different perspectives as to the content of the curriculum, with progressivists believing in careful planning of the child's educational experiences while the libertarian stress non-interference and natural growth underpinned by pupil choice and personal freedom.

The growth in AE provision that has taken place over the last 40 years (Sliwka, 2008) could be depicted as a return to the time before mass schooling, with Horace Mann reminding us that the 'pioneering efforts to centralise public schooling were opposed from the start by religious leaders who viewed education to be a personal, family and community endeavour not a political programme to be mandated by the state' (Sliwka, 2008:1). Many of these pioneers who initially opposed the intro- duction and delivery of state education referred to Jean-Jacques Rousseau's book 'Emile', which was published in 1762 and argued that education should follow the child's innate growth patterns rather than respond to the demands of society (Sliwka, 2008). An early example of this rejection of state schooling can be seen by Bronson Alcott (Levin, 2006), who started the Temple School in Boston in 1834 because of the focus by early American schools upon rote memorisation and recitation.

Other early pioneers include as follows:

- *John Dewey*: an American pioneer who, along with a number of others, formed the progressive education movement.
- *Ellen Key*: a Swedish educator who was one of the first advocates of child-centred education.
- *Maria Montessori*: an Italian paediatrician who opened Casa de Bambini, a school for early years.
- *Rudolf Steiner*: an Austrian philosopher who founded the first Waldorf School in 1919.

By the 1960s, there was a change in philosophy regarding the provision of AE, from educa- tional pioneers who were heavily influenced by Rousseau to something that became part of a social movement, which was led and informed by a new wave of writers, including Ivan Illich in Europe, John Holt in the United States and Paulo Freire in Brazil (Sliwka, 2008), all of whom ques- tioned the values and methods that were being adopted within state education.

In recent years, school systems within the OECD can be seen to have loosened their grip on education and have allowed for greater autonomy within education and provided government funding for new forms of schooling (such as charter schools in the USA, free schools in the UK and designated character schools in New Zealand). This increased autonomy could be seen as a direct result of a neoliberalist philosophy that has informed government policy and aspired to a reduction in the size of the public sector through the introduction of market forces (Wiseman, 2016). This marketization has required a move away from local and central government with a focus upon parental choice within an educational market place. As a result of this increased autonomy, Sliwka (2008) believes that we will continue to see many of the 'experimental' teaching practices that were developed within AE settings becoming embedded within mainstream pro- vision and is evidenced with the current inclusion of student-centred, independent and project- based learning: key elements of AE provision.

Global networks of alternative education

The rise of AE provision has led to a development of a number of global networks. These include as follows:

Montessori schools

These are among the most well-known of all AE provision. However, the name is not copyrighted, so multiple models/interpretations exist. General characteristics of Montessori schools can include a special set of didactic teaching materials, pupil involvement in the selection of topics, multi-age classrooms and class groups, longer time blocks, a collaborative learning environment, student mentors, absence of testing and grades and individual and small group instruction in both academic and social skills. (Montessori Education, UK)

Waldorf schools

These can also be known as Steiner schools and are based on the philosophy of Rudolf Steiner, which focusses on the ethos of

> an unhurried and creative learning environment where children can find the joy in learning and experience the richness of childhood rather than early specialisation or academic hot-housing. The curriculum itself is a flexible set of pedagogical guidelines, founded on Steiner's principles that take account of the whole child. It gives equal attention to the physical, emotional, intellectual, cultural and spiritual needs of each pupil and is designed to work in harmony with the different phases of the child's development. The core subjects of the curriculum are taught in thematic blocks and all lessons include a balance of artistic, practical and intellectual content.
>
> *(Steiner Waldorf Schools Fellowship, 2016)*

Round square schools

These schools are based upon the theories of educational philosopher Kurt Hahn who believed in an experiential learning philosophy in preparation for life. The schools are based upon six ideals that include Internationalism, Democracy, Service, Environmentalism, Leadership and Adventure (Round Square, 2016).

Escuelas nuevas

There are over 20,000 schools across Columbia and other Latin American countries, the Philippines and Uganda. Their focus is upon improving the education of children from families on low incomes in rural areas. They are embedded within their local community within which parents are expected to take an active part. Characteristics of the schools include collaborative, participatory and personalised teaching methods (The Center for Education Innovation).

Individual/group task

- Visit the following websites to find out more about these 'global networks'.
  www.montessorieducationuk.org/
  www.steinerwaldorf.org/steiner-education/what-is-steiner-education/
  www.roundsquare.org/
  www.educationinnovations.org/program/escuela-nueva
- What qualities do you think you would need to have in order to teach in these schools?

Alternative education across the world

The provision of AE varies from country to country. The reasons for this variation depend on a variety of historic, economic and social issues, which are particular to the country in question.

Alternative education in the USA

AE became an established feature of the US education system in the 1960s and is seen by Lange and Sletten as being rooted within the civil rights movement. They state that 'the mainstream public educational system of the late 1950s and early 1960s was highly criticized for being racist and exclusively designed for the success of the few' (2002:9). Raywid shares this view and describes the state schools of the 1960s and 1970s as 'cold, dehumanising, irrelevant institutions, largely indifferent to the humanity and the 'personhood' of those within them' (1981:551). Young agrees, believing that the education of the time saw academic excellence as being defined 'solely in narrow cognitive terms at the expense of equity' (1990:9), which favoured those students who benefitted from a highly traditional upbringing. However, in 1965, US President Johnson declared 'war' on poverty and changed the focus from excellence to equity. Following this, and with funding from the government, a raft of AE programmes was spawned with two broad categories becoming evident: those within public education and those outside. Freedom schools are an example of those outside the education system in which 'groups' attempted to gain control of the 'oppressive educational processes' (Lange and Sletten, 2002:9). The free school movement was another type of provision that emphasised individual achievement and fulfilment and allowed pupils both the freedom to learn and freedom from restrictions. A.S. Neil, a pioneer in the free school movement, explains the philosophy behind these schools, stating: 'my view is the child is innately wise and realistic, if left to himself without adult suggestion of any kind, he will develop as far as he is capable of developing' (Young, 1990:10). Within the free school movement, assessment of the learning environment was seen as being more important than the achievement of, or progress to, learning outcomes.

Individual/group task

- How does the American 'free school movement' of the 1960s differ from the 'free schools', which were introduced by Michael Gove, within the UK, in 2010?

In the first decade of the AE movement, during the 1960s, the numbers of pupils grew from 100 to 10,000 with the introduction of voucher schemes and magnet and charter schools (Lange and Sletten, 2002). The National Center for Education Statistics (NCES, 2002) undertook the first national survey of public AE provision, serving 'at-risk' students, and found that there were 10,900 public alternative schools, serving 612,000 students within the academic year 2000–2001, with 39% of all school districts offering some type of AE. However, despite this initial growth, by the 1980s, many of the schools had not survived and as a result, the philosophy was seen to change 'from the progressive and open orientation in the 1970s to more conservative and remedial in the 1980s' (Young, 1990:20), which were geared around children who were disruptive and/or falling behind their peers in educational standards. This provision was seen to focus upon large urban areas where inequality was rife.

However, despite the closure of many AE providers, the public education sector can be seen to have taken on elements of alternative provision that lay outside the education system and mainstreamed these. Lange and Sletten certainly take this view and state that

> Many of the reforms currently pursued in traditional schools – downsizing the high school, pursuing a focus or theme, students and teacher choice, making the school a community, empowering staff, active learner engagement, authentic assessment – are practices that alternate schools pioneered.
>
> *(2002:7)*

This adoption of aspects of AE practices is seen within 'open schools', which were characterised by parent, student and teacher choice; autonomy in type and pace of learning and non-competitive evaluations together with a child-centred approach. The development of the open schools system is seen to have led to the creation of a range of 'alternative' school provision, which, according to Lange and Sletten (2002), included the following:

- Schools without walls – community learning with people from the locality coming in to teach;
- Schools within a school – intended to split large schools into smaller communities of belonging;
- Multicultural schools – designed to integrate culture and ethnicity into the curriculum;
- Continuation schools – for those that have dropped behind due to pregnancy, truancy, etc.;
- Fundamental schools – emphasised a 'back-to-basics' approach due lack of academic rigour in free schools;
- Magnet schools – developed in response to the need for racial integration.

Despite the adoption of elements of AE provision within the mainstream education system, every year, one in three students is seen to 'drop out' of high school (Smith and Thomson, 2014), and this is seen to be an escalating problem. 'The high drop-out and low graduation rates, as well as increasing discipline problems and disenfranchisement of students, show that the traditional school setting is not effective for teaching many of the students in today's society' (Smith and Thomson, 2014:111). As a result, a large number of AE settings were established, but unfortunately, many have not been seen to be successful. Smith and Thomson (2014) now call for more research into this area as recent government reports estimate that 3.8 million (10%) of Americans drop out of school each year and have no qualifications (the UK which has a 9% dropout rate and totals 168,000 pupils). These students make up half of those on welfare payments and over half of the prison population.

In the USA, most AE provision is now geared towards these at-risk groups with traditional schools often failing to meet their needs. Smith and Thomson (2014) identify key risk factors that are linked to this dropout rate. These are the following:

- Socioeconomic – limited parental education, poverty, unstable home life, single parent households and lack of parental support and need to earn additional money;
- Personal – working more than 12 hours per week, legal problems, pregnancy, substance misuse and language barriers;
- School-related factors – attendance, performance, behaviour and special educational needs (SEN).

The one-size-fits-all model of public education could now be seen as 'an antiquated approach' that is 'becoming less effective and common sense indicates that educators need to come up with means of adapting education to the differing needs of modern day students' (D'Angelo and Zemanick, 2009:212). AE within the USA, however, is often viewed 'with negative stigmas as dumping grounds or warehouses for at-risk students who are falling behind, have behavioural problems, or are juvenile delinquents' (Kim and Taylor, 2008:207) and therefore fails to offer a true alternative to state education.

Effective practices for use in AE settings (USA)

Tobin and Sprague (2000) identified eight practices appropriate for AE settings for children with emotional and behavioural difficulties from an exhaustive review of school-based interventions. These are the following:

- Low students to teacher ratio (less than 20:1);
- Highly structured classroom with behavioural classroom management;
- Positive methods to increase appropriate behaviour;
- School-based adult mentor;
- Functional behavioural assessment. Identifying trigger and motivations for poor behaviour;
- Social skills instruction;
- Parent involvement;
- Positive behavioural interventions and supports. Framework for preventing and responding to poor behaviour to provide a predictable structure and routine with reinforcement dependent upon students' performance of desired behaviour.

These are seen to be suitable for children at risk, implementable within a school setting and producing positive outcomes.

Alternative education in the UK

On September 1st, 2011, the then Secretary of State for Education, Michael Gove, made reference in a speech to a group of children he called the 'educational underclass', which were identified as those 'pupils who are outside mainstream education and fail to achieve academically and grow up without the skills to become successful adults and members of society' (Taylor, 2012:2). In the same year, Gove commissioned a review, to be undertaken by Charlie Taylor (the government's expert adviser on behaviour), on the quality of alternative provision within the UK, which he saw as an important but ignored area within the English education system. This report produced some alarming findings.

Taylor was 'critical of a flawed [education] system that fails to provide suitable education and proper accountability for some of the most vulnerable children in the country' (2012:4), stating that 'the government cannot continue to hold these children [outside of mainstream education] in their peripheral vision' warning the government that they will pay a 'heavy price' (2012:4) if they continue to fail these children. As a result of this lack of attention, there is little/no reliable data available as to the numbers of pupils who attend alternate provision in the UK, with the

Department for Education (Taylor, 2012) estimating that there are 14,050 pupils in pupil referral units (PRUs) and 23,020 in other alternative settings on full- or part-time placements.

The children who attend this provision are seen to do so for a wide range of reasons, but predominately they are children with behavioural difficulties, in years 10 and 11, who have either been permanently excluded from school and have been placed by a local authority or referred by individual schools in an attempt to change their behaviour (Taylor, 2012). However, in his report, Taylor portrays the children who access this provision as 'victims' rather than 'offenders' who are in need of specialist education and states that

> It is important to note that many children who are referred to PRUs and alternate provision come from the most deprived backgrounds. They often come from chaotic homes in which problems such as drinking, drug-taking, mental health issues, domestic violence and family breakdown are common. These children are often stuck in complex patterns of negative, self-destructive behaviour and helping them is not easy or formulaic. Many also have developed mental health issues. To break down these patterns they need the time, effort, commitment and expertise of dedicated professionals working in well-organised, well-resourced and responsive systems.
>
> *(Taylor, 2012:4)*

Children in AE are therefore seen to be twice as likely as the average pupil to qualify for free school meals, to have a tendency for poor attendance in school and to be known to social services and the police. As set out within the Taylor review (2012), 79% of pupils in PRUs have SEN with two-thirds of pupils being boys. The academic outcomes for pupils are generally poor and settings are not seen to pay sufficient attention to improving the academic attainment of their pupils, with some AE providers doing little more than keeping their pupils off the streets.

Despite the complex difficulties of many children in alternative provision, it remains alarming that, in 2011, only 1.4% of children achieved five or more GCSEs at grades A*–C (including English and Maths) compared to 53.4% of their peers in all schools (ibid). However, with no requirement to deliver the National Curriculum, little information shared about the child's needs, little or no assessment and poor expectations for progress or likely reintegration into mainstream schooling, it is unsurprising that so few children make any progress within alternative educational provision within the UK (Taylor, 2012).

A.S. Neil's Summerhill democratic school in England

An example of high-quality AE provision within the UK can be found within A.S. Neil's Summerhill school in Suffolk, a coeducational boarding school. The school was founded in 1921 and continues to be an influential model for progressive, democratic education.

Summerhill is the oldest children's democracy in the world and is also probably the most famous alternative or 'free' school. The system that Summerhill employs does not focus upon education but adopts an alternative view of parenting that attempts to eliminate much of the friction that is experienced by many modern families. Its approach is summarised by its principal, Zoë Neill, in the following extract taken from its website.

'Summerhill is a real place, not a utopia. Living in a community of around 100 people is not always easy. Everybody is learning about themselves, and on a bleak January day, with the east wind blowing, things are sometimes not wonderful! But Summerhill in summer time is lush, green and not unlike never-never land. It is more of a family or tribe than a school-full of companionship, laughter and real feelings. For many Summerhill pupils it becomes the most meaningful experience in their lives'.

Alternative education in Australia

In 2008, the Australian Federal Labor government introduced the yearly National Assessment Programme in Literacy and Numeracy (NAPLAN) for all pupils in years five, seven and nine, with the performance of individual schools being published on the Australian Curriculum, Assessment and Reporting Authority (ACARA) website: My School. 'The high stakes nature of these tests and the publication of results have led to government reviews, cheating by teachers and principals and a re-focussing of curricula and pedagogies in schools towards the perceived demands of the tests' (Francis and Mills, 2012:252). The focus upon testing of this type can be seen to be exacerbated by a neoliberal policy context, evident in many Western economies, which attempts to increase market forces and reward those features that serve to widen and perpetuate social inequality (ibid). 'Not surprisingly, selection and methods of access to 'good' schools favour middle class parents who are advantaged in these processes by both material and cultural capital' (Francis and Mills, 2012:256). Therefore, 'a broad-scale self-fulfilling prophecy is perpetuated, as working-class pupils disengage' (ibid), requiring AE provision to provide an opportunity to help 'reconnect' these pupils who find themselves 'disconnected'.

AE in Australia is provided through what is referred to as 'second chance' or 'flexi' schools, which cater for pupils who primarily come from families in poverty or those on a low income. These schools tend to have an increased awareness of 'student voice' and an increased flexibility in the structure and type of provision on offer. A list of the different types of provision available is identified by Francis and Mills (2012), who researched AE provision in South East Queensland, and is presented below.

- *Fernvale Education Centre*: a church-funded school for girls suffering from serious family and personal problems;
- *Woodlands Flexi School*: a regional school overseen by a high school and supported by community organisations for pupils who live in low-income rural homes;
- *Cave Street Flexi School*: a very small school located in a house within an urban area that consists of one teacher and a social worker catering for young people up to 16 years of age;
- *Victoria Meadows Flexi School*: an inner-city school with children from 5 to 25 years of age that is cofunded by a church, city council and a learning centre. It is a multicultural school with many of the pupils living independently.

There was a broad range of socioeconomic reasons that led to children accessing the provision listed above, with many of the students being highly transient and/or homeless, or being required to earn money to boost their family income. Despite the reasons for this disengagement from mainstream schools, what is interesting to discover from Francis and Mills (2012) research is that the students who attended this alternate provision were highly motivated and had a sense of commitment to the education they were accessing. The reasons for this [re] engagement were due to a number of factors that are as follows:

- *The learning programme*: 'Common across the research sites was the endeavour to cater to the needs of the students who chose that particular place'. Some were classed as schools, whereas others 'centres' and 'work sites' (McGregor and Mills, 2012:853);
- *The environment*: 'issues in respect to attendance, uniforms, assessment deadlines and behaviour were handled with greater flexibility and on-going staff-student dialogue' (McGregor and Mills, 2012:854);
- *Voluntary attendance*: leading to many of the centres having waiting lists;
- *The teaching relationship*: building a sense of community was seen as a key reason as to why children remained within these schools as well as accepting the students for who they are. 'The issue of teacher-student relationships and the teaching strategies that flowed from that was a dominant theme within the data from our study.' Students used the following terms as positive features: 'caring, small, community, family, respectful, equal, supportive, non-judgmental, mutual responsibility' (McGregor and Mills, 2012:857).

The findings of the research undertaken above therefore present a positive view of current AE within South East Queensland. However, they conclude with a warning regarding the development of future provision. 'We would be concerned if "alternative" or "flexi schools" became sites where students who were deemed to be "a problem" were "offloaded" and where a limited "dead-end" curriculum was offered in a way that constructed that such schools as offering a remedial form of education' (2012:860).

Melissa Roderick (2003): Produced a typology of AE that placed student's educational needs to the fore rather than the demographic or programme characteristics and is set out below.

Type 1: Students that have 'fallen off the track' because they have got into trouble and need a short-term recovery programme.

Type 2: Students that have prematurely moved into adulthood.

Type 3: Students who have fallen behind at school and are older but returning to gain necessary qualifications. (In the USA, this is seen as the most well-provided for; mainly found within large urban areas.)

Type 4: Students who have fallen behind because they have a particular educational need.

Homeschooling: a history and alternative educational movement all its own

Apple (2010) informs us that homeschooling is growing rapidly in the USA and now accounts for more than 2.2% of the student population. He sees this growth as being driven by a number of 'groups', the largest with overtly Christian/ideological commitments who believe that state education cannot meet their children's particular needs and/or may impose the beliefs of the state upon their child. Apple claims that these groups create 'horror stories' about state education, through which parents become concerned that their child may become 'infected' via peer interaction; against this background, homeschooling becomes seen as a form of inoculation.

Apple (2010) claims that many of those who engage in homeschooling often have a fundamental mistrust of the state, but despite this mistrust is often adept at taking advantage of government funding. This can be seen in the development of 'home school charter programs that connect independent families through the use of the web' (Apple, 2010:147). However, not all homeschoolers are Christian Conservative; a school district in California – in a bid to solve a financial crisis, for example – is currently employing home charter schools. In this example, Apple sees technologically linked homes as being recast as 'public' education that transforms the meaning of 'public', suggesting that this may be a vision of the future, something he views with concern, given the possibility of large numbers of children growing up in relative isolation where no alternative viewpoint exists.

This pattern of growth is also evident in Europe, and while still totalling less than 1% of the total student population, numbers are increasing in Belgium, Denmark, France, England, Ireland, Italy, Norway and Portugal (Blok, 2004). Gaither (2009) identifies several factors that have led to this increase in homeschooling since the 1980s. These include the following:

* Post-war mass suburbanisation and improvements in housing stock;
* Rise of feminism as inspiration for counterculture approaches;
* Disillusionment with public education and increased bureaucracy;
* Secularisation together with fears over bullying and standardised testing.

Homeschooling is not available everywhere, however; it is illegal in Germany and Brazil and has been recently outlawed in Russia. It was also, until relatively recently, illegal in the Netherlands, with its government believing that 'home-schooling conflicted with the interests of children' (Blok, 2004:41). Today, homeschooling in the Netherlands remains almost non-existent following a century of compulsory education that has 'established a tacit assumption that parents are incompetent to teach their own children' (ibid), despite a lack of evidence to support this. The availability of homeschooling across the globe is seen as reflecting differing government ideals and in particular the balance between privatisation of schooling and the surveillance of its population (Bielick *et al.*, 2001). Even in the UK, homeschooling is becoming increasingly scrutinised and can be seen to go against the grain of the government's introduction of mass free childcare in order to encourage parents to return to work.

Although data are limited regarding the demographic background of homeschooled children, they are viewed as a privileged group with parents generally being better educated, having higher incomes and possessing a very strong sense of commitment to education (Blok, 2004). Estimates by Bielick *et al.* (2001) claim that between 75–90% of all homeschoolers are white, Collom and Mitchell (2005) adding that 90% are female. Blok also believes that parents are naturally good at teaching their own children as they are culturally attuned to their child both in terms of behaviour and language and are aware of their child's areas of interest. They are also particularly motivated, flexible and are not limited by institutional barriers that often lead to a much more effective use of time. This claim is perhaps not without merit, as a number of educational theorists advocate one-to-one teaching, with Bloom regarding 'the science of teaching as a quest for methods of group instruction which are as effective as one-to-one tutoring' (Blok, 2004:49).

Conclusion

Despite many of the negative features highlighted within this chapter, the introduction of mass state-funded education has undoubtedly brought with it many significant social and economic benefits. However, throughout the relatively brief history of mass schooling, change and transformation have been constant, as government after government sees state education as a vehicle for the achievement of their own political ideologies and policy objectives rather than the experiences of the 'learner'. As a result, state education cannot and does not serve the needs of all students, and AE has emerged from a recognition of this need. The history of AE has therefore mirrored and run parallel to mass education but has been less subject to change due to its philosophical and ideological roots, which have always considered the individual child rather than the perceived political demands of the economy and society.

This chapter sheds some light on this history as well as the current practice of AE, which, in the USA, was initially driven by the civil rights movement but transformed into a state-sponsored safety net for school 'dropouts' who are in danger of leaving school with no qualifications and contributing to the ever-growing prison population. In the UK, the Taylor report presents a grim portrayal of alternate education that highlights poor-quality provision and low aspirations for pupils. Australia, however, illustrates a much more positive picture with high-quality programmes effectively engaging the disaffected and excluded. Despite this variation in practice, which is evident across the globe, one thing seems clear: more respect, more research and more investment is needed within the UK, as we move to a more fragmented marketised educational landscape within which it is becoming increasingly difficult to differentiate between mainstream and AE provision.

Individual/group task

- The chapter refers to a number of pioneers and theorists who have shaped and informed AE provision. Go back through the chapter and identify these and carry out some research, focussing upon their theoretical, ideological and/or philosophical beliefs.
- Once you have undertaken this research, reflect upon their ideas in relation to your own attitudes to education. How do they compare? What do you agree with/disagree with?
- Following this, what do you think the purpose of education is and/or should be and how would you like to see it shaped in the future?

Recommended reading

Apple, M. (2010) Doing the work of god: home schooling and gendered labor. In M. Apple, S. Ball and L.A. Gandin (Eds.) *The Routledge International Handbook of the Sociology of Education*. London: Routledge.

Baroutsis, A., Mills, M., McGregor, G., Riele, K. and Hayes, D. (2016) Student voice and the community forum: finding ways of 'being heard' at an alternative school for disaffected young people. *British Educational Research Journal*, 42(2), 438–453.

Francis, B. and Mills, M. (2012) Schools as damaging organisations: instigating a dialogue concerning alternative models of schooling. *Pedagogy, Culture & Society*, 20(2), 251–271.

Harber, C. (2004) *Schooling as Violence: How Schools Harm Pupils and Societies*. London: RoutledgeFalmer.

McGregor, G. and Mills, M. (2012) Alternative education sites and marginalised young people: 'i wish there were more schools like this one'. *International Journal of Inclusive Education*, 16(8), 843–862.

Sliwka, A. and Yee, B. (2015) From alternative education to the mainstream: approaches in Canada and Germany to preparing learners to live in a changing world: from alternative education to the mainstream. *European Journal of Education*, 50(2), 175–183.

References

Apple, M. (2010) Doing the work of god: home schooling and gendered labor. In M. Apple, S. Ball and L.A. Gandin (Eds.) *The Routledge International Handbook of the Sociology of Education*. London: Routledge.

Baroutsis, A., Mills, M., McGregor, G., Riele, K. and Hayes, D. (2016) Student voice and the community forum: finding ways of 'being heard' at an alternative school for disaffected young people. *British Educational Research Journal*, 42(2), 438–453.

Barr, R.D. (1981) Alternatives for the eighties: a second decade of development. *The Phi Delta Kappan*, 62(8), 570–573.

Bielick, S., Chandler, K. and Broughman, S.P. (2001) *Homeschooling in the United States: 1999*. Washington, DC: National Center for Education Statistics.

Blok, H. (2004) Performance in home schooling: an argument against compulsory schooling in the Netherlands. *International Review of Education*, 50(1), 39–52.

Collom, E. and Mitchell, D. (2005) Home schooling as a social movement: identifying the determinants of homeschoolers perceptions. *Sociological Spectrum*, 5(3), 273–305.

D'Angelo, F. and Zemanick, R. (2009) The twilight academy: an alternative education program that works. *Preventing School Failure: Alternative Education for Children and Youth*, 53(40), 211–218.

Francis, B. and Mills, M. (2012) Schools as damaging organisations: instigating a dialogue concerning alternative models of schooling. *Pedagogy, Culture & Society*, 20(2), 251–271.

Freire, P. (1993) *Pedagogy of the Oppressed*. New York: Continuum.

Gaither, M. (2009) Homeschooling in the USA. *Past, Present and Future Theory and Research in Education*, 7(3), 331–346.

Harber, C. (2004) *Schooling as Violence: How Schools Harm Pupils and Societies*. London: RoutledgeFalmer.

Hayes, D. (2012) Re-engaging marginalised young people in learning: the contribution of informal learning and community-based collaborations. *Journal of Education Policy*, 27(5), 641–653.

Kim, J. and Taylor, K.A. (2008) Rethinking alternative education to break the cycle of educational inequality and inequity. *The Journal of Educational Research*, 101(4), 207–217.

Lange, C.M. and Sletten, S.J. (2002) *Prepared for: Project FORUM*. National Association of State Directors of Special Education, Alexandria, VA.

Levin, M. (2006) *Alternative Education*. Available at: www.thecanadianencyclopedia.ca/en/. (Accessed 23rd August 2016).

McGregor, G. and Mills, M. (2012) Alternative education sites and marginalised young people: 'I wish there were more schools like this one'. *International Journal of Inclusive Education*, 16(8), 843–862.

Miller, R. (2007) *A Brief History of Alternative Education*. Available at: www.educationrevolution.org/history. (Accessed 20th July 2016).

National Center for Education Statistics (NCES) (2002) *Public Alternative Schools and Programs for Students at Risk of Education Failure: 2000–01*. Statistical Analysis Report. U.S. Department of Education ED Pubs. Available at: http://nces.ed.gov/pubs2002/2002004.pdf. (Accessed 23rd May 2016).

Raywid, M.A. (1981) The first decade of public school alternatives. *The Phi Delta Kappan*, 62(8), 551–554.

Roderick, M. (2003) What's happening to the boys? Early high school experiences and school outcomes among African American male adolescents in Chicago. *Urban Education*, 38(5), 538–607.

Round Square (2016) Available at: www.roundsquare.org. (Accessed on 17th July 2016).

Sliwka, A. (2008) The contribution of alternative education. In OECD, *Innovating to Learn, Learning to Innovate*, Paris: OECD.

Sliwka, A. and Yee, B. (2015) From alternative education to the mainstream: approaches in Canada and Germany to preparing learners to live in a changing world: from alternative education to the mainstream. *European Journal of Education*, 50(2), 175–183.

Smith, A. and Thomson, M. (2014) Alternative education programmes: synthesis and psychological perspectives. *Educational Psychology in Practice*, 30(2), 111–119.

Steiner Waldorf Schools Fellowship (2016) Available at: www.steinerwaldorf.org/steiner-education/what-is-steiner-education/. (Accessed 16th July 2016).

Taylor, C. (2012) *Improving Alternative Provision*. DfE. London: HMSO. Available at: www.gov.uk/government/uploads/system/uploads/attachment_data/file/180581/DFE-00035-2012.pdf. (Accessed 20th August 2016).

Tobin, T. and Sprague, J. (2000) Alternative education strategies: reducing violence in school and the community. *Journal of Emotional and Behavioral Disorders*, 8(3), 177–186.

Wiseman, P. (2016) Stability and change during periods of re-organisation: a cultural historical investigation into children's services (in England). *International Journal for Cross-Disciplinary Subjects in Education (IJCDSE)*, Special Issue, 5(1), 2394–2400.

Young, T. (1990) *Public Alternative Education*. New York: Teachers College Press.

3 Pedagogical outlooks underpinning early-years education and workforce training in England and Hungary

Tunde Rozsahegyi and Mike Lambert

Introduction

England and Hungary, 1000 miles apart, share characteristics of Western democracy and have, respectively, been part of the European Union since 1973 (then the European Economic Community) and 2004. England's history and traditions, however, reflect influences of empire and the USA, as well a role as the largest constituent country of the United Kingdom. Hungary's, on the other hand, mirror characteristics of Central and Eastern Europe, three decades of socialist government after the Second World War, and more recent democratic, decentralised and market-oriented development (Halász, 2015).

According to census data, England's population is around 53 million, steadily increasing due mainly to net migration. Hungary's is around 10 million, decreasing due principally to low birth rate. About 80% of the population declares itself to be 'white British' in England and 'Hungarian' in Hungary. In both countries, a large proportion lives in the capital cities, London and Budapest.

Drawing mainly on English-language sources, this chapter invites readers to compare early-years provision and workforce training in these two countries. Differing understandings of the notion of 'pedagogy' are discussed and pedagogical outlooks are identified and examined. There is more extended consideration of two particular sets of perspectives, the first relating to care, education and 'upbringing', the second to curriculum. Readers are asked to consider all these elements in relation to their own professional experiences and to reflect on implications for practice and professional development.

Early-years provision

England

The first 'infant school' in England, with children aged from three to six, was established in London in 1818. More than a century later, the influential 1933 Hadow Report (Board of Education, 1933) found 55 recognised nursery schools, 30 of these run by local authorities and 25 by voluntary bodies, and recommended that nursery education should be made widely available, especially in poorer districts. Four decades later, however, the Plowden Report (Central Advisory Council for Education (England), 1967:116) found that large-scale nursery education remained 'an unfulfilled promise'. Substantial development eventually came with social programmes of the New Labour government 1997–2010 and further changes since then.

Currently, children aged three and four are legally entitled to 15 hours of free provision for 38 weeks of the year. In 2013, this was extended to disadvantaged two-year-olds, around 40% of the age group. According to the Department for Education, at the start of 2016, 68% of eligible two-year-olds, 93% of three-year-olds and 97% of five-year-olds were benefitting from some funded early education (DfE, 2016). There is an intention to increase the 15-hour entitlement to 30 hours per week for all three- and four-year-olds with working parents from September 2017.

Many different kinds of locations offer provision, including registered childminders, children's centres and nursery classes in schools. Privately run facilities are a major element – according to DfE (2016), 96% of two-year-olds, 64% of three-year-olds and 21% of four-year-olds attend private, voluntary and independent provision. From age four, children can apply for a place at a reception class in a publicly funded primary school. Compulsory primary education starts at age five – the Elementary Education Act of 1870 fixed this age nearly 150 years ago.

Hungary

According to OECD (2004), Hungary had the first kindergarten in central Europe in 1828, and by 1938, over a quarter of children aged between three and six were attending this kind of provision. In 1965, 3,227 kindergartens were in operation, usually with extended hours, which allowed both parents to go to work. Legislation in 1993 recognised kindergarten as an official part of the education system with the same status as elementary and secondary education. OECD concluded that Hungary's 'legislative, regulatory and administrative structures in both childcare and kindergarten are generally very comprehensive' (2004:21).

The system includes childcare centres (*bölcsőde*) for children aged from 20 weeks to three years – the first opened in Budapest in 1852 (OECD, 2004). While access is an entitlement for all, only around 13% of infants currently attend (Hungarian Institute for Educational Research and Development, 2015), the low take-up rate explained by a tradition of caring for young children within the family, generous maternal leave, early admission age to preschool facilities, lack of provision in some parts of the country and cost, although some municipalities charge only for meals.

Legislation and criteria for licensing family day-care homes were developed in the early 1990s. Development has been slow, however: in 2007, there were 205 licensed providers, of which only a quarter were publicly financed (Korintus, 2012).

Kindergarten (*óvoda*) starts at age three, and under legislation, in 2015, all children from this age must attend (Hungarian Institute for Educational Research and Development, 2015). Previously, the compulsory starting age was five. Nearly, all kindergartens are publicly funded by national or local government; attendance is free (although meals must usually be paid for) and is for around 9 hours a day (National Information: Hungary, 2010). The number operated by churches, private groups or foundations, where fees may be payable, has expanded in recent years: 9% of relevant children attended these in 2013 (Hungarian Institute for Educational Research and Development, 2015).

Formal primary schooling starts at age six, or sometimes seven, depending on birthdate and maturity. The aim of this flexibility is to take into account children's individual differences when starting school (Pákozdi, 2012).

Workforce training

England

The 1933 Hadow Report recommended that nursery teachers should have 'special instruction in nursery care' (Board of Education, 1933:190) and that 'helpers' should be provided to assist them. Decisive moves towards this position, however, had to wait until the next century. Since HM Government (2005), and continuing in the light of the hard-hitting Nutbrown review (DfE, 2012), political developments have sought to create a more formally and consistently trained workforce for children from birth to age five, and one led by educators with graduate-level training.

Specialised three-year initial teacher training for 'Early Years Teachers' was introduced in 2013, having been delivered in other forms under the label of 'Early Years Professional Status' since 2007. These graduate-level professionals lead and support other staff in early-years settings, including 'Early Years Educators' for whom qualification at level 3 (GCE Advanced Level) standard was introduced in 2014 (Abrahamson, 2015).

There is a requirement that publicly maintained nurseries and centres should have an Early Years Teacher, while independent settings have tighter staff-child ratios if a qualified teacher does not work directly with the children (DfE, 2014). Pay, terms and conditions are less favourable than those for qualified teachers working with older children (Kalitowski, 2016).

Hungary

The first training institution providing one year further education for work with young children was established in 1837 (Varga *et al.*, 2015). Currently, those working with under-threes in childcare and those working in kindergartens have separate training (OECD, 2006).

The lead staff in the former, the *bölcsőde*, is the 'childcare worker' (*gondozónő*). The graduate-level training programme for these 'pedagogues' (teachers) was launched in 2009 (Dávid and Podráczky, 2012). Other staff are 'technical assistants' (*technikai dolgozók*), who have no compulsory course (National Information: Hungary, 2010).

In the kindergarten, the lead staff is the 'kindergarten pedagogue' (*óvodapedagógus*), pre-school teachers required by the 1990 Hungarian Education Law to have a Bachelor's degree in early-childhood education. OECD (2006:347) reported that 'two-thirds of staff in kindergartens working directly with children are tertiary-trained pedagogues'. They work alongside 'kindergarten assistants' (*dajka*) who may have a diploma or bachelor's degree and a further certificate gained through compulsory in-service training (National Information: Hungary, 2010). OECD (2006) reported that 60% of these had training at vocational-college level. Their conclusion was that 'over 90 per cent of total [kindergarten] staff are fully trained' (2006:343), although most were ageing and the number of younger training-college candidates declining. Virtually, all early-childhood workers are female (Cameron and Moss, 2007), and some titles, such as *gondozónő*, imply this (the suffix, *nő*, means 'woman').

> **Discussion: Provision and workforce training**
>
> Look carefully at this information about early-years provision and workforce training in England and Hungary. Address these questions:
>
> 1   How is provision similar? How does it differ?
> 2   How is training similar? How does it differ?
> 3   What might such similarities and differences tell us about traditions and attitudes in these two countries to the care and education of young children?

Pedagogy and outlooks

Elsewhere, we have defined the notion of pedagogy as the 'shared formulation and understanding of educational ideas, even beliefs, which underpin both policy and practice' (Rozsahegyi and Lambert, 2016:15). Such ideas may vary according to the age or nature of those being taught and the contexts in which this takes place. 'Pedagogical outlooks', which underlie early-years care and education and workforce training in England and Hungary, are now discussed, the word 'outlooks' intended as a generic term, encompassing values, ideas and curricular perspectives.

England

Historically, Simon (1981) and Alexander (2004) questioned the extent to which education in England had any established pedagogy at all. Simon explained this by citing the influence of traditional public-school concern for children's character development rather than for actual learning. Alexander's update found a continuing dearth and a subordinate relationship to the overriding importance of curriculum: 'The pedagogy of principle has yet to be rescued from the pedagogy of pragmatism and compliance' (2004:29). Parker-Rees (2007:14) wrote: 'It is perhaps odd ... that our understanding of pedagogy is still dominated by a rather narrow, systemising approach to the assembly and profiling of individual intellectual abilities', while Stephen (2010:17) found a lack of explicit engagement with pedagogy to be 'characteristic of early years education' in the Anglo-American tradition as a whole.

Others, however, have been more willing to recognise evidence of the concept in relation to actual practice. For instance, Siraj-Blatchford *et al.*, whose report was influential in advancement of early-years education in England, were happy to associate pedagogy closely with curriculum: 'Different early years practices are informed by different educational philosophies and values and by the different assumptions that are held about learning, child development, appropriate styles of instruction and curricula' (2002:28). A Department for Education research brief on pedagogy in the early years (Wall *et al.*, 2015) has made similar connections. Using this perspective, it is possible to identify particular outlooks in England's approaches to early-years education and workforce training. Here are three of these:

Child-centred outlooks

'Child-centred' ideals have long been proposed as fundamental to Anglo-American education and a vital element to be assimilated in educator training. The reforming American psychologist, John Dewey, compared it to other approaches:

> The old education ... may be summed up by stating that the center of gravity is outside the child. It is in the teacher, the textbook, anywhere and everywhere you please except in the immediate instincts and activities of the child himself ... Now the change which is coming into education is the shifting of the center of gravity ... the child becomes the sun around which the appliances of education revolve; he is the center about which they are organized.
> *(1900:51)*

This kind of advocacy has had plenty of criticism, most stridently in the 1970s by Cox and Boyson (1975). While overenthusiasm has largely been moderated, a strong focus on the child more than the teacher, and on learning more than teaching, remains, and can frequently be identified in the way in which English educators are trained and the way in which they portray their beliefs. Smedley (1997:22) called the notion 'part of early years culture', albeit one which should be 'not routinely accepted as a dogma'.

Individualistic outlooks

It is interesting to note that the aspiration above is towards 'child-centred', rather than 'children-centred' education. The singular noun reflects individualistic values that are also prevalent. There is constant insistence that children have different rates and ways of learning, and different 'potential' and needs, all reflecting an individualistic approach common in postmodern Western educational systems.

Early care and education is not exempt from this. For instance, Basford writes: 'Babies and children develop in individual ways and at varying rates ... your practice needs to be developmentally appropriate' (2008:5), and '[They] are, firstly, individuals, each with a unique profile of abilities' (2008:10). The view from Miell (1995), quoted by Brooker and Broadbent (2003:33), personalises this outlook:

> Developing a sense of self is often seen in Western cultures as the long process of becoming a self-aware individual – becoming aware, for example, of what you look like, your gender, what makes you happy and sad, what roles you play ... All the things which delineate you as an individual.

Responsibility and accountability

Concern for the individual child is accompanied by concern that all accept and address their responsibility in relation to growth and learning. First, the learner, her or himself, is 'a unique and self-actualising agent' (Taguchi, 2010:15), echoing emphasis in capitalist societies on personal obligation to make a success of one's life. More strongly expressed are expectations on families and public services to support and promote each child's development: the 'team around the child' (Siraj-Blatchford et al., 2007). Schools and education authorities have in particular been made increasingly accountable for their actions, most notably through inspection, self-evaluation and public reporting of outcomes (Ofsted, 2015).

Hungary

Educators and others in Hungary are less reluctant than those in England to employ the term 'pedagogy' (*pedagógia*) when discussing their work. A kindergarten teacher is an *óvodapedagógus*, kindergarten pedagogue. Educators in training study 'History of Pedagogy', 'Psychology for Pedagogy' and, on early-years courses, 'Pedagogy for Kindergarten'. Strategies for teaching have a different name: *Módszertan*, 'Methodology'.

This is not surprising, as the discourse of social and educational pedagogy is traditionally rooted in Central Europe, and further east in the former Soviet Union. Pedagogical ideas have come, for instance, from the Soviet Belarusian psychologist, Lev Vygotsky, and the lesser known Soviet Ukrainian pedagogue, Vasyl Sukhomlinsky. Drawing from these and other influences, here are three pedagogical outlooks pertinent to Hungarian early-years education and workforce training:

Collective values

Hungary draws on less individualistic, more collective pedagogical traditions than England. Under socialist government between 1945 and 1989, education reflected the idea that a citizen's duty was more to the community and the state than to oneself. While the child's growth of identity was important, 'a preference for a community way of life should become a characteristic of each child's personality' (Millei, 2011:41). Despite the incorporation of more capitalist values and practices within society as a whole since then, collective sentiments remain a central pedagogical outlook.

Socialisation

Education in Hungary, as in England, can be and is described as 'child-centred' (for example, OECD, 2004). However, in Hungary, the interactive relationship between child and others (other children, parents, educators, community) receives greater emphasis in pedagogical thinking. Vygotsky's perspectives emphasised social interaction as the route for children's development and learning. Sukhomlinsky expressed the need to nurture the child's 'inner need for human fellowship' (in Cockerill, 2009:31), the platform being processes 'of experiencing wonder at the many facets and inexhaustibility of human nature' (2009:11).

The role of educators

Even more significantly, in Hungary, adults are seen to lead children's development in this respect. This process is reliant on moral personality as much as on particular procedures, emphasising the social rather than technical role of educators in shaping children's lives: 'We educate first and foremost, not with this or that variety of methods or techniques, but through the influence of our own personality, of our individuality' (Cockerill, 2009:7).

Discussion: Outlooks in training

James is training to be an early-years educator in England. When asked to identify a pedagogical outlook underlying his work and learning, he chooses a phrase used by the New Labour Government a decade earlier: 'Every child matters'. He explains that every child should develop and learn as an individual, and that each child's efforts, potential and particular ways of learning deserve attention and support.

Eszter is training to be an early-years educator in Hungary. For her, an important pedagogical outlook is that children's overall development is led by the personality and example of adults, most notably the teacher or educator. Furthermore, development and learning are first and foremost addressed not for each child on a separate basis but as features of activity for a whole group of other children and adults.

What are your opinions of these pedagogical outlooks? To what extent do you see them underpinning your own experiences in early-childhood education and workforce training? What challenges do educators face when seeking to strengthen and maintain such outlooks?

Care, education, 'upbringing'

Discussion now extends to two pedagogical outlooks, which warrant separate scrutiny. The first relates to perspectives on care, education and, in Hungarian terms, 'upbringing'.

England

In England, childcare for the very youngest children has traditionally been a private concern, with governmental or municipal support focussed on cases of crisis or severe disadvantage. The Government's *Birth to Three Matters* framework (DfES, 2002) was an effort to regard it as a more public responsibility and to focus attention on healthy development of children within childcare arrangements. Now, the early-years curricular framework (DfE, 2014) relates to all children from birth to five, and, as noted at the start of this chapter, arrangements for training increasingly so as well. Overall, however, the sector endures a gap in status compared with the rest of the educational system, evidenced, for instance, in differential workforce pay and conditions noted above.

Technical characteristics of the English educational system can also be seen to affect adversely the early-years sector. A comparative study by Broadfoot et al. (2000:3), for instance, found in England 'a discourse rooted in a rationalist vocabulary of scientific measurement – of standards and scales; of objective judgements and comparisons'. Early-years professionals have often resisted this discourse, but, nevertheless, both provision and workforce training are patrolled by the same long-standing and robust 'Ofsted' inspection system as other parts of the educational system. While perhaps creating unity, this also brings dominant school values to an early-years sector, which may feel it needs something rather different. Leach (2011), for instance, has critically reflected that such operational measures take educators away from thinking innovatively about how to influence and envigorate growth and development of children and how to engage parents in that process.

Hungary

Hungary has similar issues, emerging most noticeably in separate models of *bölcsőde* (childcare centres) and *óvoda* (kindergarten). With attendance at kindergarten now compulsory from the age of three, this provision has a status approaching that of education for older children. This does not apply to the *bölcsőde*, however, where low take-up by families is accompanied by low pay and status for its workforce (Cameron and Moss, 2007).

In terms of pedagogy, however, Hungary has an important, unifying concept for early care, development and learning, that of *nevelés*. The closest translation of this word is 'upbringing', or perhaps 'nurturing', terms largely absent from professional early-years literature in England, as both commonly refer in English discourse to the role of parents, rather than to that of society as a whole.

For Korintus (2012:4), *nevelés* is a holistic, all-inclusive concept, encompassing not just care (*gondoskodás*) and education (*oktatás*) 'but also health, behaviour, and social skills – everything needed in life'. It conveys the notion that when you provide care (as a parent or professional), you also directly or indirectly nurture and teach children as well. In this sense, *nevelés* relates to the notion of 'pedagogy', examined above. Indeed, Vygotsky's (1991:31) seminal definition (in Russian) related pedagogy to this concept: *'Pedagogika – nauka o vospitanii detyei'* – pedagogy is the science of the upbringing of children. Kraevskii (2002), writing about Russia, and Smith (2013) about Scotland, similarly delineated upbringing as a pedagogical task, one that exceeds narrow transmission of knowledge, skills and experience, the aim being rather: '...to inculcate particular qualities of personality (humanness, morality, independence, the ability to be creative, and so on)' (Kraevskii, 2002:84).

Discussion: 'Upbringing' or 'care and education'?

What is your understanding of these terms? How might a holistic notion of 'upbringing' differ from dual notions of 'care' and 'education'? How are these concepts reflected in your own experiences in early-years provision and workforce training?

Curriculum

The second outlook to receive extended attention relates to the curricular experiences of children during their early care and education.

England

The 1933 Hadow Report recommended that between the ages of two and five, children should be 'surrounded with objects and materials which will afford scope for experiment and exploration' (Board of Education, 1933:179). Ideas presented should be 'very simple and few at a time;

oral lessons should be short and closely related to the child's practical interests' (1933:182). Today's curricular basis is provided by the 'Early Years Foundation Stage' (EYFS) framework for children from birth to five, originally presented in 2007 and regularly updated. This 'sets the standards that all early years providers must meet to ensure that children learn and develop well and are kept healthy and safe' (DfE, 2014:5).

The EYFS is not a programme or syllabus, rather it is a delineation of appropriate standards, areas and goals for learning, and requirements for assessment in the early years. The four 'guiding principles' that should 'shape' activities and experiences are 'every child is a unique child'; 'children learn … through positive relationships'; they 'learn and develop well in enabling environments' and they develop and learn in different ways and at different rates' (DfE, 2014:6). These resonate with recommendations of earlier government-commissioned, evaluative studies, which highlighted correlation between the quality of social interactions and positive outcomes in children's development. They are a reminder, too, of the alignment of pedagogy with practice, which was noted earlier in this chapter.

Play

The main pedagogical platform in the EYFS is 'play', although writers have highlighted limitations in how this is advocated. Leach, for instance, was sceptical about any links with particular learning outcomes, suggesting that play cannot underpin the curriculum, as 'children play because that is what children do' (2011:27).

'Schoolification'

With its early entry into formal schooling (England's starting point of age five, in practice sometimes four, is among the lowest in the world), it is perhaps not surprising that activities redolent of the national school curriculum, such as early reading and writing, find their way into the curriculum for very young children, accompanied by strong focus on monitoring of outcomes. OECD (2006:62) called this tendency (as others have done) 'schoolification'.

The issue can be conceptualised as the integration of children's cognitive or intellectual development, on the one hand, and social or moral development, on the other, and what sort of balance best helps children first to grow, then eventually benefit from formal education in school. The complaints are that an intellectual focus has crowded out wider concerns, more appropriate and necessary for the very young child. A positive conclusion is that the English outlook seeks to combine both of these concerns in a humanistic approach – a desire to see children do well at their education and to develop as fair, reasonable and responsible human beings, as well. The issue, however, continues to cause apprehension (for example, Clausen, 2015), with calls for an opposite influence, either extending activity appropriate for early years into the school curriculum or a higher school starting age overall (Palmer, 2009; Morton, 2013).

Hungary

Two separate National Core Programmes provide the curricular basis for care and education (or *nevelés*) in Hungary. The curriculum for children under three is the Hungarian Core

Programme for Childcare (Szociálpolitikai és Munkaügyi Intézet, 2008), the other is the Hungarian Core Programme of Kindergarten Education (Oktatási Hivatal, 1996), originally formulated by Bakonyi and Szabadi (1971) and most recently updated in 2013 (Hungarian Institute for Educational Research and Development, 2015). Each kindergarten setting must develop this framework by 'adopting or adapting one or creating their own' (Villányi, 2012:10), taking into account in particular local needs and traditions. Accredited curricula that can help with this process include some well-known elsewhere, for instance, Steiner-Waldorf and Montessori (European Commission/EACEA/Eurydice, 2015), as well as others less commonly recognised. These include an 'activity-based' programme, which prioritises children's cooperation and communication; a 'Development of Movement' programme, which promotes a physically active lifestyle and 'Green Kindergarten', which incorporates principles of sustainability and ecological education (Villányi, 2012). In this respect, Varga *et al.* (2015:8) have claimed that 'Hungary offers an example of where early childhood education and care providers are offered relative autonomy in their approach, when contrasted to the heavily regulated systems that are present in the UK'. This autonomy, albeit relative, is evidence of how Hungarian education has become more diverse since the more prescribed and centralised system under socialism.

Overall, Hungarian curricula have reflected rather more established perspectives than the more recently developed English equivalent. The kindergarten curriculum incorporates play, health habits, physical education, mathematics, mother tongue, literature, art, music and knowledge of social and natural worlds, including the world of work. This reflects the traditional notion of education in which 'everything is important – the lessons, the development of diverse interest, and the interpersonal relationship between the students in the group' (Cockerill, 2009:29), as well as the idea that education should prepare young children for their contribution to common good and growth of society (Millei, 2011). While ultimately focussed on achieving children's readiness for school at age six or seven, the Hungarian emphasis seems to be to do this without unduly imitating the academic concerns associated with schooling itself.

Play

Lakatos (2012) explains how the National Core Programme of Kindergarten Education gives high priority to playing as the primary form of children's kindergarten activity. She recommends that teachers should position themselves between 'overcontrol' and 'zero involvement', relying on 'their methodological culture and the knowledge of children in deciding when to interfere, when to play together and when to help, always respecting the principles of free play, first and foremost of which is that the ruler of this domain is the child' (2012:5).

Folk traditions

Lakatos' description of play may sound similar to its equivalent in England, and indeed elsewhere. One aspect where it differs, however, is the greater emphasis given in Hungarian practice to promoting traditional songs, group games and regional customs within children's activity. According to Varga *et al.* (2015), the 1891 *Law of Infant Care* stated that there was no place for scholastic education in kindergartens, but that emphasis should be placed on folk traditions and use of natural elements found in Hungary. O'Donnell's (2001) international review noted similarly, pointing out how the *Core Programme* document recommended use of games, poems, music, singing, drawing, modelling, crafts and movement in order to achieve its aims with young children. Despite fluctuations over many years, the importance of these 'Hungarian peculiarities' (Varga *et al.*, 2015:111) remains very evident in curriculum and workforce training today. An even more specialised focus on these is another accredited option for kindergartens when developing their curriculum (Villányi, 2012).

Discussion: Curriculum

England has one curricular framework, relevant for work with young children from birth to five. Hungary has two: one for children up to the age of three, the other for three- to six-year-olds. In your view, which approach is more appropriate? What are the implications of this for training of the workforce?

Conclusion

This chapter has examined a range of pedagogical outlooks underpinning early-years education and workforce training in the two countries. By no means, everything is different between them, and where there is a difference, it may be in emphasis, rather than complete. This is hardly surprising – the general aims of helping young children to grow and develop are similar, and it would be odd if there were huge disparities in how it was felt this should be achieved.

However, there are differences as follows: more long-standing state commitment to young children in Hungary, more rapid, recent development in England; individualistic values in England, more collective outlooks in Hungary; concepts in one country largely absent from professional discourse in the other. There may be other differences, too, which readers have picked out from this text or which emerge from further scrutiny.

Both countries, of course, have challenges to be faced and addressed. In England, one might include the continuing creation of a consistently trained workforce throughout the sector, as well as determining a firm set of pedagogical values to underpin their work. The debate over how an early-years curriculum relates to demands of compulsory schooling reflects continuing uncertainty. The UK's imminent withdrawal from the European Union might also affect opportunities for professionals to learn from thinking and practice elsewhere.

Hungary's challenges are no less onerous. They include establishing equal educational opportunities for disadvantaged groups, most notably children with disabilities and those of Roma heritage (Hungarian Institute for Educational Research and Development, 2015). There is also the task of organisationally and financially sustaining and unifying a comprehensive early care and education system, including recruitment and maintenance of a more diverse and younger workforce (OECD, 2004).

This scrutiny of similarities, differences and challenges in England and Hungary has therefore created a nuanced comparison of outlooks in the two countries. This chapter ends by inviting readers themselves to consider what might be learnt from those that have been examined.

Discussion: Lessons for early education and workforce training

If you are English, what might be learnt from Hungarian outlooks? If you are Hungarian, what might be learnt from English outlooks? If you are neither of these, how might the early education and workforce training, which you have experienced benefit from understanding of the pedagogical outlooks identified and discussed in this chapter?

Recommended reading

Faulkner, D. and Coates, E.A. (2013) Early childhood policy and practice in England: twenty years of change. *International Journal of Early Years Education*, 21(2/3), 244–263. Available at: http://oro.open. ac.uk/38133/64/ECPCombined.pdf.
This article 'offers a chronological account and critical appraisal of changes to … services in England over the past 20 years'. Four main areas are covered: policies to reduce social inequality; professionalization of the workforce; changes to pedagogy and curriculum; and the impact of research.

Hidashi, J. (2010) A successful kindergarten model in Hungary. *Child Research Net*. www.childresearch.net/ projects/ecec/2010_08.html.
Drawing on official documents, the author provides a very readable summary of provision and workforce training in Hungary and considers challenges for further development.

Miller, L. and Cameron, C. (Eds.) (2014) *International Perspectives in the Early Years*. London: Sage.
This book critically examines a range of themes, including the relationship between early-years and primary education, inclusive access to public services for Roma people, and gendering of the workforce.

References

Abrahamson, L. (2015) *The Early Years Teacher's Book: Achieving Early Years Teacher Status*. London: Learning Matters/SAGE.
Alexander, R. (2004) Still no pedagogy? Principle, pragmatism and compliance in primary education. *Cambridge Journal of Education*, 34(1), 7–33.
Bakonyi, P. and Szabadi, I. (1971) *Az Óvodai Nevelés Programja*. Budapest: Tankönyvkiadó, Országos Pedagógiai Intézet.
Basford, J. (2008) The early years foundation stage: principles into practice. In J. Basford and E. Hodson (Eds.) *Teaching the Early Years Foundation Stage*. Exeter: Learning Matters.
Board of Education (1933) *Infant and Nursery Schools* (The Hadow Report). Report of the Consultative Committee. London: HMSO. Available at: www.educationengland.org.uk/documents/hadow1933/ hadow1933.html. (Accessed 1st September 2016).
Broadfoot, P., Osborn, M., Planel, C. and Sharpe, K. (2000) *Promoting Quality in Learning: Does England Have the Answer?* London: Cassell.
Brooker, L. and Broadbent, L. (2003) Personal, social and emotional development: the child makes meaning in a social world. In L. Brooker (Ed.) *Learning in the Early Years: A Guide for Teachers from 3 to 7*. London: Paul Chapman.
Cameron, C. and Moss, P. (2007) *Care Work in Europe: Current Understandings and Future Directions*. London: Routledge.
Central Advisory Council for Education (England) (1967) *Children and Their Primary Schools, Vol. 1: The Report* (The Plowden Report). London: HMSO.
Clausen, S.B. (2015) Schoolification or early years democracy? A cross-curricular perspective from Denmark and England. *Contemporary Issues in Early Childhood*, 16(4), 355–373.
Cockerill, A. (2009) *Each One Must Shine: The Educational Legacy of V.A. Sukhomlinsky*. Sydney: EJR Language Service Pvt Ltd.
Cox, C.B. and Boyson, R. (1975) *Black Paper 1975: The Fight for Education*. London: Dent.

Dávid, M. and Podráczky, J. (2012) Teacher training and in-service training: conveying the basic values and learning how to implement them. In Hungarian Institute for Educational Research and Development (2012) *Early Childhood Education and Care: Specificities of the Hungarian System*. Budapest: HIERD.

Dewey, J. (1900) *The School and Society*, 2nd edition. Chicago, IL: University of Chicago Press.

DfE (2012) *Foundations for Quality: The Independent Review of Early Education and Childcare Qualifications* (The Nutbrown Review). London: Department for Education.

DfE (2014) *Statutory Framework for the Early Years Foundation Stage: Setting the Standards for Learning, Development and Care for Children from Birth to Five*. London: Department for Education.

DfE (2016) *Provision for Children under Five years of Age in England, January 2016*. Statistical First Release (SFR) 23/2016. Available at: www.gov.uk/government/uploads/system/uploads/attachment_data/file/532575/SFR23_2016_Text.pdf. (Accessed 1st September 2016).

DfES (2002) *Birth to Three Matters*. London: Department for Education and Skills.

European Commission/EACEA/Eurydice (2015). *Early Childhood Education and Care Systems in Europe. National Information Sheets 2014/15*. Eurydice – Facts and Figures. Luxembourg: Publications Office of the European Union. Available at: http://eacea.ec.europa.eu/education/eurydice. (Accessed 2nd September 2016).

Halász, G. (2015) Education and social transformation in Central and Eastern Europe. *European Journal of Education* 50(3), 350–371.

HM Government (2005) Children's workforce strategy: a strategy to build a world-class workforce for children and young people. Consultation document. Available at: www.education.gov.uk/consultations/downloadabledocs/5958-dfes-ecm.pdf. (Accessed 3rd September 2016).

Hungarian Institute for Educational Research and Development (2015) *Education for All 2015 National Review Report: Hungary*. UNESCO. Available at: http://unesdoc.unesco.org/images/0022/002299/229933E.pdf. (Accessed 2nd September 2016).

Kalitowski, S. (2016) *Towards an Early Years Workforce Development Strategy for England*. Bromley: PACEY Professional Association for Childcare and Early Years. Available at: www.pacey.org.uk/working-in-childcare/workforce-development-policy-briefing-jan16.pdf. (Accessed 2nd September 2016).

Korintus, M. (2012) The holistic meaning of 'nevelés' in Hungarian language: ECEC terminology in Hungarian. In Hungarian Institute for Educational Research and Development, *Early Childhood Education and Care: Specificities of the Hungarian system*. Budapest: HIERD.

Kraevskii, V.V. (2002) Upbringing or education? *Russian Education and Society*, 44(8), 81–94.

Lakatos, M. (2012) Basic principles of free play as reflected in the National Core Curriculum of Kindergarten Education. In Hungarian Institute for Educational Research and Development, *Early Childhood Education and Care: Specificities of the Hungarian System*. Budapest: HIERD.

Leach, P. (2011) The EYFS and the real foundations of children's early years. In R. House (Ed.) *Too Much, Too Soon? Early Learning and the Erosion of Childhood*. Stroud: Hawthorn Press.

Miell, D. (1995) Developing a sense of self. In P. Barnes (ed) *Personal, Social and Emotional Development of Children*. Oxford: Blackwell.

Millei, Z. (2011) Governing through early childhood curriculum, 'the child', and 'community': ideologies of socialist Hungary and neoliberal Australia. *European Education*, 43(1), 33–35.

Morton, K. (2013) Research shows growing concerns over 'schoolification' of early years. *Nursery World*, 27 September 2013. Available at: www.nurseryworld.co.uk/nursery-world/news/1119569/research-growing-concerns-schoolification. (Accessed 4th September 2016).

National Information: Hungary (2010). *EASE Early Years Transition Programme*. Available at: www.ease-eu.com/documentation.html. (Accessed 4th September 2016).

O'Donnell, S. (2001) *International Review of Curriculum and Assessment Frameworks. Thematic Probe: Early Years Education*. Slough: National Foundation for Educational Research.

OECD (2004) *Early Childhood Education and Care Policy: Country Note for Hungary*. Paris: OECD.

OECD (2006) *Starting Strong II: Early Childhood Education and Care*. Paris: OECD.

Ofsted (2015): *Early Years Inspection Handbook*. Available at: www.gov.uk/government/publications/early-years-inspection-handbook-from-september-2015. (Accessed 5th September 2016).

Oktatási Hivatal (1996) *Az Óvodai Nevelés Országos Alapprogramja*. Budapest: 363/2012. (XII. 17.) Kormányrendelet.

Pákozdi, M. (2012) Flexible start of school. In Hungarian Institute for Educational Research and Development, *Early Childhood Education and Care: Specificities of the Hungarian System*. Budapest: HEIRD.

Palmer, S. (2009) Four years bad. Six years good. Seven years optimal. *Literacy Today*, 61, 7. Available at: www.suepalmer.co.uk/modern_childhood_articles_four_years.php. (Accessed 6th September 2016).

Parker-Rees, R. (2007) Liking to be liked: imitation, familiarity and pedagogy in the first years of life. *Early Years*, 27(1), 3–17.

Rozsahegyi, T. and Lambert, M. (2016) Pedagogy for inclusion? In Z. Brown (Ed.) *Inclusive Education: Perspectives on Pedagogy, Policy and Practice*. Abingdon: Routledge.

Simon, B. (1981) Why no pedagogy in England? In B. Simon and W. Taylor, *Education in the Eighties: The Central Issues*. London: Batsford.

Siraj-Blatchford, I., Clarke, K. and Needham, M. (2007) *The Team around the Child: Multi-agency Working in the Early Years*. Stoke-on-Trent: Trentham Books.

Siraj-Blatchford, I., Sylva, K., Muttock, S., Gilden, R. and Bell, D. (2002) *Researching Effective Pedagogy in the Early Years*. Norwich: HMSO.

Smedley, S. (1997) Personality, professionalism and politics: what does it mean to be an early years teacher? In S. Robson and S. Smedley (Eds.) *Education in Early Childhood: First Things First*. London: David Fulton/ Roehampton Institute.

Smith, M. (2013) Forgotten connections: reviving the concept of upbringing in Scottish child welfare. *Scottish Journal of Residential Child Care*, 12(2), 13–29.

Stephen, C. (2010) Pedagogy: the silent partner in early years learning. *Early Years*, 30(1), 15–28.

Szociálpolitikai és Munkaügyi Intézet (2008) *A Bölcsődei Nevelés-Gondozás Alapprogramja*. Budapest: Szociálpolitikai és Munkaügyi Intézet.

Taguchi, H.L. (2010) Rethinking pedagogical practices in early childhood education: a multidimensional approach to learning and inclusion. In N. Yelland (Ed.) *Contemporary Perspectives on Early Childhood Education*. Maidenhead: Open University Press.

Varga, A.N., Molnár, B., Pálfi, S. and Szerepi, S. (2015) Hungarian perspectives on early years workforce development. In V. Campbell-Barr and J. Georgeson (2015) *International Perspectives on Early Years Workforce: Critical Approaches to the Early Years*. Northwich: Critical Publishing.

Villányi, J. (2012) The types of kindergarten curricula. In Hungarian Institute for Educational Research and Development (2012) *Early Childhood Education and Care: Specificities of the Hungarian System*. Budapest: HEIRD.

Vygotsky, L.S. (1991) Pedagogika i Psikhologiya. In V.V. Davydova (Ed.) *Pedagogicheskaya Psikhologiya*. Moscow: Pedagogika.

Wall, S., Litjens, I. and Taguma, M. (2015) *Pedagogy in Early Childhood Education and Care (ECEC): An International Comparative Study of Approaches and Policies*. London: Department for Education/OECD.

4 Spiritual, moral, social and cultural education in Dutch and English primary schools

Sarah Elsey

Introduction

This chapter provides an understanding of the links between practice and policies in *spiritual, moral, social and cultural* (SMSC) education in primary schooling in the Netherlands and Britain. It includes findings from a small-scale research study in English and Dutch schools designed to investigate, illustrate and compare the practical realities of teaching a SMSC curriculum with case studies of good practice.

In England, Wales and Northern Ireland, SMSC falls within the provision of *personal, social, health and economic* (PSHE) education. But the landscape is changing and the National Curriculum (DfE, 2013) states that SMSC provision should be interwoven within other key areas of learning, while the 2015 Ofsted framework for schools recommends that SMSC development will be a significant focus in inspections (Ofsted, 2015). In Dutch primary schools, however, these key issues are housed in 'social and environmental studies', which also covers geography, history, biology, citizenship, road safety and political studies.

Historical context

This section provides an overview of primary policy and practice in the education systems of the Netherlands and England, Wales and Northern Ireland.

The Netherlands

In the late 1970s, in the Netherlands, educators witnessed the gradual reconfiguration of primary education that resulted in the Primary Education Act of 1981, now known as WPO (Wet Primair Onderwijs, law for primary education, Netherlands Statutes, 1998). The vision was to provide a child-centred education to cater for pupils' emotional, social and cognitive needs. The WPO came into force on 1 August 1998, replacing the Primary Education Act (1981) and the Special Education Interim Act (1995). The earlier Education Act (1969) stated that every child must attend school from the first school day of the month following its fifth birthday. Children are expected to attend primary school full time until they are 12 years old. The Dutch education system is characterised by the two overarching principles of 'freedom of education' and 'equal state support' for public and private schools (Karsten, 1994). A number of regulatory frameworks ensure that education is inclusive and available for all.

'Freedom of education', a key feature of the Dutch system, is guaranteed under Article 23 of the Constitution. This refers to the freedom to found schools, to organise the teaching in schools and to determine the philosophical principles on which they are based. This freedom is, however, limited by the standards set by the Ministry of Education, Culture and Science. These standards, which apply to both public and private education, prescribe the subjects to be studied, and other administrative elements such as the qualifications that teachers are required to have, planning and reporting obligations and the right for parents and pupils to have a say in school matters.

The WPO was revisited in the 1980s to ensure that education would continue to focus on the holistic development of children with equal regard for their cognitive and emotional learning and a maintained emphasis on child-centred learning. In 1985, the WPO lowered the starting age for compulsory education from six to five years, abolished separate nursery schools and brought provision for four- and five-year-olds into primary education (*Basisschool*). Although education is not compulsory until age five, nearly all children attend school from the age of four.

England, Wales and Northern Ireland

In England, Wales and Northern Ireland, before changes to the National Curriculum in 2013, PSHE helped schools to achieve their statutory obligations, in particular, the requirement of all state schools to deliver a balanced and broadly based curriculum. Under section 78 of the Education Act (2002), an underpinning principle was that educators were to provide an education that 'promotes the spiritual, moral, cultural, mental and physical development of pupils at the school and of society' and 'prepares pupils at the school for the opportunities, responsibilities and experiences of later life'. Two years later, 'well-being' was added to the Children Act (2004) and the 'well-being requirement' introduced. Well-being is defined in the Act as the promotion of physical and mental health; emotional, social and economic well-being; engagement in education, training and recreation; recognising the contribution made by children to society and protection from harm and neglect. Both the Education Act (2002) and the Academies Act (2010) confirmed that PSHE contributes to schools' statutory duties to provide a balanced and broadly based curriculum. The Academies Act (2010), as in 2002, stipulated that provision should promote pupils' spiritual, moral, cultural, mental and physical development and prepare them for the opportunities, responsibilities and experiences of later life. These are also in line with the Ofsted judgements (2015) in relation to personal development, behaviour, welfare and safeguarding.

In February 2013, the DfE launched a consultation on a revised National Curriculum that came into effect in September 2014. While PSHE continues to sit outside of the statutory National Curriculum, the DfE made it clear in their 'framework document for consultation' that 'all schools should make provision for personal, social, health and economic education (PSHE), drawing on good practice' (DfE, 2013). Elements of sex and drugs education were to remain within the science curriculum.

Evidence from the literature concludes that well-delivered PSHE programmes have an impact on both academic and non-academic outcomes for pupils, particularly the most vulnerable and disadvantaged (Weare and Gray, 2003; PSHE Association, 2016). As stated previously, PSHE is a non-statutory subject in England, but despite this, the majority of English schools include it within their curriculum (Ofsted, 2015). The obligations felt by most practitioners are to continue to provide learning environments with a range of opportunities that ensure children progress both emotionally and socially. All practitioners thus have a duty to report to parents on this area of development. In order to do this, some form of teacher judgement needs to take place.

The PSHE Association (2016) suggests that there should be regular opportunities for learners to reflect and identify what has been learnt. They should also be able to set expectations for their own learning and become aware of their abilities. Furthermore, it suggests that more emphasis should be placed on achievements and progression rather than on failure. Moss and Brookhart (2012:24) advise that targets and levels should be personal and 'teachers should always check for understanding' and ask 'children to put their own learning goals in their own words'.

Nicky Morgan, Secretary of State for Education from July 2014 to July 2016, stated that PSHE as a whole was not compulsory for schools, despite many campaigning for it to be so. This decision was made, despite concerns being flagged regarding the quality of PSHE, (MacDonald, 2009). In 2015, Caroline Lucas, the Green Party's MP, tabled a bill to make the subject compulsory, saying, 'As well as being an essential part of safeguarding our children, PSHE has huge potential in relation to employability and academic attainment. PSHE teaches young people the skills they need to make good choices and to think things through' (BBC, 2015). As discussed previously, PSHE has to be taught to a high standard so that children's development is not hindered or affected enabling them to develop into confident individuals.

Individual/group task

- Teachers are said to bring their own beliefs and values into the classroom. What are your values and beliefs and where do these stem from?
- Who else influences and shapes children's beliefs and values?

Comparative research project on SMSC

The small-scale project was intended to compare the provision of SMSC in primary education in England and the Netherlands. Questionnaires were sent to seven schools in the West Midlands and three in the Randstad region of the Netherlands. The schools are part of the author's professional network, and, as such, the findings are illustrative. The examples included present distinctive elements of SMSC practice and provide starting points for further reflection. The questionnaire responses were collated and analysed using a process of thematic coding. In the interests of confidentiality, all information about the schools, staff and children is reported here anonymously.

Instances of good practice from primary schools in both countries illustrate that schools have their own distinctive philosophies and pedagogies. The examples of practice are unique to the educational settings but there is one thread that is common throughout – the overall ontological views around the provision for social and emotional development of those primary school children. The findings are reported here under a series of themes, each with references to the background literature.

Theme 1 – school mission

All members of the Dutch and English school leadership teams in the study furnish and share a mission statement with all stakeholders in order to provide a collective understanding of 'why we are here'. Many schools have developed mission statements that encapsulate the fundamental values of the school. These are shared and echoed around the school in the classrooms and during whole-school weekly collaborative events such as assemblies. Some schools also outline the expectations of staff, parents and children in their role of working towards a supportive caring environment. A respondent from English School A commented:

> Linking heavily with our school's mission statement, our school drives five key values which apply to all staff and children. Our 'acronym' values underpin our school ethos, around tolerance, respect, ownership, happiness and cooperation. These values link to SMSC too and are promoted in each class, in each lesson, in each aspect of the children's academic journey.

English School C echoed this, commenting 'our mission statement is – all God's children learning and achieving together. We refer to this daily through our professional manner and teaching but also we have other values to share to including British Values'.

With the subject not being statutory in England, some teachers in the study – despite their passion – made it clear that due to timetabling constraints, PSHE is often marginalised. One PSHE lead said the main concern was about the non-statutory nature of PSHE in her school, leading to staff either not engaging with PSHE at all or engaging at a minimum level due to other curriculum pressures, 'the things the government has defined as being important'. As a result, there is a 'disincentive for schools to focus on non-statutory subjects such as PSHE', as one teacher commented. Therefore, PSHE's existence in any given school can be dependent upon the head teacher's views on allocating time to pupils' wider well-being.

Individual/group task

- What can you foresee happening in the future if SMSC remains non-statutory?

Theme 2 – teaching resilience

In January 2016, the UK Prime Minister, David Cameron, said in his life chances speech (DfE, 2016), 'our aim in politics should be to give every child the chance to dream big dreams, and the tools-the character, the knowledge and the confidence that will let their potential shine brightly'. There have been milestones where the UK government has been investing in the principles of developing character building. Nicky Morgan said, 'all schoolchildren will be taught a "curriculum for life" to give them the "emotional resilience" to cope with the modern internet age' (The Telegraph, 2015).

Rowley and Cooper (2009:151) state that 'resilience should be taught in a cross-curricular way through a range of approaches'. For example, in the history curriculum, children learn how 'their own lives are affected by historical influences', which is linked to the history key concept, 'cause and consequence' (Cooper, 2005; DfE, 2013) and in geography, they learn how they are affected by 'geographical and environmental factors'.

Resilience is the 'capability to recover from a crisis, setback or disaster' (Meichenbaum, 2006:4). This suggests that traumatic events can impact a child's education, whether at school or home (Goddard *et al.*, 2013). Garmezy's theory on resilience includes diverse aspects such as cognitive skills, motivation and other protective facts, which can be implemented to support children (Masten *et al.*, 1990). Werner (2013) explained the term 'protective factors' as individual or environmental characteristics, conditions or behaviours that reduce the effects of stressful life events. Garmezy also put forward three factors that appear common in resilience – an individual input largely associated with temperament and intelligence, family support and external support from outside the family such as schools (Goddard *et al.*, 2013).

One teacher in English School E believed

> that our values can and will be often challenged and we have to be understanding of that. That others may not share the values we hold but we need to stay true to ourselves and operate with integrity and honesty. Children's resilience is crucial as this helps them deal with differing opinion and unexpected and challenging situations.

English School A's senior management team added in a similar vein:

> As a school we like children to see that learning is a challenge and sometimes may be tricky. But we also show that things are tricky for us as teachers as we are their role-models whilst in school. We show the children that it is alright to get things wrong as we all do. We try and teach children to persevere and have determination to go back and try again. If everything was easy we would all be perfect. It's about trying your best and being yourself.

In the Netherlands, a teacher commented on the support provided through key questioning as a whole class ethos:

> Encouraging children to accept that 'failure' is OK as it is part of the learning process. In my classroom we often refer to 'What's the worst that can happen?' when answering questions. When they realise that it is all right to make errors their contributions are more forthcoming.

Individual/group task

Research the Child and Adolescent Mental Health Service (CAMHS) and School Attendance Project (2016), and consider these questions:

- What are the characteristics of a resilient child?
- What are the challenges that face any practitioner working with these children?
- Have you any experience of how primary schools support the teaching of resilience?
- Teaching resilience could be perceived as an abstract notion, but Dutch schools encourage children to be independent and have 'bouncebackability'. How does the pedagogy of Montessori (widespread in the Netherlands) support this?

Theme 3 – opportunities for children to understand societal values and be 'global citizens'

Researchers, experts and teachers agree on the importance of the school culture for the development of values and norms (Higgins-d'Allessandro and Sadh, 1997), but it is clear there is little consensus on the terminology employed. Various terms are used, each with their own tradition and theoretical position (Veugelers, 2000). For instance, the English literature refers to 'values education', 'character education', 'moral education', 'personal and social education', 'citizenship education', 'civic education', 'religious education' and 'democratic education'. Values are expressed through subjective judgements (attitudes) and through behaviour (Berkowitz and Gibbs, 1983; Veugelers and Vedder, 2003). Teachers are supposed to prepare children to function in a democratic society: to educate them for citizenship (Klaassen, 1996). Citizenship in the view of Dutch researchers relates not only to the public domain but also to the areas of work (Veugelers, 1995), care (Dam and Volman, 1998) and international orientation (Karsten, 1999).

At the turn of the twenty-first century, England redesigned the curriculum, moving learning towards a more personalised approach in a bid to prepare children better for their place in society and an ever-changing economic landscape. In 2003, the 'Every Child Matters' agenda (DfES, 2003) emphasised that the curriculum should focus more on creative aspects, and with this the child-centred philosophy of the Plowden Report (Central Advisory Council for Education, 1967) had arguably come full circle. It also saw a renewed emphasis on inclusion for pupils with special needs. In 2015, the Education Secretary additionally asked for values to be covered in PSHE lessons in schools. In England, since November 2014, schools must promote 'British values' through SMSC, and this aspect was to be assessed through inspection. Ofsted (2015) expect to see a school ethos and climate that promote 'British values' at every level; SMSC provision has become a key factor when deciding a school's status as 'outstanding', 'inadequate' or somewhere in between. According to Ofsted (2015), 'fundamental British values' are democracy, the rule of law, individual liberty, mutual respect for and tolerance of those with different faiths and beliefs and for those without faith. The Government set out its definition of British values in the 2011 Prevent Strategy, and these values were reiterated in 2014 Government documentation (DfE, 2015).

When asked for their views on teaching primary children about 'values', the seven English respondents agreed that parents and home life was an area of consideration for the practitioner. One English respondent (School A) stated, 'their (children's) current values, their experiences to date, their home life and other social aspects contributed to who they are'. A teacher from School D in the Netherlands said, 'You have to consider the values their parents may hold and also what the current affairs are as these can all be influencing factors on young children'. One English respondent linked values to religion: 'That all children are unique and we do have to consider religions and nationalities, but as a Church school we are all about the learning and giving children a good and happy education'. One Dutch respondent explained, '...we work with the method "kanjertraining" and we teach the children to realise and respect those goals'. ('Kanjertraining' is a Dutch system for helping children with relationships.)

Democracy encourages pupils to understand others' views, values and feelings, showing them they have a right to be part of their school. This is delivered by pupils being able to vote for a leader to voice their own opinions across to their fellow peers and teachers in school. It helps pupils 'to be well prepared for the democratic process that rules the country' (School A). It can impact on the pupils' 'social development as they have to speak their views therefore projecting their opinions whilst standing their ground to prove their point' (School C). This encourages children to become 'confident in expressing their views and develop a skill of public-speaking that will help in the future' (School E). A respondent from School B added, 'We have a student council and each class has two representatives – they are responsible for feeding back to the rest of the class and they have key responsibilities within that that they must fulfil'.

Schools shared examples of how children are taught to respect the right of individuals to have their voices and opinions heard, and how classes develop their own rules charter, which they sign to ensure ownership and cooperation. Children's views are heard through such initiatives as Eco-schools, (Foundation for Environmental Education (FEE), 2011; Keep Britain Tidy, 2016), school council, circle time and questionnaires. Some schools have a house and deputy captain to represent pupil voice and children are given opportunities to make decisions about things that affect them in school, such as equipment they would like to be purchased. In the Netherlands, the schools shared good practice where the children's voice was heard through circle time and children's committees from all years throughout the school.

'Individual liberty' enhances pupils' confidence and ability to choose between right and wrong and make their own decisions inside and outside school. Lessons delivered in schools are designed to enable children to lead learning as they are encouraged to explore other objectives set and taught (Goddard *et al.*, 2013). Children are expected to take responsibility for their own actions and to understand the consequences their actions might have. Educators provide safe boundaries for children to enable them to make informed choices. In School D, a teacher explained how 'pupils are encouraged to know, understand and exercise their rights and personal freedoms being a Rights and Respecting School'. A respondent from Dutch School B also commented that 'within the school community, all pupils are given the freedom to make choices, this may be about the way they wish to present their work, involvement in home learning projects, choices about clubs and activities they wish to engage in'.

Participants were asked for their views on the impact that teaching values in schools has on children, and their responses were unanimous in both countries. One English respondent suggested this was '…enormous! Teaching and modelling key values for young children is absolutely paramount for their development'. The sentiment is echoed by a Dutch participant:

> It gives children a sense of achievement and goodness about themselves as they know that each child is individual and special. Therefore, they then portray this manner onto others when playing, learning and socialising outside of school.

Another teacher from Dutch School D stated that it '…improved self worth and gave them a sense of belonging that we are all working towards a common goal and it gives them the opportunity to contribute to that'.

'Value-forming education' is arguably an essential element of the teaching practice of every teacher – not just for school subjects like religious education and philosophy (Veugelers and de Kat, 2002). Within the framework of their school subject, teachers – through their pedagogical actions – provide their own interpretation of 'value-forming education'. Teaching can never be value-free: teachers' values are reflected by their subject matter, their explanations and their behaviours (Goodlad *et al.*, 1990; Gudmundsdottir, 1990).

Respondents were additionally asked whether they believed that home-life values impact behaviours towards others in school. The response from one teacher in Dutch School F: 'Absolutely. The values/beliefs/attitudes the children's parents have will directly influence children in a primary setting, particularly the younger children as they are even more impressionable and often haven't formulated their own values or conclusions about the world around them'. School D concurred: 'teachers have a key responsibility here too: impressionable children can often pick up on the beliefs and attitudes that their teacher has; therefore, it is crucial that teachers act as role models with regards to positive values'.

Respondents in both countries agreed that 'values are the core beliefs and attitudes that guide our behaviours and decisions in situations of any context'. A School B participant said, 'the values we hold define us as people', while a School E teacher added 'the values we nurture in our children are fundamental to how they develop and how they view the challenging world'.

In 2005, the Dutch Parliament agreed legislation that outlined the task schools have in promoting and stimulating active citizenship and social integration, 'directed towards pupils' understanding of an acquaintance with the various backgrounds and cultures of their fellow pupils' (Wagenvoorde, 2015:205). The former minister of education, Maria Van der Hoeven, demonstrated her commitment to increasing social cohesion by incorporating social integration into the WPO Act. The Dutch government gives greater autonomy to schools, which have increasing freedom to develop their own policies. The inclusion in the act of concepts such as active citizenship and social cohesion form the basis of curriculum design in Dutch schools.

Six values widely acknowledged in the Netherlands and used by the Inspectorate to make an assessment of provision are freedom of speech, equality, sympathy, tolerance and rejection of bigotry and discrimination. Oomen (2009:111) criticises the six values and states that 'social-liberal rights such as political rights, freedom of religion, the right of a fair trial and participation rights are not included'.

A teacher in one Dutch school said that 'the whole year-group follows the school's mission statement, which is an ongoing statement in the whole school and all teachers discuss this regularly. I see values as key messages that are deeply embedded, and are core to everything we do'. Her colleague added 'it's not what is right or wrong, but a way in which we see ourselves as a school which caters for all nationalities, religions and backgrounds therefore giving the children the best experiences and opportunities to learn'.

Individual/group task

One English school states in its PSHE and Citizenship Policy, '....we assess children's knowledge and understanding through discussion and questioning techniques. We will assess how well the children can use the knowledge and understanding in developing skills and attitudes'.

1   How can values be assessed?
2   Should a school or a teacher be allowed to assess students on values that they 'ought' to have developed?
3   To what extent can a teacher gauge the values that a child has acquired in assessing his/her opinions and behaviour?
4   What ethical considerations are pertinent here?

Good SMSC practice in the Netherlands

The stated goals of the Dutch curriculum include the provision of an uninterrupted develop-ment process for pupils, adapted in accordance with their progress; an education geared towards emotional, intellectual and creative development and the necessary knowledge and social, cultural and physical skills. The delivery is very much what the educator recognises as the appropriate teaching and learning strategies for those children in their care. The Dutch government formulates key learning goals that schools have to teach, though they are free to meet them in the way they see fit. There is thus less political control over subject content than in England. Educators are trusted to provide a curriculum appropriate for the learners they are responsible for. The learning goals are further specified in a set of core objectives. Core objectives in the Netherlands may be considered as general indicators of common educational content or general guidelines. This allows schools to choose the teaching and learning activities and materials they see fit considering the needs of their pupils. Two com-monly used schemes of work in primary schools are 'Alles-in-1' (Alles-in-1, 2016) and 'DaVinci' (DaVinci, 2016).

The resources in the Alles-in-1 scheme take into account children's different capabilities, tal-ents and ways of learning. The Dutch curriculum clearly states that the core subjects need to be taught in an integrated way as much as possible. Alles-in-1 covers key concepts in PSHE: art, Dutch and English. This thematic approach has positive effects on the children as learners (Rowley and Cooper, 2009; Alexander, 2013). Their curiosity and eagerness to learn increases, and practitioners and parents are involved in enabling these capacities. The vision for 'Alles-in-1' (2016) translates to 'coherent education for everyone who wants it'.

The DaVinci method (DaVinci, 2016), as shared by the Dutch practitioners in the study, (School D and School F) is the latest approach to teaching world exploration for all primary year groups. This curriculum provides an education in which all core objectives are addressed in a coherent way, bringing together Dutch history, world citizenship and civic education. Teachers do not teach subjects such as geography, history, biology and religion as separate entities but teach one cross-curricular lesson per week. Children make the connections between the ac-tivities and resources used, as they are confronted with the various themes. All the resources provided can be adapted to the vision of the individual teacher or school and allow children to develop metacognitive skills. By exploring the natural world from birth and interacting with it and their peers, children learn about their own identity. Guiding children through these pro-cesses enables children to remain enthusiastic and to have an open attitude towards their environment. Children are shown that no event in the world stands on its own, as they are given tools they can use in their future, which aim to allow them to contribute to bringing about a peaceful global society.

Individual/group task

- The Dutch curriculum (WBO) has statements for the children and teachers to aspire to at the end of each phase (foundation, infant and junior). In what ways do you think this would benefit children's SMSC development?

Good SMSC practice in England, Wales and Northern Ireland

In 1999, the National Curriculum outlined the elements to be taught within PSHE as a statutory subject in key stages 1 and 2. With the revamp of the curriculum, it was decided that PSHE was no longer to be statutory, leaving the decision on whether to teach it to the schools. The PSHE Association (2016) states that the purpose of PSHE is to help learners 'acquire the knowledge, understanding and skills they need to manage their lives, now and in the future'. The research participants were asked about which parts of the English curriculum support SMSC planning and development. Their responses revealed a range of discrete and thematic activities. English School D commented that 'although we don't have separate planning for SMSC, all teachers are encouraged to bear SMSC in mind when planning for all subjects'.

Teachers in the English sample were clear about what is expected of them and are given the autonomy to design lessons that incorporate these elements. They agreed that schools must meet the standards for SMSC set out in the Education Regulations. Children need to have experience of many key aspects of SMSC. Some of the most notable being helping pupils develop their self-esteem, self-confidence and self-knowledge; distinguishing between right and wrong; taking responsibility for one's actions and contributing meaningfully to the wider aspects of life; appreciating and understanding their own and others' cultures and promoting tolerance and harmony. A respondent from School C said:

> As we are a Church of England School, we are expected to display and model this professionally ourselves daily but as a lesson we teach/discuss this at least once a week within the classroom for PSHE and twice a week in the classroom for RE (Religious Education).

There was also emphasis on whole-school thinking and working collaboratively. Willis and Wolstenholme (2016), in a systematic review focussing on the effectiveness of school-based interventions, concluded that a promotional rather than a preventative approach was more effective, as were initiatives aimed at changing the school environment rather than brief classroom-based individually focussed programmes. In schools where there is a collaborative approach, the children had a deeper understanding of the values underpinning society.

Three of the English schools in the study discussed using a scheme of work called 'Social, Emotional Aspects of Learning' (SEAL-DfES, 2005) that encourages opportunities for children to develop the social skills of communication and teamwork in order to help build 'character'. The SEAL scheme gives teachers a framework of ideas for teaching key aspects or domains of emotional intelligence. During PSHE, Citizenship and SEAL activities, children can reflect on their own values, attitudes and feelings and explore the complex and sometimes conflicting values they encounter in their lives. The English respondents all expressed the view that PSHE/SMSC was an area that makes a significant contribution towards supporting schools in meeting statutory responsibilities to promote well-being, achieve the curriculum aims and promote community cohesion.

Stacey (2015) states that

> SEAL should be recognised as more than a curriculum. It is a way of working, a pedagogy that develops independent learners and good communities... if they can manage their behaviour... maintain motivation through setbacks and disappointments then the school has embedded these principles successfully.

(2015:7)

A PSHE coordinator agreed with the accessibility of the scheme, saying, 'the SEAL programme enabled teachers to have a dialogue with pupils about behaviour and refer to the issues raised in the SEAL materials'. Another class teacher added:

> It's given me strategies to deal with things, behaviour and emotional issues... Having the whole class focus helps to refer back to when there are issues. Behaviour issues were recorded in a book and that still happens now. What has changed is that I now also include the emotions of the child... I have got a fuller picture.

A teacher from English School A commented that 'teachers were more aware of children's circumstances and realised that children can't just forget what has just gone on and they do bring their baggage with them'.

'The Rule of Law' is the second area of 'British values' and encourages children to recognise their behaviour and the consequences it holds by examining the reasoning behind the laws. This is delivered in schools via a reward-and-sanction system that pupils follow. Through simple classroom rules and promises, pupils are able to understand how the 'The Rule of Law' sets clear boundaries. An English School C teacher revealed how they implement this in their school:

> The importance of laws, whether they be those that govern the class, the school or the country are consistently reinforced throughout the school and behaviour expectations are reinforced through class and school assemblies. Visits from authorities such as the Police, Fire Service help reinforce this message.

School A recognises its role in preparing children for life in modern Britain, the tolerance of those of different faiths and beliefs based on 'British values'. Through worship, class discussions, RE and PSHE, this is achieved by enhancing pupils' understanding of their place in a culturally diverse society and by providing opportunities to experience such diversity, reinforcing messages of tolerance and respect. School D explained that 'members of different faiths or religions are encouraged to share their knowledge to enhance learning within classes and the school. They actively promote celebrations of different faiths and cultures'. School C said, 'The school worship committee (solely children) play an active part in specific worship themes and one visit to a religious building at some point in the year'.

Conclusion

Children can benefit enormously from high-quality PSHE. The direct comparisons of provision in these different settings highlight the key principles of the different curricula, which have the same goal of developing and strengthening children's resilience and well-being. Examples of good practice illustrate the varied ways practitioners endeavour to provide children with 'tools' and strategies to cope with everyday conflicts and unfamiliar situations in and out of school, enabling them to manage their response to issues and dilemmas.

For both England, Wales and Northern Ireland and the Netherlands, the overall success of this area is that proponents of PSHE argue for its importance in helping pupils to be 'confident as individuals, responsible as citizens and successful as learners' (Waters, 2011:77). Moreover, recent literature has discussed the ways in which PSHE can 'bridge the gap between positive health outcomes and educational attainment' (Hayman, 2014:248).

Individual/group task

- What are the similarities and differences between the provision of SMSC in schools in England, Wales and Northern Ireland and the Netherlands?

Recommended reading

Elsey, S., Coleyshaw, L. and Royle. K. (2015) *Qualitative Evaluation of SUMO and PENN Interventions.* Available at: https://static1.squarespace.com/static/54524d42e4b0350d40bea003/t/5648729be4b0315c2dd303bd/1447588507773/HEADSTART_Evaluation_V4%5B2%5D.pdf.

An insight into two programmes promoting resilience in Primary Schools (SUMO) and Secondary Schools (PENN).

Formby, E., Coldwell, M., Stiell, B., Demack, S., Stevens, A., Shipton, L., Wolstenholme, C. and Willis, B. (2010) *Personal, Social, Health and Economic (PSHE) Education: A Mapping Study of the Prevalent Models of Delivery and Their Effectiveness.* London: DfE.

Hart, A. and Heaver, B. (2015) *Resilience Approaches to Supporting Young People's Mental Health: Appraising the Evidence Base for Schools and Communities.* Available at: www.youngminds.org.uk/assets/0002/4058/BB_YPMH_Final2.pdf.

A useful evaluation of resilience programmes in different educational settings.

References

Alexander, R. (2013) *Versions of Primary Education.* Chicago, IL: Routledge.

Alles-in-1 (2016) *Meaningful Education that Fascinates!* Available at: http://alles-in-1.org. (Accessed 12th August 2016).

BBC (2015) *Make PSHE Lessons Compulsory, Says Green Party MP.* Available at: www.bbc.co.uk/news/education-33521259. (Accessed 12th July 2016).

Berkowitz, M. and Gibbs, J.C. (1983) Measuring the developmental features of moral discussion. *Merrill-Palmer Quarterly,* 29, 399–410.

Central Advisory Council for Education (England) (1967) *Children and Their Primary Schools Vol. 1: The Report (The Plowden Report).* London: HMSO.

Cooper, H. (2005) *The Teaching of History in Primary Schools.* London: David Fulton Publishers.

Dam, G.T. and Volman, M. (1998) Care for citizenship: an analysis of the debate on the subject care. *Curriculum Inquiry,* 28(2), 231–246.

DaVinci (2016) *The DaVinci Method.* Available at: www.demethodedavinci.nl/visie-en-uitgangspunten (Accessed 20th August 2016).

DfE (2013) *The National Curriculum in England: Key Stages 1 and 2 Framework Document.* London: Crown Copyright.

DfE (2015) *Prevent Duty Guidance for England and Wales.* Home Office. Available at: www.gov.uk/government/publications/prevent-duty-guidance. (Accessed 8th July 2015).

DfE (2016) *Cameron's Speech 'On Life Chances'. Part of: Education of disadvantaged children Support for Families Mental Health Service Reform.* Available at: https://www.gov.uk/government/speeches/prime-ministers-speech-on-life-chances. (Accessed 22nd August 2016).

DfES (2003) *Every Child Matters-Green Paper.* London: Crown Copywright.

Foundation for Environmental Education (2011) *The History of Eco-Schools.* Available at: www.eco-schools.org.uk/about-us (Accessed 16th June 2016).

Goddard, G., Smith, V. and Boycott, C. (2013) *PSHE in the Primary School: Principles and Practice.* Abingdon: Routledge.

Goodlad, J., Soder, R. and Sirotnik, K. (1990) *The Moral Dimensions of Teaching.* San Francisco, CA: Jossey-Bass.

Gudmundsdottir, S. (1990) Values in pedagogical content knowledge. *Journal of Teacher Education,* 41(3), 44–52.

Hayman, J. (2014) Personal, social, health and economic education: the bridge between public health and education. *International Journal of Health Promotion and Education*, 52(5), 245–249.

Higgins-d'Allessandro, A. and Sadh, D. (1997) The dimensions and measurement of school culture: understanding school culture as the basis for school reform. *International Journal of Educational Research*, 27(7), 553–569.

Karsten, S. (1994) Policy on ethnic segregation in a system of choice: the case of the Netherlands. *Journal of Education Policy*, 9(3), 211–225.

Karsten, S. (1999) Neoliberal education reform in the Netherlands. *Comparative Education*, 35(3), 303–317.

Keep Britain Tidy (2016) *Eco-School in Primary Schools*. Available at: www.keepbritaintidy.org. (Accessed 12th September 2016).

Klaassen, C. (1996) The moral dimensions of citizenship education. In J. Timmer and R. Veldhuis (Eds.) *Political Education: Towards a European Democracy*. Amsterdam: Instituut voor Publiek en Politiek.

Macdonald, S.A. (2009) *Independent Review of the Proposal to Make Personal, Social, Health and Economic (PSHE) Education Statutory*. London: DCSF.

Masten, A.S., Best, K.M. and Garmezy, N. (1990) Resilience and development: contributions from the study of children who overcome adversity. *Development and Psychopathology*, 2(4), 425–444.

Meichenbaum, D. (2006) Resilience and posttraumatic growth: a constructive narrative perspective. In L. Calhoun and R. Tedeschi (Eds.) *Handbook of Posttraumatic Growth: Research and Practice*. Mahwah, NJ: Lawrence Erlbaum Associates.

Moss, C.M. and Brookhart, S.M. (2012) *Learning Targets: Helping Students Aim for Understanding in Today's Lessons*. London: Sage Publications.

Ofsted (2015) *School Inspection Handbook: Handbook for Inspecting Schools in England under Section 5 of the Education Act 2005* (as amended by the Education Act 2011). Manchester: Crown Copyright.

Oomen, B. (2009) Mensen-en kinderrechten: de gemiste kans van het burgerschapsonderwijs. *Nederlands Tijdschrift voor het Onderwijsrecht*, 2, 100–117.

PSHE Association (2016) https://www.pshe-association.org.uk/.

Rowley, C. and Cooper, H. (Eds.) (2009) *Cross-Curricular Approaches to Teaching and Learning*. London: Sage Publications.

Stacey, J. (2015) *PSHE-SEAL Scheme of Work*. Ealing: Health Improvement Team. Available at: www.egfl.org.uk/sites/default/files/Services_for_children/PSHE/PSHE-SEAL-CIT%20scheme%20of%20work-July2015.pdf. (Accessed 15th September 2016).

The Telegraph. (2015) http://www.telegraph.co.uk/women/sex/better-sex-education/11462769/Nicky-Morgan-unveils-lessons-for-life-for-all-children.html. Accessed 27th March 2017.

Veugelers, W. (1995) Teachers and values regarding labour. *Curriculum Studies* 3(2), 169–182.

Veugelers, W. (2000) Different ways of teaching values. *Educational Review*, 52(1), 37–46.

Veugelers, W. and de Kat, E. (2002) Student voice in school leadership: promoting dialogue about students' views on teaching. *Journal of School Leadership*, 12(1), 97–108.

Veugelers, W. and Vedder, P. (2003) Values in teaching. *Teachers and Teaching: Theory and Practice*, 9(4), 377–389.

Wagenvoorde, R. (2015) *Is Citizenship Secular? Conceptualising the Relation between Religion and Citizenship in Contemporary Dutch Society* (Vol. 2). Münster: LIT Verlag.

Waters, L. (2011) A review of school-based positive psychology interventions. *The Australian Educational and Developmental Psychologist*, 28(2), 75–90.

Weare, K. and Gray, G. (2003) *What Works in Developing Children's Emotional and Social Competence and Wellbeing?* London: DfES.

Werner, E. (2013) What can we learn about resilience from large-scale longitudinal studies? In S. Goldstein and R. Brooks (Eds.), *Handbook of Resilience in Children*. Chicago, IL: Springer.

Willis, B. and Wolstenholme, C. (2016) *Social Health and Economic (PSHE) Education under the Coalition Government: Research Report*. Sheffield: Centre for Education and Inclusion Research.

5 The technical and vocational provision in England

A comparative study with the Austrian secondary system

Sean Starr

Introduction

The education sector continues to be linked by policy-makers to social mobility, particularly in its role in providing the training and skills associated with workforce development and economic growth (Lubienski, 2009). In this respect, legislators look to cultivate and innovate to find ways of meeting these demands, and for better strategies and educational initiatives aimed at educating those communities and students who are underserved, or even essentially excluded, by national education systems, not only to draw on these forgotten groups of human capital but also as a matter of social justice (Johanningmeier, 2009). Such innovations within the education sector can improve outcomes, often without utilising greater levels of resources (Gorard, 2010). While there are a number of policy strategies available for pursuing these goals, one of the more popular approaches in recent years has been to leverage market-style mechanisms, with the introduction of a variety of educational provision in the English school sector. One area that is currently being redeveloped in England is the apprenticeship dimension.

This chapter reviews the reintroduction of apprenticeships in England, with a focus on education into employment. This is achieved by comparing English secondary schools with the Austrian system. The Austrian system was chosen due to its having over 40 years of very diverse educational provision, including a significant vocational and apprenticeship programme. The features and characteristics of the two systems are described; how the two systems ensure widening access to the labour markets is investigated.

Context of technical, vocational education and training

There has been an incremental move in many countries towards more comprehensive school systems where an increasing proportion of students are given the opportunity to pursue education in more academically oriented schools (Slaughter and Rhoades, 2009). Technical and vocational education and training (TVET) has been neglected in England, regardless of the student's interests, passion or abilities. As a consequence, it has received limited attention compared to other parts of the education system and is often regarded as inferior (Wolf, 2011), seen as having lower status or as a second choice after professional education (OECD, 2011). Many people, therefore, dismiss promising and meaningful career paths in areas where employment demand is greater, simply because of the stigma attached to technical and vocational occupations.

Direct migration from compulsory schooling to the working environment was the norm for many young people in England, until the collapse of the youth labour market in the late 1970s. Hence, school-to-work transitions have become extended (Rikowski, 2001), with the current leaving age for compulsory education or training in England being 18. Increasing the compulsory element of education may support skill formation for societal, organisational and individual needs, something which is arguably a global concern (Hiebert and Borgen, 2002). In this context, Powell and Solga (2010:705) suggest that for policy-makers 'one of the crucial challenges is the question of whether to invest in general post-secondary education or in specific vocational training'.

Despite what appears to be a growing interest in TVET in England, defining what it means is not straightforward and reflects a wider problem of 'shifting and often messy conceptualisations' of TVET (Avis, 2012:4). TVET is a broad concept, usually defined at a European level as preparing learners for jobs related to a specific trade, occupation or vocation (Colley *et al.*, 2003). Therefore, TVET may serve as an entry point to employment or further/higher education and is described as the combined process of education and training, recognising the common objective of employment as its immediate goal. Cable (2010) suggested, for example:

> For many individuals and for the country there may be more to be gained from vocational education [....] which is in many respects, the area where we will tackle some of our key deficits as a country in intermediate skills. Apprenticeships rather than degree courses? [....] apprenticeships are delivering vocational education every bit as valuable for their students and the wider economy as the programmes provided by universities.

In England, there is now an understanding that dualism between academic and vocational learning is required to meet the demands of society, as Hayes (in Wolf 2011:6) suggests:

> Little makes more difference to people's lives than the empowerment they receive from education. But for those young people whose aptitudes and talents are practical, expectations are too often limited and opportunities restricted. For far too long vocational learning has been seen as the poor relation of academic learning.

Individual/group task

- What evidence is there that some countries are trying to bring general and vocational education closer together in at least one way? What is the value of doing this?

A brief comparison of the main features and characteristics of the English and Austrian educational systems

Austria and England have widely differing approaches to education and, as a result, very different systems. The education systems of Austria, Germany and Switzerland are structurally similar (Pilz, 2012) and highly selective. Austria follows a coordinated market economy renowned for its extensive dual-apprenticeship training systems at upper secondary level (Hall and Soskice, 2001). Secondary school systems that are essentially selective contrast markedly with England's, which is largely comprehensive. The greater prevalence of selection by schools provides one explanation for why social segregation is higher in those countries than in England (Jenkins *et al.*, 2006).

Austria belongs to the collective skill system cluster where initial vocational training is organised through the cooperation of employer organisations, including the state as well as intermediary associations such as employers' associations and trade unions (Busemeyer and Trampusch, 2012). Austria is also characterised by an institutional divide between the vocational education and training (VET) system and the academic system (Lasonen and Manning, 2001). This division between VET and academic, called the 'educational schism' (Baethge, 2006; Graf, 2015), has become increasingly contested due to a complex set of interrelated socioeconomic factors resulting in an increasing demand for higher skills. On the other hand, the English educational rhetoric is based on the assumption that the academic system is a superior educational currency (Chankseliani *et al.*, 2016), directed primarily towards preparation for university education, even though the majority of students move directly into the labour force (Heinz *et al.*, 1998).

Individual/group task

- What evidence, if any, is there that technical and vocational schools are more suitable to those of lower ability?

The majority of English students leave the primary phase at age 12 and remain in secondary until they are 16, at which point they may stay on at their current school (depending on provision) or move to a college (technical/sixth form). During the transition between primary and secondary schooling, there is the possibility of selection to grammar schools in some areas of England, but the proportion in grammar schools is only 5% of the student population (Bolton, 2016), compared to 34% in 2010 in Austria (Herzog-Punzenberger *et al.*, 2012) who attend a grammar equivalent (allgemeinbildende höhere Schule – AHS).

Austrian secondary education is divided into a junior and a senior level: the Unterstufe (for children aged 10–14) and the Oberstufe (14–18/19). Schools are also organised into general and academic secondary schools, with upper and lower secondary education levels. Those of average ability or below attend general schools called Hauptschule (general secondary school), while those of higher academic ability attend AHS.

If a student has reached a certain level of achievement at a Hauptschule, he or she may be transferred directly to AHS. Since September 2016, a new type of school has been introduced called 'new secondary school' (Neue Mittelschule – NMS). NMS is a comprehensive school for 10–14-year-olds and offers a wide range of learning programmes. In principle, the curriculum of the lower cycle of AHS applies; students obtain individual support and tailored instruction. Hauptschulen are being phased out and converted to NMS.

After successfully completing the four-year junior secondary school, children transfer to upper secondary education. Given that schools in Austria are compulsory for nine years, students can finish their secondary education at the end of the ninth grade (age 14); however, there is an expectation that they should enrol at a vocational school combined with an apprenticeship.

The Oberstufe covers general secondary education and secondary vocational education. The school system is divided into a general education branch and a vocational branch. Therefore, children either attend an academic secondary school upper level (AHS-Oberstufe) or a School for Intermediate Vocational Education (berufsbildende mittlere), a College for Higher Vocational Education (höhere Schule), a Pre-Vocational School (Polytechnische Schule), or part-time schools.

Though the English system is not as fluid in terms of transition and transfer opportunities within secondary school (particularly from the age of 12 to 14), there are eight different school types that make up the English secondary education system: independent schools, grammar schools, academy schools (which can be subdivided into sponsored academy, converted academy, free school, UTC or studio school), city technology colleges, voluntary-aided schools, foundation schools, voluntary-controlled schools and comprehensive schools. Each school type is characterised by a unique set of features regarding their autonomy and governance, though the curriculum offer is often very similar in many schools. In England, assessments at the end of primary school are used to support any identification of progress, with movement based on 'choice' rather than academic ability. In Austrian schools, assessments between primary and lower secondary phase/lower secondary and upper secondary determine the nature of school attended.

Curriculum offer

The curriculum offer in England is determined by the national curriculum and supported by governmental accountability measures, which focus on academic subjects. At the end of secondary education, the same public academic examinations are taken in all school types, if appropriate. At the age of 16, all students have the opportunity to take General Certification of Secondary Education (GCSE) examinations. If the student decides to pursue academic education beyond this point, it involves studying for 'A-level' examinations. All secondary and further education providers may also look at alternative curriculum pathways and offer vocational qualifications. While most TVET is through an integrated curriculum, such curricula may be more demanding to teach and their success may depend on adequate training and preparation for teachers and trainers (Viceník, 2000).

The Austrian education system is run by the individual federal states and therefore there is no national curriculum standard as such. Intermediate and upper secondary technical and vocational schools/colleges offer pupils the possibility of choosing between different study courses. Within certain limits, providers can also determine the pupil numbers required for creating new classes and dividing existing ones. The content of the curriculum is different for academic schools, reflecting the notion of dualism (Graf, 2013) or hybridisation (Powell and Solga, 2010). Nevertheless, all Austrian states abide by uniform requirements for the school leaving examination (Abitur) for AHS students and recognise the credentials certifying completion of school. While the Austrian system offers a standardised, competency-based matriculation examination or matriculation (Matura) and diploma examination, within the academic schools, the final examination Reifezeugnis or Reifeprüfungszeugnis (final examination certificate) grants access to all forms of higher education, while the vocational/apprenticeship routes lead to a certificate that provides the apprentice with access to two different vocational careers. On the one hand, it is a prerequisite for admission to the Master Craftsman Exam and for qualification tests, and on the other hand, it gives access to higher education.

Individual/group task

- What do you think would be key features of a curriculum that ensures doors are opened for all students?

Widening access and youth unemployment

Guidance and support needs to be of a high quality to ensure efficiency in the labour market signalling back into education and training, and to ensure pathways are well matched to learners' attainments and aspirations. Failure in the system could possibly be attributed to early school-leaving rates. These rates can be linked to unemployment, social exclusion and poverty. The early school-leaving rate, from European Commission (2015) data in Austria was well below the EU average (7.3% compared to 11% in 2015) and below the Europe 2020 target of 9.5%. The rate fell continuously over from 10% in 2006. The UK had a slightly different picture with an early school-leaving rate of 10.8% in 2015, which is a reduction from 14.8% in 2010.

In England, youth unemployment increased from 14% in 2007, to 22% in 2011 and in 2016, was nearly back to levels found in 2007 with 15% in 2015 (Eurostat, 2016). Austria has proven more resilient and has one of the lowest rates of youth unemployment – around 9% in 2007, 8% in 2011, and a slight increase to 11% in 2015 (ibid).

With youth unemployment currently at a record high, the need to create routes into employment for school-leavers is of paramount importance. Being unemployed when young leads to a higher likelihood of long-term impact in later life in terms of subsequent lower pay, higher unemployment, reduced life chances (Mroz and Savage, 2001; Bell and Blanchflower, 2011; Strandh et al., 2014), lower lifetime earnings (Buckley, 2015) and greater mental health problems in late life (McQuaid, 2014).

The low rates of youth unemployment in Austria highlight the dual system's effectiveness in interacting with the world of work, and the institutional support that young people receive to make the transition between the two (OECD, 2011). In contrast, apprenticeships in England are seen as an 'either/or' choice compared with completing a degree (Lodovici et al., 2013). This is partly because governments have prioritised access to university as part of their social mobility strategies; therefore, there is a large pool of university graduates from which to recruit (Wolf, 2011). Apprenticeships could be considered the preferred tool for ensuring those without a degree are not being left behind (Fuller and Unwin, 2010).

Policy-makers across Europe increasingly stress the importance of high-quality vocational education (Lanning and Rudiger, 2012). In Austria, 40% of school-leavers enter apprenticeship training upon completion of compulsory education at age 15 (Nindl, 2012), while in England, only 25% of 16–18-year-olds are currently in apprenticeships (Delebarre, 2016). For Austria, this number has been stable since the 1950s (Deissinger, 2002) while this has steadily reduced in England from 2010 (Delebarre, 2016). Furthermore, Austrian apprentices have an estimated completion rate of 85%, taking account of dropout and failure of the final examination (IBW, 2009). In 2008/09, the overall success rate (completion of all Framework Elements) for England was 72.2% (Steedman, 2010).

Apprenticeships in England are for students aged 16 or over and combine working with studying for a work-based qualification from GCSEs or equivalent up to degree level. They play a vital part in addressing youth unemployment and the skills challenge, and continue to facilitate the transition from school to work, leading to higher employment probabilities than equivalent full-time schooling (Brunello, 2009). They also help in addressing the UK's productivity challenge, with investment in skills being responsible for around a fifth of productivity growth (O'Mahony, 2012).

Apprenticeships and the labour market

A key 'policy error' in England was the assumption that qualifications are the main change instrument (Oates, 2013), with the same qualifications being used across different categories: that qualifications can be used as the 'building blocks' of the curriculum rather than specific well-designed curricula being put in place that then use appropriate qualifications for certification of key elements (Machin and Vignoles, 2006). This is not evident in some other high-performing systems, including Austria (Tinklin *et al.*, 2004). As such, off-job provision is in a secondary role but provides wider learning, which could otherwise not be delivered through workplace learning. The state has an interest in this wider learning, which provides enhanced labour mobility and human capital.

In England, employer demand for apprentices has been persistently low and is heavily scarred by the legacy of Youth Training Scheme (Fuller and Unwin, 2003). Repeated attempts to revive the system have been frustrated by the weak institutional framework for apprenticeships, which is characterised by low involvement or commitment from key stakeholders. There is also evidence that the quality of apprenticeships in England varies widely across sectors and that it is much lower in those sectors where apprenticeships are not traditional. Apprenticeships in Austria are bound up with a notion of the importance of participation in work and occupational life. A sense of craft and skill at work is not only important in traditional apprenticeship sectors, such as manufacturing, or in highly skilled occupations. While there are many examples of good apprenticeships in England, too often a focus on meeting the immediate skills needs of employers means that the role of vocational education is largely restricted to assessing competence in specific job roles.

Austria has more than 250 apprenticeship trades, ranging from car mechanics and hairdressers to clerks and retail sales advisers. Austrian employers make significant input into course design and content, making sure the skills they need are developed. In England, there are at present 203 apprenticeship frameworks that guide the industry-specific competencies, technical skills, theoretical concepts and relevant knowledge required to obtain a vocational qualification. Approximately, one third of all apprenticeships in England are in engineering, vehicle maintenance and construction. The remaining two thirds are offered in service sector occupations.

In the Austrian model, the principal relations in the apprenticeship are between the individual apprentice and an employer (Steedman, 2010). Provision is of long duration, and pay rates are lower than those earned by experienced workers. This provides the necessary internal economics to make the model attractive to employers. The trade-off within the system focuses on the lower trainee pay rate, which the trainee tolerates due to the personal capitals they gain during the learning, and which ultimately leads to enhanced progression and wage return. This relationship was very different in England (until 2013). The principal relations were between private training providers and the apprentice, with employers in a secondary role, providing work experience. Alongside this relationship were the assumptions that 'minimum time to certification' is efficient, injects people rapidly into the labour market and reduces the burden on the public purse. This is based on a serious neglect of the role and internal economy of 'classical apprenticeship' (Steedman, 2010; Ryan *et al.*, 2011). This seriously weakens the curriculum content and learning outcomes (Hiebert and Borgen, 2002).

Individual/group task

- Is it possible to develop 'distinctive' and valued TVET education that has currency? What needs to change in the English system to achieve this, in your view?

Governance of apprenticeships

England does not yet have a coherent partnership between government, employers, trade unions and apprentices. The split in responsibility for apprenticeship between two ministries (the Department for Education and the Department for Business, Innovation and Skills) makes change more difficult to achieve and, from 2013, groups of employers have been able to develop apprenticeships, working together to design standards and assessment approaches (DfE, 2015). In Austria, the federal government stands aside from the administration and management of apprenticeships. Employer and trade union organisations largely determine the content of apprenticeship certificates. Occupational skills are acquired on employers' premises in the workplace. The federal government determines the strategic direction and objectives of apprenticeships and legislates to provide a framework that sets out and safeguards the rights of apprentices and employers.

The British government, by contrast, has left issues of standards and length of apprenticeships in the hands of employers while insisting on employed status for apprentices. Much anecdotal evidence suggests that this distribution of responsibility has led to high costs and poor returns for apprentices, in particular in the newer service sector programmes. This lack of employer and trade union commitment has led to the government becoming the dominant partner in the funding, management and promotion of apprenticeships.

In the dual-system countries, the government defines apprentice and employer rights and responsibilities and regulates them by statute. The resulting regime is designed to ensure high-quality training with a strong transferable element and to protect both apprentice and employer from excessive cost. Employers in England appear to be unwilling to pay apprentices, who, after all, have full employee status, a wage that allows the employer to recoup the production lost when apprentices are training. As a consequence, there is no minimum duration for an apprenticeship in England, with the decision left largely to the individual employer. The average time it takes to complete an apprenticeship in England is just one year, compared to an average of three to four years in Austria (Steedman, 2008). In 2011, the British government introduced, for the first time, a statutory minimum number of guided learning hours for apprenticeships. However, the amount specified – 280 hours a year, with a minimum of 100 hours or an average of two hours per week off-the-job – is still very low compared to Austria, where apprentices study for at least one day a week in off-the-job learning in a vocational college, in addition to their on-the-job training. This is to ensure that young people gain transferable skills that support mobility and progression in the labour market. The Austrian dual educational components aim to be strong enough to support entry into other sectors or higher education (Steedman, 2011). These wider aims for apprenticeships in Austria are reflected in much higher requirements for the general and technical- or knowledge-based components.

Apprenticeship funding

In all apprenticeships, employers are normally expected to enter into a contract of employment with an apprentice and, having done so, to take responsibility for paying the agreed wage and other costs. The dual Austrian system in its purest form shares the costs of apprenticeship training between government (which funds general education), apprentices (who accept reduced earnings) and employers (who bear the costs of occupational training). In Austria, the cost of apprentices is reduced further by government-sponsored employer incentives in the form of either direct subsidies for apprenticeships and/or tax deductions (OECD, 2009). These policies are often justified with the argument that, in the absence of public intervention, the market produces less than the optimal proportion of apprentices (Brunello, 2009).

The main difference between the UK system and those successful schemes abroad appears to be a few 'modest' government subsidies worth a fraction of the overall cost, which employers expect to pay for the apprentices' training and wages (Lodovici *et al.*, 2013). In contrast in England, the government funds 100% of the costs for training 16–18-year-olds; if the apprentice is 19+, the government funds up to 50%. Government funding to cover the cost of apprentice training is not paid directly to the employer unless the company has 5000 employees or more. From April 2017, the UK government will introduce a levy on businesses from which it expects to raise around £3 billion a year. The objective of the levy is to give employers more control over where, and how, money is spent on apprenticeships. Employers in the UK with an annual wage bill of more than £3 million will be charged a levy of 0.5% of their full UK payroll, regardless of whether they make use of the funding available for apprenticeships. Any business paying into the levy will be given an allowance of £15,000 per tax year to offset against any levy payment made. Businesses with an annual wage bill under £3 million will be able to draw from the levy fund to access subsidised apprenticeship training but new funding rules will apply. The CBI does not support this levy, due to the risk that it will be unsuccessful. This is supported by Wolter and Ryan (2011) and Brunello (2009) who imply that this type of funding may cause deadweight losses and result in substitution effects.

Cost-benefit of apprenticeships

The social benefits of apprenticeships arguably outweigh their initial costs to employers, individual apprentices and public budgets (McIntosh, 2007). Furthermore, Quintini and Martin (2007) show that in European countries where apprenticeship systems are most developed, young people have better labour market outcomes than in other countries. Austria was found to be among the countries with the lowest share of youth experiencing repeated periods of unemployment.

Moreover, in Austria, more than half of those leaving school found a job without experiencing any period of unemployment.

The dual system demonstrates that high-quality, cost-effective training can be provided by employers in the workplace. Providing training gives employers a direct stake in decisions about training content and increases incentives to become directly involved in decision-making. Ryan (2001) and Steedman (2005) point out that this result may be due to better matching of training to labour market demand achieved in apprenticeship programmes, where training is contingent on a job offer from the employer. However, while most regulated apprenticeship systems offer young people much improved employment prospects, they are not always able to guarantee higher pay or career prospects in the medium run (Quintini *et al.*, 2007).

Using pooled data from the Labour Force Surveys of 2004 and 2005, McIntosh (2007) found that completing an apprenticeship is associated with a 16–18% wage increase, compared to unskilled workers. However, apprenticeships appear to reduce female pay significantly (Ryan, 2001). While in Austria, with respect to low educational attainment, apprenticeships show wage gains in almost all studies and countries analysed. Positive effects on wages were found by Hofer and Lietz (2004) and by Fersterer *et al.* (2008). Hofer and Lietz find that unskilled workers earn 10–12% less than former apprentices.

Conclusion

The current generation of young Britons leaving education has never gone into the labour market with more years of schooling and higher levels of qualifications, yet they are losing out in the struggle for employment. If England is going to offer more specialised routes into the workplace, whether via a traditional education, specialised education or a more employer-led route, curriculum programmes should link to national standards, including those from industry. Furthermore, where they exist, the provision should not narrowly replicate workplace experience; its function is to provide broader learning, which cannot be provided by the workplace, to consolidate learning in the workplace and to ensure that skills and knowledge related to future professional practice are developed.

With the introduction of more specialised TVET provision in England, it may possibly allow for routes to represent 'vocationalised' general education. Acute specialism is then integrated, when the precise aspirations of the learner are identified. Therefore, they go into more specialised training or back onto a general education route (European Commission, 2015). This type of system will offer students and parents many choices. This is already well established and a distinctive feature of the Austrian educational system, with extensive cooperation prevailing between the technical and vocational community and educational institutions. The dual education system, which combines theoretical and practical teaching, is applied in preparing for careers requiring apprentice training as well as in higher vocational schools.

Though the English system can be deemed more efficient than educationally effective (Dolton *et al.*, 2014), such efficiency is not immediately concerned with raising international assessments. This could be for the simple reason that the English system has constraints that prevent it from moving to the next level. With unlimited funding available, much more could be done to increase educational outcomes, but this is unrealistic: national budgets are limited, and spending needs to be prioritised accordingly in order to deliver value for money. One could suggest that extensive resources are already being deployed and therefore it could be the case that underlying flaws exist in the education delivery model. The system has the potential to increase outputs for limited additional inputs by making policy changes, such as the additionality of education provision provided by technical/vocational and apprenticeship provision. Therefore, the addition of TVET may allow for increased participation in wider society. However, Austria's performance is better in quality measures than in terms of efficiency. This may be because they can prioritise outcomes over cost, or perhaps because their system generates other outcomes that aren't captured by PISA rankings. Or, more simply, it may be because the system is over-resourced beyond a threshold required to drive quality increases. In addition, schools can develop alternative compulsory subject areas that enable the students to design their school career in line with individual talents and interests. Furthermore, optional educational programmes and subjects may be specified within the scope of the school's autonomy to provide important additional qualifications for practice.

The reintroduction and expansion of apprenticeships could support labour market progression prospects and clearer routes to upskilling young people. It would also address the skills shortages that are apparent in some parts of the economy, particularly those associated with STEM (science, technology, engineering, maths) subjects. Each vocational stream consists of a number of different occupations, and each occupation consists of a number of different jobs. This type of model is more akin to a horizontal model (Wheelahan, 2013), which supports movement between organisations.

Though vertical diversity may be attractive (as in the Austrian system), it can promote sentiments associated with 'elite, excellence and quality', which legitimise winners and stigmatise those of average ability or lower (Teichler, 2008). It has not yet been possible to identify the net effect of widening access to schools that provide a more academically oriented general education on overall educational outcomes (OECD, 2000; Maurin and McNally, 2007). There is a danger in the developing English model that vocational education will be interpreted in theory and practised as 'trade' education: as a means of securing technical efficiency in specialized future pursuits. Education would then become an instrument of perpetuating the existing industrial order of society, instead of operating as a means of its transformation. The desired transformation is not difficult to define in a formal way. It signifies a society in which every person shall be occupied in something, which makes the lives of others better and worth living (Dewey, 2012). Therefore, the focus on academic and vocational provision is not simply a technical matter of designing and implementing a better system, it is, above all, a governance process. Associated stakeholders have a considerable influence over the progress of hybridisation and qualification currency, especially in more flexible systems. As a consequence, they have some discretion in how they value the outcomes of education. Ultimately, there is not a simple rule that suggests a route system (Austrian model) is bad and a unitary system is good (English model).

Recommended reading

Graf, L. (2015) The rise of work-based academic education in Austria, Germany and Switzerland. *Journal of Vocational Education and Training*, 68(1), 1–16.

References

Avis, J. (2012) Global reconstructions of vocational education and training. *Globalisation, Societies and Education*, 10(1), 1–11.

Baethge, M. (2006) Das deutsche Bildungs-Schisma. In *SOFI-Mitteilungen*, 34, 13–27.

Bell, D. and Blanchflower, D. (2011) Young people and the great recession. *Oxford Review of Economic Policy*, 27(2), 241–267.

Bolton, P. (2016) *Grammar School Statistics*. Available at: http://researchbriefings.parliament.uk/Research-Briefing/Summary/SN01398#fullreport. (Accessed 15th July 2016).

Brunello, G. (2009) *The Effect of Economic Downturns on Apprenticeships and Initial Workplace Training: A Review of the Evidence*. Available at: https://www.oecd.org/edu/skills-beyond-school/43141035.pdf. (Accessed 15th October 2016).

Buckley, P. (2015) *An Unbalanced Age: Effects of Youth Unemployment on an Aging Society*. Available at: https://dupress.deloitte.com/dup-us-en/economy/issues-by-the-numbers/effects-of-youth-unemploy-ment-us.html. (Accessed 16th October 2016).

Busemeyer, M. and Trampusch, C. (2012) *The Political Economy of Collective Skill Formation*. Oxford: Oxford University Press.

Cable, V. (2010) *A New Era for Universities. Oral Statement to Parliament*. Available at: https://www.gov.uk/government/speeches/a-new-era-for-universities. (Accessed 21st July 2012).

Chankseliani, M., Relly, S. and Laczik, A. (2016) Overcoming vocational prejudice: how can skills competitions improve the attractiveness of vocational education and training in the UK? *British Educational Research Journal*, 42(4), 582–599.

Colley, H., James, D., Diment, K. and Tedder, M. (2003) Learning as becoming in vocational education and training: class, gender and the role of vocational habitus. *Journal of Vocational Education and Training*, 55(4), 471–498.

DfE (2015) *Future of Apprenticeships in England: Guidance for Trailblazers*. Available at: https://www.gov.uk/government/uploads/system/uploads/attachment_data/file/487350/BIS-15-632-apprenticeships-guidance-for-trailblazers-december-2015.pdf. (Accessed 17th September 2015).

Deissinger, T. (2002) *Apprenticeship Systems in England and Germany: Decline and Survival. Towards a History of Vocational Education and Training (VET) in Europe in a Comparative Perspective*. Available at: www.cedefop.europa.eu/en/publications-and-resources/publications/5153-0. (Accessed 5th September 2015).

Delebarre, J. (2016) *Apprenticeship Statistics: England (1996–2015)*. Available at: www.parliament.uk/briefing-papers/SN06113.pdf. (Accessed 10th July 2016).

Dewey, J. (2012) *Schooling for Democracy*. London: Create Space Independent Publishing Platform.

Dolton, P., Marcenaro-Gutierrez, O. and Still, A. (2014) *The Efficiency Index: Which Education Systems Deliver the Best Value for Money?* GEMS Education Solutions. Available at: www.edefficiencyindex.com (Accessed 8th July 2016).

European Commission (2015) *Education and Training Monitor 2015, Country Analysis*. Available at: http://ec.europa.eu/dgs/education_culture/repository/education/library/publications/monitor15_en.pdf. (Accessed 10th August 2016).

Eurostat (2016) *Unemployment Statistics*. Available at: http://ec.europa.eu/eurostat/statistics-explained/index.php/Unemployment_statistics. (Accessed 5th December 2016).

Fersterer, J., Pischke, J.S. and Winter-Ebmer, R. (2008) Returns to apprenticeship training in Austria: evidence from failed firms. *Scandinavian Journal of Economics*, 110(4), 733–753.

Fuller, A. and Unwin, L. (2010) Change and continuity in apprenticeship: the resilience of a model of learning. *Journal of Education and Work* 25(5), 405–416.

Gorard, S. (2010) Education can compensate for society – a bit. *British Journal of Educational Studies*, 58(1), 47–65.

Graf, L. (2013) *The Hybridization of Vocational Training and Higher Education in Austria, Germany and Switzerland*. Opladen, Germany: Budrich UniPress.

Graf, L. (2015) The rise of work-based academic education in Austria, Germany and Switzerland. *Journal of Vocational Education and Training*, 68(1), 1–16.

Hall, P. and Soskice, D. (2001) *Varieties of Capitalism*. Oxford: Oxford University Press.

Heinz, W.R., Kelle, U., Witzel, A. and Zinn, J. (1998) Vocational training and career development in Germany: results from a longitudinal study. *International Journal of Behavioural Development*, 22, 77–101.

Herzog-Punzenberger, B. (2012) *Nationaler Bildungsbericht Österreich* Available at: https://www.bifie.at/system/files/buch/pdf/NBB2012_Band2_gesamt_20121217.pdf.

Hiebert B. and Borgen, W. (2002) *Technical and Vocational Education and Training in the 21st Century: New Roles and Challenges for Guidance and Counselling.* Paris: UNESCO.

Hofer, Hand Lietz, C. (2004) Labour market effects of apprenticeship training in Austria. *International Journal of Manpower,* 25, 104–122.

Institut für Bildung der Wirtschaft-IBW (2009) *Lehrlingausbildung im Überblick.* Available at: www.ibw.at/components/com_redshop/assets/document/product/1334055114_ibw_research_brief_nr54.pdf. (Accessed 12th October 2016).

Jenkins, S., Micklewright, J. and Schnepf, S. (2006) Social segregation in secondary schools: how does England compare with other countries? *Oxford Review of Education,* 34(1), 21–37.

Johanningmeier, E. (2009) *Equality of Educational Opportunity and Knowledgeable Human Capital: From the Cold War and Sputnik to the Global Economy and No Child Left Behind.* Charlotte, NC: Information Age Publishing.

Lanning, T. and Rudiger, K. (2012) *Youth Unemployment in Europe: Lessons for the UK.* Available at: https://www.researchonline.org.uk/sds/search/download.do%3Bjsessionid=8EB0BC2ACB09A1B9DD9ED6AA24C78047?ref=B27130. (Accessed 10th October 2016).

Lasonen, J. and Manning, S. (2001) How to improve the standing of vocational compared to general education. A collaborative investigation of strategies and qualifications across Europe. In P. Descy and M. Tessaring (Eds.) *Training in Europe. Second Report on Vocational Training Research in Europe 2000: Background Report.* Luxembourg: Office for Official Publications of the European Communities.

Lodovici, M., Comi, S., Origo, F., Patrizio, M., Torchio, N., Speckesser, S. and Montalt, J. (2013) *The Effectiveness and Costs-Benefits of Apprenticeships: Results of the Quantitative Analysis.* Available at: http:ec.europa.eu/social/BlobServlet?docId=11352&langId=en. (Accessed 17th October 2016).

Lubienski, C. (2009) *Do Quasi-Markets Foster Innovation in Education? A Comparative Perspective.* Available at: http:www.oecd.org/edu/workingpapers. (Accessed 1st May 2010).

Machin, S. and Vignoles, A. (2006) *Education Policy in the UK.* Available at: http://cee.lse.ac.uk/ceedps/ceedp57.pdf. (Accessed 10th April 2016).

Maurin E. and McNally, S. (2007) *Educational Effects of Widening Access to the Academic Track: A Natural Experiment.* Available at: http://cee.lse.ac.uk/ceedps/ceedp85.pdf. (Accessed 16th July 2016).

McIntosh, S. (2007) *A Cost-Benefit Analysis of Apprenticeships and Other Vocational Qualifications.* Available at: http:www.education.gov.uk/publications/eOrderingDownload/RR834.pdf. (Accessed 18th October 2016).

McQuaid, R. (2014) *Youth Unemployment Produces Multiple Scarring Effects.* Available at: http://blogs.lse.ac.uk/politicsandpolicy/multiple-scarring-effects-of-youth-unemployment/. (Accessed 20th October 2016).

Mroz, T. and Savage, Timothy H. (2001) *The Long-Term Effects of Youth Unemployment.* Available at: https://www.epionline.org/wp-content/studies/mroz_10-2001.pdf. (Accessed 19th October 2016).

Nindl, S. (2012) *Facilitating Access to Apprenticeship and Integration into Labour Market: Training Guarantee and Youth Coaching.* Available at: http:ec.europa.eu/social/BlobServlet?docId=10753&langId=en. (Accessed 11th December 2016).

Oates, T. (2013) *Towards a New VET – Effective and Vocational Training.* Available at: www.cambridge-assessment.org.uk/images/122543-towards-a-new-vet-effective-vocational-education-and-training.pdf (Accessed 19th July 2015).

OECD (2000) *Making Transitions Work: From Initial Education to Working Life.* Available at: www.oecd.org/edu/innovation-education/transitionfrominitialeducationtoworkinglife-homepage.htm. (Accessed 9th September 2015).

OECD (2009) *Learning for Jobs: OECD Reviews of Vocational Education and Training: England and Wales.* Available at: https://www.oecd.org/unitedkingdom/43947857.pdf. (Accessed 3rd July 2016).

OECD (2011) *Education at a Glance 2011: OECD Indicators.* Available at: https://www.oecd.org/education/skills-beyond-school/48631582.pdf. (Accessed 3rd September 2015).

O'Mahony, M. (2012) Human capital formation and continuous training: evidence for EUcountries. *Review of Income and Wealth,* 58, 531–549.

Pilz, M. (2012) Modularisation of vocational training in Germany, Austria and Switzerland: parallels and disparities in a modernisation process. *Journal of Vocational Education and Training,* 64(2), 169–183.

Powell, J. and Solga, H. (2010) Analyzing the nexus of higher education and vocational training in Europe: a comparative-institutional framework. *Studies in Higher Education,* 35(6), 705–721.

Quintini, G., Martin, J.P. and Martin, S. (2007) *The Changing Nature of the School-to-Work.* Available at: http://econpapers.repec.org/RePEc:iza:izadps:dp2582. (Accessed 7th October 2016).

Rikowski, G. (2001) Education for industry: a complex technicism. *Journal of Education and Work*, 14, 29–49.

Ryan, P. (2001) The school-to-work transition: a cross-national perspective. *Journal of Economic Literature*, 39, 34–92.

Ryan, P., Wagner, K., Teuber, S. and Backes-Gellner, U. (2011) *Financial Attributes of Apprenticeship Training in Germany, Great Britain and Switzerland*. Dusseldorf: Hans Böckler Stiftung.

Slaughter, S. and Rhoades, G. (2009) *Academic Capitalism and the New Economy*. Baltimore: Johns Hopkins University Press.

Steedman, H. (2005) *Apprenticeship in Europe: Fading or Flourishing*? London: Centre for Economic Performance.

Steedman, H. (2008) *Time to Look again at Apprentice Pay? Getting Cost-Sharing Right*. Wath-upon-Dearne: Sector Skills Development Agency.

Steedman, H. (2010) *The State of Apprentice in 2010*. Available at: http://cep.lse.ac.uk/pubs/download/special/cepsp22.pdf. (Accessed 11th October 2016).

Steedman, H. (2011) *Apprenticeship Policy in England: Increasing Skills versus Boosting Young People's Job Prospects*. London: Centre for Economic Performance.

Strandh, M., Winefield, A., Nilsson, K. and Hammarström, A. (2014) Unemployment and mental health scarring during the life course. *European Journal of Public Health*, 24(3), 440–445.

Teichler, U. (2008) Diversification? Trends and explanations of the shape and size of higher education. *Higher Education*, 56(3), 349–379.

Tinklin, T., Hodgson, A., Howieson, C., Raffe, D. and Spours, K. (2004) Post-16 curriculum and qualifications reform in England and Scotland: lessons from some international comparisons. *Journal of Education and Work*, 17(4), 441–465.

Vicenik, P. (2000) National conclusions: Czech Republic. In S. Manning (ed.) *Dually-Oriented Qualifications: AKnowledge Base Related to the Leonardo da Vinci Projects*. Berlin: WIFO. Available at: INTEQUAL/DUQUAL. www.b.shuttle.de/wifo/duoqual/=base.htm. (Accessed 9th September 2015).

Wheelahan, L. (2013) *The Weak Link between Education and Jobs. Bridging the Divides: Transitions from Secondary to Tertiary and into Employment*. Paper presented in Auckland on 2–3 July 2013. Available at: www.manukau.ac.nz/__data/assets/pdf_file/0015/110067/The-Weak-Link.pdf. (Accessed 10th July 2015).

Wolf, A. (2011) *Review of Vocational Education – The Wolf Report*. Available at: https://www.gov.uk/government/uploads/system/uploads/attachment_data/file/180504/DFE-00031-2011.pdf. (Accessed 2nd July 2012).

Wolter, S. and Ryan, S. (2011) Apprenticeship. In E. Hanushek, S. Machinand L. Woessmann (Eds.) *Handbook of the Economics of Education*. North Holland: Elsevier.

6 The rise of private supplementary tutoring

Contemporary issues and international perspectives on shadow education in China

Roy Y. Chan, Hei-Hang Hayes Tang and Patrick Delaney

Introduction

Shadow education, also known as private supplementary tutoring (PST), has spread widely all over the world (Manzon and Areepattamannil, 2014). Notably, China (Mainland and Hong Kong) has experienced massive shadow education growth in the past two decades (Zhang and Bray, 2016), where PST is often viewed as an effective way for young adults to achieve higher test scores such as the Hong Kong Diploma of Secondary Education Examination (HKDSE) and the National College Entrance Examination (NCCE), commonly known as the Gaokao (Bray *et al.*, 2015). While numerous scholars have called for new empirical research on shadow education (Trent, 2016), research on PST has often lagged behind the expansion and diversification of the phenomenon (Liu and Bray, 2016). Furthermore, little is known about whether such activity helps students succeed in the HKDSE and NCCE, and to what extent these activities prepare them for higher education participation after high school (Bray and Lykins, 2012).

Generally, the HKDSE and the Gaokao provide the primary gateway for students to obtain a post-secondary education (Zhang, 2016). Today, a significant number of Chinese high school students prepare for the HKDSE and the Gaokao by participating in PST activities. Typically, PST refers to the outside tutoring services offered by the private sector and paid for by families. Often seen as the third most important education sector, critics have argued that the increasing demand for PST is the result of several economic and social factors including the perceived low quality of mainstream education, depleted teacher salaries, introduction of high-stakes examinations, socioeconomic status, gender and inadequate content learned at schools (Zhang and Bray, 2016). Additionally, PST has continued to expand rapidly as a result of fierce competition in the global labour market. While some have noted that shadow education provides a steady income to private tutors, others have complained that much PST is highly driven by students' desire to pass high-stakes examinations set by the school or system level (Au *et al.*, 2010). Furthermore, PST is often driven by the 'educational desire' (Tang, 2015) of parents to develop their child's general learning capacities and enhance self-esteem.

This activity is highly evident across East Asia, where Confucian values often emphasise diligence and effort that are further fuelled by globalisation and privatisation of education as families become increasingly aware of the fierce competition in the labour market (Salili, 2005). Normally, the driving force behind globalisation is predominantly free market capitalism. Maringe

(2010:24) states 'globalization is a multidimensional concept in which the social, cultural, technological, political and ideological aspects of life become increasingly homogeneous'. In other words, the growth and spread of shadow education 'is deeply embedded in the culture' (Bray, 2009:24) as a response to the globalisation of academic capitalism. School systems in China are increasingly competitive, which prompts an intensifying demand for and supply of private tutoring. Thus, shadow education is viewed as a 'hidden' form of education privatisation as a result of high-stakes testing and school system change within the curriculum. As Bray (2009:5) noted, 'as the curriculum changes, so does the curriculum change in the shadow'. And as more friends participate in private tutoring, the more likely students are to partake in shadow education activities (Baker and LeTendre, 2005).

Therefore, this chapter seeks to explore the determinants of private tutoring participation not only for education policy-makers and university planners but also for parents and students. Because many Chinese students are driven by the significant demands of college admission, this chapter adds to an ongoing policy discussion on the expansion and prevalence of shadow education and its implications for high-stakes testing and NCCE preparation. As long as the HKDSE and the Gaokao serve as the principal gatekeeper to Chinese higher education institutions, parents and students will continue to be motivated to pay for shadow education activities in the years ahead. Thus, it is our hope that our chapter will raise serious concerns about college entrance examination and admission effects on PST.

The landscape of PST and college test preparation

In recent years, shadow education has accomplished significant private capital investment from families across the income range. Most notably, recent research by Global Industry Analysts, Inc. (2012) shows that for all levels of primary and secondary schooling, the entire world will spend over US$102.8 billion each year on shadow education by 2018 (Forbes, 2012). Additionally, some research indicates that parents invest in shadow education because they fear losing out in the globally competitive workforce if they do not invest in PST to improve their child's competitiveness in high-stakes entrance examinations (Xue and Ding, 2009). In other words, shadow education arises from competitive educational environments, particularly in East Asian countries with high-stakes examination cultures and stratified education systems (Tang, 2015). Because Confucianist culture in East Asia often prides itself on examination scores to determine an individual's academic achievement (particularly success from secondary to higher education), there are several good reasons why private tutoring benefits these national contexts and can be instrumentally beneficial to individuals.

Historically, public education in East Asia has long been regarded as a public good benefiting not only individuals but also the whole of society. Today, however, the growth in market forces has turned education into a private good and, often times, a commodity for purchase and trade (Tilak, 2008). This market shift is particularly evident in the case of shadow education, whereby major tutoring companies in China and other Asian societies offer classes in lecture theatres with overflow rooms served by video links typically before or after the regular school day, at weekends, on public holidays and during school vacations. Furthermore, private tutoring companies may offer lessons that are more individualised than mainstream education, and occasionally, assist low-performing students to work at their own pace without the feeling of falling behind. In addition, PST may extend students' capital acquisition and accumulation and contribute to their lifelong learning (DiMaggio, 1982). Moreover, shadow education may provide steady incomes for local tutors and teachers who decide to offer PST to gain extra income outside their regular classes. Nonetheless, while some factors of private tutoring are deemed positive, other elements can be seen as problematic.

For instance, PST growth has often been criticised for reproducing social and economic inequalities in mainstream schooling and wider society (Bray and Lykins, 2012). While in some exceptional cases, there are educational groups and agencies that provide free tutoring to disadvantaged students, most tutoring services are focussed on profit-making or return on investment whereby tutors serve higher-achieving wealthy students (Bray *et al.*, 2014). In addition, some scholars have noted that the rise of shadow education negatively affects the dynamics of teaching and learning (e.g. curriculum, student performance) in formal schools, students' engagement in the classroom, as well as student performance in both classroom activities and examinations (Bray, 2009). That is, PST may damage students' independent-learning abilities, restrict students' leisure time and affect formal educational systems in terms of both equity and quality (UNESCO, 2015). Thus, new research is much needed to understand the motivations and consequences of shadow education in other developed countries, such as Japan (Yamamoto and Brinton, 2010), Hong Kong (Zhan *et al.*, 2013), Vietnam (Dang, 2007), Macau (Ho *et al.*, 2008) and South Korea (Kim and Lee, 2010). As mainstream schooling often does not teach students testing skills needed for high-stakes examinations, more students will continue to enrol in shadow education to avoid fear or regret of not participating or succeeding in the future.

History of shadow education

Historically, PST has often stirred much controversy over educational quality and equality (Mori and Baker, 2010). Typically, much comparative research in both developing and transitional countries has focussed on issues such as access to higher education, funding, student mobility and the impact of globalisation (Manzon, 2011). Rarely, however, has comparative research examined the global challenges of shadow education in understanding inequalities in college access and participation between urban and rural regions.

To enumerate, shadow education, first coined during the early 1990s in Malaysia (Marimuthu *et al.*, 1991), Singapore (George, 1992) and Japan (Stevenson and Baker, 1992), was used as a metaphor to describe any tutoring activities conducted outside formal schooling. UNESCO's International Institute for Educational Planning (IIEP) first published a cross-national study of private tutoring in 1999. Most notably, the report finds that PST has a long tradition in elite privileged families and that its history is as long as that of formal schooling. For example, South Korea is known for its *hagwons*, Japan for its *juku* and Taiwan for its *buxiban* (Kang, 2010). All of these activities are often referred to as 'cram schools', whereby for-profit institutions 'offer(s) supplementary instructions and practice exams in the classroom and provide their own curriculum, publications and textbooks like a mainstream school' (Bray, 2009:25).

Today, cram schools are often learning centres or institutes that prepare students for better examination performance. These institutes often flourish when high-stakes testing serves as a gatekeeper to future educational opportunities (Buchmann, 2002). Bray (2003:17) divides cram schools into four categories: (1) private tutoring only exists because mainstream education exists; (2) size and shape of private tutoring changes, as size and shape of the mainstream system changes; (3) the public has focussed more on the mainstream than on its shadow and (4) the features of the shadow system are much less distinct than those of the mainstream system. That is, the primary purpose of cram schools is to improve grades and performance in high-stakes examinations. Other purposes may include improving student confidence, increasing classroom motivation and fostering intellectual capital. Despite the increasing attention from policy-makers and planners to address the expansion of PST in East Asia, much private tutoring often goes unnoticed in today's commercialised world (Trent, 2016).

For instance, the highly renowned PST company *Kumon* now claims to serve over 4 million students in 45 countries, including China, India, Indonesia, South Korea, Malaysia, Myanmar, Singapore, Thailand and Vietnam (Kumon, 2016). Similarly, *Modern Education*, a highly renowned cram school in Hong Kong, announced plans to expand their tutoring services into Mainland China (Kwo and Bray, 2014). As such, one can argue that shadow education is highly marketised service in East Asia and has a backwash effect on regular schools (Mori and Baker, 2010). Wealthy families can afford greater amounts of PST than students in low-income families and thus have higher chances of mobility and career success (Bray *et al.*, 2015).

Shadow education in China

PST has emerged significantly across China (Xue and Ding, 2009; Zhang, 2014). China has, in fact, experienced massive shadow education growth in the past two decades, which will account for more than half the world's enrolment by the year 2050 (Altbach, 2013). More recently, however, private tutoring centres have sprung up focussing on foreign standardised tests such as the SAT, GRE and TOEFL. The demand for college test preparation in China is often the result of perceived student weaknesses or limitations of the schooling system. Chinese parents believe that investing in shadow education is the most important prerequisite leading to an individual's success in the labour market (Baker and LeTendre, 2005).

As noted earlier, Confucian values in East Asia often place education as the highest priority, and parents expect their child to have as much education as possible, regardless of gender, socioeconomic status and geographical location (Zhang, 2014). While many Chinese families care immensely about the success of their child's progress, little research has yet to examine whether shadow education enhances students' educational achievement from secondary to post-secondary levels or their transition from post-secondary to employment. Furthermore, limited studies have yet to explore how PST influences students' NCCE performance.

Historically, studies have noted that the reasons Chinese students engage in PST relate to the large disparities in education quality, test-oriented education, the high cultural value of education, as well as schoolteachers' need to increase income. In addition, Xue and Ding (2009) noted that the one-child family policy has further fuelled demand. Specifically, they found that 73.8% of Chinese students received tutoring in elementary schools, 65.6% in middle schools and 54% in high schools. In a similar study, Bray *et al.* (2014) concluded that 92.1% of senior high school students in Hong Kong enrolled in tutoring 'to improve examination scores', followed by other pressures to perform well in examinations. Bray *et al.* (2014) emphasised that examinations, and the consequences of success or failure, are the dominant driver of demand for private tutoring in China.

China's high-stakes examination system has often been criticised for exacerbating inequalities between urban and rural regions, as well as limiting students' imagination, creativity and critical thinking skills (Zhang, 2016). This cause is often the result of the growing unequal access to high-quality tutors between large urban/high-income eastern regions and small rural/midwestern regions. For instance, Kwok (2010) claimed that high-income households had greater demands for PST than middle- and low-income households: 62.5%, 57.9% and 47.1%, respectively. Similarly, Zhang (2014) found that, in Chongqing, only 22.1% of rural students received some kind of private tutoring compared with 65% of urban students, in part because of the availability of tutors. Comparatively, Lei (2005) suggested that over half of urban students in China are more likely to engage in PST than their rural counterparts.

Academic achievement and shadow education in China

Relatively, few studies on academic achievement in China have been conducted in the past decade (Ho *et al.*, 2008), and fewer still have been reported in English by Western-influenced researchers (Byun, 2014). Historically, studies on the effectiveness of private tutoring on academic achievement have often been contradictory. For example, some studies have reported a positive impact of private tutoring in Japan (Stevenson and Baker, 1992), Taiwan (Liu, 2012) and Kenya (Buchmann, 2002), while others have found a negative impact on achievement in Korea (Lee and Shouse, 2011), Singapore (Cheo and Quah, 2005) and Nepal (Thapa, 2011). A more recent study by Byun (2014) found that PST for test purposes made some difference in achievement gains in South Korea, but that other types of tutoring had made little difference. Similarly, Sohn *et al.* (2010) found a positive relationship between expenditures on PST and academic performance in Seoul, but that the relationship deteriorated when adjusting for student background. However, in a similar study, Xue and Ding (2009) found a negative correlation in data from 4,772 students. In addition, Kang (2010) suggested that there were modest effects from investment in private tutoring among 1,752 students tracked by the Korean Education and Employment Panel. Consequently, research on private tutoring has often painted mixed results. Despite its contested benefits, some parents and students still believe that investment in shadow education is worthwhile to reassure themselves they are doing everything they can to assist their child in succeeding in examinations.

It is interesting to note that Bray (2003) argued that international governments have adopted four different stances on shadow education: (type I) to ban, (type II) to ignore, (type III) to regulate and (type IV) to encourage. He argued that China falls under type III in that the government regulates tutoring centres and requires tutors to be as qualified as mainstream teachers (People's Republic of China, 2004) but prohibits the latter from using their position as teachers for profit or personal gain (People's Republic of China, Ministry of Education 2013:Item 5). However, these laws are in practice difficult to enforce, despite such measures as those enacted, for example, by the Shanghai provincial government to curtail this phenomenon by offering teachers a merit-pay salary and thus reducing the economic incentive to tutor students outside of formal schooling (Shanghai Education Commission, 2009).

This all presents a problem in Chinese society, as the mainstream curriculum does not include preparation for the SAT or other similar exams. Students wishing to study abroad have overwhelmingly begun attending private tutoring centres for their SAT preparation classes. Byun and Park (2012) examined the effectiveness on student achievement defined through SAT scores in relation to the weekly amount in hours and the overall duration of the study. Specifically,

160 East Asian American students were given a questionnaire asking about their SAT tutoring history, family income and SAT scores. The results suggest that tutoring has a trivial effect on SAT scores, with the law of diminishing returns kicking in at 20 hours per week and at 24 months of classes. The authors did not control for endogenetic variables such as student motivation or attitude towards learning, unlike Zhang (2013) in his analysis of 40,000 students taking the NCCE in Jinan, Shandong, China. This sampling method thus allows this to be considered a city-wide representative sample of 11th and 12th grade students attending regular public high schools in Jinan. The data indicate that urban students are considerably more likely to participate in private tutoring than their rural counterparts and are more satisfied with their tutors as well. Zhang found that tutoring has mixed effects on student achievement dependent on students' location, urban or rural, and on the subjects tutored. With an average overall effect as not significant on achievement, private tutoring was found to have a significant negative correlation with rural students in Maths, Chinese and overall NCCE score, but underperforming urban students or urban students from lower quality schools may receive a significantly positive effect from private tutoring. It is not surprising that UNESCO's *2013/2014 EFA Global Monitoring Report* (2014:271) stated that 'private tutoring, if unchecked or uncontrolled, can be detrimental to learning outcomes, especially for the poorest students who are unable to afford it'. Aside from Zhang (2013), Zhang and Bray (2015) focussed on the demand side of tutoring and its prevalence among 860 grade nine students and 773 parents in Chongqing, China. Their results indicate that 70% of the sampled students representing both urban and rural areas of Chongqing reported having received tutoring during their schooling. More than half reported receiving more than four hours during regular school seasons, and a quarter reported receiving more than 15 hours per week.

Attempting to analyse shadow education's effect on student achievement, researchers throughout the world have used a variety of methods with mixed results. An individual study on one form of shadow education in one location of one student population is hardly representative of a similar student population in a different location or that of a different student population. It appears the results of one study have few if any, implications outside of the study from the available literature outlining such research. Research within China on the effects of shadow education is very limited due to available data sets and many participants' unwillingness to speak about their involvements on both the demand and supply sides, partly due to the common phenomenon of teachers tutoring their own students.

Inequality and shadow education

Shadow education can have a detrimental effect on both the economic efficiency and educational inequality in modern society (Byun, 2014). Notably, Hallak and Poisson (2007:258) asserted that 'shadow education has become a source of distortion that adversely affects mainstream education'. Similarly, Grodsky (2010:476) states that 'shadow education contributes to education inequality such as school segregation and tracking or ability grouping within schools that fall under the control of educational organizations'. In other words, students with more highly educated parents are often more informed regarding college test preparation compared to those from disadvantaged backgrounds. Consequently, shadow education creates inefficiencies and excludes certain social groups. Students taking the NCCE have found themselves investing in more PST as a result of highly competitive entrance examinations (Tsegay and Ashraf, 2016).

Thus, the NCCE system plays an instrumental role in social mobility, social equity and stability of the nation, while at the same time reproducing and maintaining inequality in college access and enrolment (Tsang, 1994).

Similarly, in the USA, Buchmann *et al.* (2010) found that family background and income inequalities have shaped students' likelihood of engaging in test preparation and that both variables have significant implications for college enrolment. The authors noted the recent emphasis on standardised testing in the USA has increased the demand for shadow education and potentially widened the socioeconomic achievement gap. Hence, Baker and LeTendre (2005) argued that private tutoring centres in countries like the USA are more likely to exacerbate inequalities in college access and to affect a nation's ability to provide high-quality education to the general public.

For instance, if low-achieving poor students underperform academically after participating in shadow education, then they will be at a far greater disadvantage in preparing for college examinations compared to high-achieving wealthy students. Similarly, if low-achieving poor students do realise a difference in academic achievement as a result of shadow education, then such activity carries important implications concerning educational opportunity and social stratification (Bray and Kwo, 2014).

Prestige-oriented views and status groups

As noted, Chinese high school students participate in shadow education to improve their chances in college entrance examinations with a view to entering higher education and attending elite institutions. Numerous studies have indicated that shadow education participation serves as a status-oriented or symbolic exercise of higher status through attending prestigious institutions (Lee and Shouse, 2011). Bray (2003) hypothesises that shadow education is more prevalent in countries where high-stakes testing exists and where there is a strong link between educational credentials and occupational prestige. Notably, he emphasises that students' prestige-oriented views of college entrance are likely to be influenced by the tightly structured, credential-driven framework of East Asian society. Lee and Shouse (2011) coined the term 'prestige orientation' to describe the degree to which students feel it is important to attend a top-ranked university. They suggest that prestige orientation affects parental spending on PST and that shadow education participation serves not just a functional purpose but also a symbolic purpose. In other words, adolescents who graduate from prestigious high schools are more likely to find higher occupational opportunities and social status than those from lower prestige schools.

Aside from parental spending, Karen (2002) suggested that familial background affects students' attendance at prestigious institutions. Similarly, Davies and Guppy (1997) concluded that high school graduates from low-resourced families are less likely to attend highly selective colleges and universities than those from wealthier families. Students from affluent families are more likely to hold prestige-oriented views (e.g. desire to attend elite higher education) than those from lower-income families.

'Family capital' – cultural, social, human, economic

In addition to elite status groups, shadow education can also facilitate students in gaining family capital (e.g. cultural, social, human, economic), which can benefit not only individual students but also the whole of society. For instance, PST may increase teacher income in cases where teachers are very low paid. Students from middle-income and affluent families are more likely to acquire private tutoring than students from poor families as a result of 'family capital' (Downey, 1995).

To enumerate, families with greater incomes can easily invest in greater amounts and better quality tutoring than families with lower incomes. Buchmann's (2002) study on Kenya's highly competitive educational system suggested that the use of shadow education constitutes a form of cultural capital. The author concluded that Kenyan children from wealthy families were far more likely than other children to partake in private tutoring outside of school. In other words, a major determinant of shadow education is fierce competition for enrolment in higher education. Higher education inequalities have often centred on the cultural and social capital of families that is passed along to their children.

Generally, cultural capital is conceptualised either as high-status cultural knowledge and preferences (Bourdieu, 1997), while social capital reflects positive and rewarding relationships between children, their parents and schools/teachers (Coleman, 1988). A number of studies have claimed that students' educational outcomes are strongly correlated with family resources. While cultural resources (e.g. knowledge, skills) and cultural materials (e.g. income) have little intrinsic value because higher education outcomes differ tremendously for students of different social backgrounds, Coleman (1988) emphasised that the availability of resources and parents' ability to help their child grow makes a drastic difference to the younger generation's educational success. Coleman (1998:S101) once stated, 'The function identified by the concept of social capital is the value of these aspects of social structure to actors as resources that they can use to achieve their interests'. In other words, higher levels of cultural resources play a significant role in promoting the social well-being of adolescents and, most importantly, fostering higher academic achievement and success on entrance examinations. Families with high cultural values on higher education attainment will likely invest more in PST compared to those with lower cultural values. Thus, social inequalities persist in shadow education, particularly with regard to socioeconomic, gender and rural/urban variables.

Discussion

As we've seen throughout this chapter, shadow education has significant policy implications for educational opportunity and the process of social stratification. Specifically, this comprehensive review of the literature highlights the expansion of shadow education in China, and how PST has both positive and negative implications for Chinese society and the economy. With an increasing focus on highly competitive entrance examinations, this chapter argues that PST plays a positive role in raising students' learning outcomes outside of the mainstream education system. However, this review also suggests that the inability to access high-quality private tutors can place lower-class students at a far greater disadvantage on NCCE scores compared to affluent urban students in China. Furthermore, high-income families can often afford greater quantities of PST. Consequently, this chapter argues that PST increases students' human capital potential, prestige-oriented status group and educational mobility while at the same time exacerbating social, educational and geographical inequalities in Chinese society.

Regrettably, few policy-makers and practitioners have conducted in-depth explorations of the effects of private tutoring on academic achievement and its implications for Chinese society either because of inadequate data or a lack of understanding of the consequences of shadow education. Instead of prohibiting or restricting PST, this review suggests that shadow education in East Asia is increasing as a result of highly competitive examination systems. This chapter thus suggests the importance of seeking alternative approaches to curbing shadow education in order to tease out the impact of college examination success on the demand for shadow education in China. Obviously, no single solution or modification can be recommended for China; however, East Asian countries and regions must attempt to tighten and regulate both mainstream education and the private tutoring industries to reduce the mentioned inequalities and inequities.

Conclusion

Educational leaders and policy-makers should be mindful of how shadow education in China can exacerbate or ameliorate social inequalities with regard to the college admissions process. While shadow education may not be restrained in the short-term, policy-makers and educators should build longer-term reform strategies and mechanisms that prevent families from distorting the genuine meaning of education. Specifically, institutional leaders and government officials should use appropriate instruments to promote equitable and inclusive learning, and reduce family/student reliance on PST. These factors may include as follows: (a) the possibility of financing tutoring programmes in rural cities as a flexible means of educating disadvantaged adolescents, (b) funding after-school programmes, as well as (c) starting television and other media networks in rural schools aiming to prepare students better for college examinations and high-stakes tests. Obviously, this process would require leaders to develop clearer policies and more effective regulations to encourage the positive dimensions of shadow education in order to increase the productivity of disadvantaged youths and to promote equity goals that align with UNESCO's Education for All (EFA). Implementing such initiatives into the policy realms may contribute further to the sociological aim of understanding the processes of social stratification, and the interplay of stratification and institutional processes involved in shadow education in China.

Reliable cross-national data are therefore greatly needed to allow researchers to understand the impact of policies on the demand for private tutoring. Institutional leaders and teacher-scholars should develop management policies that ensure educators cover the whole curriculum so that private tutoring does not displace classroom teaching and, more importantly, does not distort the original purpose of education in China (Trent, 2016). Despite the fact that PST activities have often been ignored by the EFA movement since the early 1990s, shadow education is now highly evident in the most recent *2013/2014 EFA Goal Monitoring Report* as noted in a section entitled 'Private tutoring versus classroom teaching: protecting the poorest' (UNESCO, 2014:271–272). The report emphasises that strategies should at least be in place to prevent the tutoring of pupils by teachers who are responsible for teaching them in their daily classes. This would ensure that full curriculum coverage is available for all, even those unable to afford supplementary tutoring.

In short, this chapter urges education policy-makers and educators to expand research efforts on shadow education in the field of comparative and international education. Furthermore, it encourages policy leaders and senior officials to hold informal dialogue on the role and function of private tutoring industries and to consider how shadow education sits in relation to UNESCO's EFA goals. New research should examine the relationship between shadow education and academic performance, and how the effects of shadow education relate to social and economic backgrounds. In addition, empirical research examining the connections between PST and well-being (e.g. student satisfaction levels, health status and labour-market outcomes) would be highly relevant. By expanding the scope of research on shadow education, our understanding of the impact of PST on Chinese education can be enhanced, and steps taken to ensure private tutoring can provide every child, regardless of their background and the type of school they attend, an equal chance of receiving a 'quality education' that aligns closely with the United Nations 2030 Agenda for Sustainable Development.

Individual/group task

- What are the advantages and disadvantages for pursuing shadow education activities in China? What are the opportunities and challenges?
- Do you think that shadow education has a significant effect on Chinese students' academic achievement? Why or why not?
- In your opinion, what policy agendas and outcomes should the government take to combat the growth of shadow education activities?
- How can policy-makers and educators help rural-poor students perform well on high-stakes entrance examination in China?

Acknowledgement

The authors would like to acknowledge Dr Trey Menefee, Dr Heidi A. Ross and Dr Laura E. Rumbley for providing feedback and comments.

Recommended reading

Bray, M., Kwo, O. and Jokic, B. (2015) *Researching Private Supplementary Tutoring: Methodological Lessons from Diverse Cultures*. Hong Kong, China: Comparative Education Research Centre (CERC), University of Hong Kong.
Park, H., Buchmann, C., Choi, J. and Merry, J. (2016) Learning beyond the school walls: trends and implications. *Annual Review of Sociology*, 42, 231–252.

References

Altbach, P.G. (2013) The prospects for the BRICs: the new academic superpowers? In P.G. Altbach, G. Androushchak, Y. Kuzminov, M. Yudkevich and L. Reisberg (Eds.) *The Global Future of Higher Education and the Academic Profession: The BRICs and the United States*. London: Palgrave Macmillan.
Au, R., Watkins, D. and Hattie, J. (2010) Academic risk factors and deficits of learned hopelessness: a longitudinal study of Hong Kong secondary school students. *Educational Psychology*, 30(2), 125–138.
Baker, D. and LeTendre, G. (2005) *National Differences, Global Similarities: World Culture and the Future of Schooling*. Stanford, CA: Stanford University Press.
Bourdieu, P. (1997) The forms of capital. In A.H. Halsey, H. Lauder, P. Brown and A.S. Wells (Eds.) *Education: Culture, Economy, and Society*. Oxford: Oxford University Press.
Bray, M. (2003) *Adverse Effects of Private Supplementary Tutoring: Dimensions, Implications and Government Responses*. Hong Kong: Comparative Education Research Centre (CERC), University of Hong Kong.

Bray, M. (2009) *Confronting the Shadow Education System: What Government Policies for What Private Tutoring?* Paris: UNESCO International Institute for Educational Planning (IIEP).

Bray, M. and Kwo, O. (2014) *Regulating Private Tutoring for Public Good: Policy Options for Supplementary Education in Asia.* Hong Kong: Comparative Education Research Center (CERC), University of Hong Kong.

Bray, M., Kwo, O. and Jokic, B. (2015) *Researching Private Supplementary Tutoring: Methodological Lessons from Diverse Cultures.* Hong Kong: Comparative Education Research Centre (CERC), University of Hong Kong.

Bray, M. and Lykins, C. (2012) *Shadow Education. Private Supplementary Tutoring and Its Implications for Policy Makers in Asia.* Manila: Asian Development Bank. Available at: www.fe.hku.hk/cerc/Publications/monograph_no_9.htm. (Accessed 19th March 2016).

Bray, M., Zhang, S., Lykins, C., Wang, D. and Kwo, O. (2014) Differentiated demand for private supplementary tutoring: patterns and implications in Hong Kong secondary schools. *Economics of Education Review,* 38(1), 24–37.

Buchmann, C. (2002) Getting ahead in Kenya: social capital, shadow education and achievement. *Research in Sociology of Education,* 13, 133–159.

Buchmann, C., Condron, D.J. and Roscigno, V.J. (2010) Shadow education, American style: test preparation, the SAT and college enrollment. *Social Forces,* 89(2), 435–461.

Byun, S. (2014) Shadow education and academic success in South Korea. In H. Park and K. Kim (Eds.), *Korean Education in Changing Economic and Demographic Contexts.* Singapore: Springer Publishing.

Byun, S. and Park, H. (2012) The academic success of East Asian American youth: the role of shadow education. *Sociology of Education,* 85(1), 40–60.

Cheo, R. and Quah, E. (2005) Mothers, maids and tutors: an empirical evaluation of their effect on children's academic grades in Singapore. *Education Economics,* 13(3), 269–285.

Coleman, J.S. (1988) Social capital in the creation of human capital. *American Journal of Sociology,* 94, 95–120.

Dang, H.A. (2007) The determinants and impact of private tutoring classes in Vietnam. *Economics of Education Review,* 26(6), 684–699.

Davies, S. and Guppy, N. (1997) Globalization and educational reforms in Anglo-American democracies. *Comparative Education Review,* 41, 435–459.

DiMaggio, P. (1982) Cultural capital and social success: the impact of status culture participation on the grades of high school students. *American Sociological Review,* 47(2), 89–201.

Downey, D.B. (1995) When bigger is not better: family size, parental resources, and children's educational performance. *American Sociological Review,* 60(5), 746–761.

Forbes. (2012) *Global Private Tutoring Market Will Surpass $102.8 Billion by 2018.* March 30, 2014. Available at: www.forbes.com/sites/jamesmarshallcrotty/2012/10/30/global-private-tutoring-market-will-surpass-102-billion-by-2018/. (Accessed 23rd May 2016).

George, C. (1992) Time to come out of the shadows. *Straits Times* [Singapore], 4th April.

Global Industry Analyst, Inc. (2012) *Private Tutoring – A Global Strategic Business Report.* Available at: www.strategyr.com/pressMCP-1597.asp. (Accessed 15th March 2015).

Grodsky, E. (2010) Commentaries: learning in the shadows and in the light of day. *Social Forces,* 89(2), 475–481.

Hallak, J. and Poisson, M. (2007) *Corrupt Schools, Corrupt Universities: What Can Be Done?* Paris: International Institute for Educational Planning, UNESCO.

Ho, S., Kwong, W.L. and Yeung, W.M. (2008) *Shadow Education and Related Services in Macau: The Phenomenon and Its Impact.* Macau: Department of Education and Youth Affairs.

Kang, S. (2010) Hagwon Curfew Backsliding. *Korea Times,* 1 April 2010. Available at: www.koreatimes.co.kr/www/news/nation/2010/04/113_63489.html. (Accessed 26th March 2014).

Karen, D. (2002) Changes in access to higher education in the United States: 1980–1992. *Sociology of Education,* 75(3), 191–210.

Kim, S. and Lee, J. (2010) Private tutoring and demand for education in South Korea. *Economic Development and Culture Change,* 58(2), 259–296.

Kumon (2016) *What is Kumon?* Available at: www.kumon.com/how-kumon-works (Accessed 26th February 2016).

Kwo, O. and Bray, M. (2014) Understanding the nexus between mainstream schooling and private supplementary tutoring: patterns and voices of Hong Kong secondary students. *Asia Pacific Journal of Education,* 34(4), 403–416.

Kwok, P.L.Y. (2010) Demand intensity, market parameters and policy responses towards demand and supply of private supplementary tutoring in China. *Asia Pacific Education Review*, 11(1), 49–58.

Lee, S. and Shouse, R.C. (2011) The impact of prestige orientation on shadow education in South Korea. *Sociology of Education*, 84(3), 212–224.

Lei, W. (2005) Expenditure on private tutoring for senior secondary students: determinants and policy implications. *Education and Economy*, 1,39–42.

Liu, J. (2012) Does cram schooling matter? Who goes to cram schools? *International Journal of Educational Development*, 32(1), 46–52.

Liu, J. and Bray, M. (2016) Determinants of demand for private supplementary tutoring in China: findings from a national survey. *Education Economics*, 25(2), 205–218. doi:10.1080/09645292.2016.1182623.

Manzon, M. (2011) *Comparative Education: The Construction of a Field*. Hong Kong: Comparative Education Research Center (CERC), University of Hong Kong.

Manzon, M. and Areepattamannil, S. (2014) Shadow education: mapping the global discourse. *Asia Pacific Journal of Education*, 34(4), 389–402.

Marimuthu, T., Singh, J.S., Ahmad, K., Lim, H.K., Mukherjee, H., Osman, S., Chelliah, T., Sharma, J.R., Salleh, N.M., Yong, L., Lim, T.L., Sukumaran, S., Thong, L.K. and Jamaluddin, W. (1991) *Extra-School Instruction, Social Equity and Educational Quality*. Singapore: International Development Research Centre.

Maringe, F. (2010) The meanings of globalization and internationalization in HE: findings from a world survey. In F. Maringe and N. Foskett (Eds.) *Globalization and Internationalization in Higher Education*. London: Continuum Publishing.

Mori, I. and Baker, D. (2010) The origin of universal shadow education: what the supplemental education phenomenon tells us about the postmodern institution of education. *Asia Pacific Education Review*, 11(1), 36–48.

People's Republic of China (2004) *Implementation Regulations of Minban Education Enhancement Law of People's Republic of China*. Beijing: Ministry of Education.

People's Republic of China (2013) *Opinions on Establishing Long-Term Mechanism for Constructing Professional Ethics of Teachers in Primary and Secondary Schools*. Beijing: Ministry of Education. Available at: www.moe.gov.cn. (Accessed 26th February 2014).

Shanghai Education Commission (2009) *Implementation of Merit-Pay Salary Reform of Primary and Secondary School Teachers in Shanghai to Prevent Fee-Paying Tutoring*. Shanghai: Shanghai Education Commission.

Sohn, H., Lee, D., Jang, S., and Kim, T.K. (2010) Longitudinal relationship among private tutoring, student-parent conversation, and student achievement. *KEDI Journal of Educational Policy*, 7(1), 23–41.

Stevenson, D.L. and Baker, D. (1992) Shadow education and allocation in formal schooling: transition to university in Japan. *American Journal of Sociology*, 97(6), 1639–1657.

Tang, H.H.H. (2015) Democratizing higher education in Hong Kong: between rhetoric and reality. In P. Blessinger (Ed.) *Democratizing Higher Education: International Comparative Perspectives*. London: Routledge.

Tilak, J. (2008) Higher education: a public good or a commodity for trade? *Prospects*, 38, 449–466.

Trent, J. (2016) Constructing professional identities in shadow education: perspectives of private supplementary educators in Hong Kong. *Educational Research for Policy and Practice*, 15(2), 115–130.

Tsang, M.C. (1994) Costs of education in China: issues of resource mobilization, equality. *Education Economics*, 2(3), 287–312.

Tsegay, S.M. and Ashraf, M.A. (2016) How do students succeed in national college entrance examination (Gao-kao) in China: a qualitative study. *International Journal of Research in Education*, 5(3), 81–90.

UNESCO (2014) *Teaching and Learning – Achieving Quality for All. EFA Global Monitoring Report 2013/4*. Paris: UNESCO.

UNESCO (2015) *Rethinking Education: Towards a Global Common Good?* Paris: UNESCO.

Xue, H. and Ding, X. (2009) A study on additional instruction for students in cities and towns in China. *Educational Research*, 348, 39–46.

Yamamoto, Y. and Brinton, M.C. (2010) Cultural capital in East Asian educational systems: the case of Japan. *Sociology of Education*, 83(1), 67–83.

Zhan, S., Bray, M., Wang, D., Lykins, C. and Kwo, O. (2013) The effectiveness of private tutoring: students' perceptions in comparison with mainstream schooling in Hong Kong. *Asia Pacific Education Review*, 14, 495–509.

Zhang, W. (2014) The demand for shadow education in China: mainstream teachers and power relations. *Asia Pacific Journal of Education*, 4(34), 436–454.

Zhang, W. and Bray, M. (2015) Shadow education in Chongqing, China: factors underlying demand and policy implications. *Korean Journal of Educational Policy*, 12(1), 83–106.

Zhang, W. and Bray, M. (2016) Shadow education: the rise and implications of private supplementary tutoring. In S. Guo and Y. Guo (Eds.) *Spotlight on China: Changes in Education under China's Market Economy*. Rotterdam: Sense Publishers.

Zhang, Y. (2013) Does private tutoring improve students' national college entrance examination performance? A case study from Jinan, China. *Economics of Education Review*, 32, 1–28.

Zhang, Y. (2016) *National College Entrance in China: Perspectives on Education Quality and Equity*. Beijing: Springer Publishing.

7 The impact of austerity in Further Education

Cross-cultural perspectives from England and Ireland

Matt O'Leary and Justin Rami

Introduction

The financial crisis of 2008 heralded the advent of an 'austerity' agenda by many international governments, characterised by a series of cuts to public spending and tax increases. Since then, austerity measures in England and Ireland have left an indelible mark on the further education (FE) landscapes in both countries. In Ireland, the global credit crunch had a crippling effect on the economy, resulting in a public finance crisis that saw unemployment rise rapidly, culminating in a financial bailout by the EU and IMF in 2010. In England, FE suffered as a consequence of the government's austerity agenda more than any other education sector. From 2010 to 2016, FE colleges endured repeated cuts to their budgets, leading to the closure of courses, departments and ongoing mass redundancies, while schools remained relatively unaffected with their funding ring-fenced. Yet the impact of this instability on the FE workforce in these two countries remains underresearched and underreported, making it all the more important to capture the voices of those who have been directly affected. From senior management to teaching and support staff, the cascading effects of austerity have been palpable at all levels. Drawing on interview and documentary data from original research conducted from 2015 to 2016, this chapter explores the impact of government austerity on the lives of the FE workforce and the communities they serve, while also reflecting on the importance of FE and its role in both countries' education systems.

This chapter starts with a brief overview of the FE sectors in each country, comparing similarities and differences between the two. It then moves on to highlighting the consequences of government austerity from a policy perspective, leading into an exploration and discussion of research data that captures what this has meant for those working in FE, its impact on their professional lives and the students they cater for. This chapter concludes by reflecting on the current status of FE and how the changes experienced as a result of austerity are likely to shape its future course.

An overview of FE in England and Ireland

There are many similarities between FE in England and Ireland but equally some notable differences between the two countries. Table 7.1 provides a snapshot of some of the key differences and similarities.

Table 7.1   A comparison of similarities and differences of FE in England and Ireland

Similarities	Differences
• *Diversity of provision* – e.g. basic skills, apprenticeships, work-based learning, community provision, offender learning	• *Sector name* – Ireland = Further Education and Training (FET); England = Further Education (FE)
• *Flexibility of provision* – full-time and part-time courses, daytime, evening and weekend	• *Age of students* – Ireland = 18+; England = 14+
• *Curriculum* – vocationally focussed rather than academically focussed curriculum	• *Governance* – Ireland = highly decentralised; England = highly centralised
• *Employability* – focus/links to employment and the demands of the labour market	• *Qualifications for teaching staff* – Ireland = mandatory qualifications include a Teaching Council approved teacher education qualification and a first degree; England = no mandatory qualifications
• *Social inclusion* – key role in promoting social inclusion through learning and training of 'non-traditional' students	• *Monitoring and evaluation* – Ireland = lack of history of established systems of monitoring and evaluation; England = long-standing history of system of monitoring and evaluation via inspections and reviews
• *Identity issues* – lack of clearly defined identity compared to schools and universities	
• *Status* – perception of being of lower status than academic route of schools and universities	

Ireland

The term FET (Further Education and Training) is used in Ireland to encompass FE, Vocational Education and Training (VET). FET is often used interchangeably with VET, depending on the perspective. FET embraces education and training that occurs after second-level schooling and mainly in the further and continuing education sector, though FET also occurs in some higher education (HE) establishments.

The most recent legislation, which marked the establishment of the National Further Education and Training Authority known as SOLAS (An tSeirbhís Oideachais Leanúnaigh agus Scileanna) and ETBs (Education and Training Boards), was in 2013 and covered FET but not VET specifically. In reality, this covers VET, which includes the PLC (Post Leaving Certificate), LCVP (Leaving Certificate Vocational Programme), LCA (Leaving Certificate Applied) awards and qualifications, adult learning, community education, vocational training, apprenticeships, on-the-job training, CPD (Continuing Professional Development), internships, other training programmes and labour activation schemes.

A distinctive feature of FET is its diversity, breadth of provision and links with other services such as employment, training, welfare, youth, school, juvenile liaison, justice and community and voluntary sector interests. Coincidentally, a wide range of government departments, statutory agencies and voluntary- and community-based organisations also provide services in this area, adding a greater complexity to the education system as a whole.

FET in Ireland is not only about employability but it also espouses the key concepts of lifelong learning. It is seen in policy and structural terms as being one of the main pillars essential to the building and maintenance of a highly skilled workforce operating within a knowledge society.

Due to the competitive entry requirements for HE, every year a fraction of students opt to remain in upper secondary education in order to improve their performance in the final year exams with the overall aim of eventually gaining entry to their chosen course in HE. Thus, traditionally, for those completing second-level education in Ireland, HE has been the preferred destination for further study or training, with 51% of Ireland's 25–34-year-olds holding a degree-level qualification (Condon *et al.*, 2014).

The FET sector is perceived by some stakeholders as being less clearly defined and of lower status than HE (e.g. ESRI, 2014). This not only echoes wider social norms but can also be seen as a reflection of the diversity of FET in terms of the perceptions of current provision. One of the stated aims of the Irish government during austerity was to implement the establishment of a new FET/VET authority (SOLAS). One of the primary objectives of this new authority is to radically enhance the image of FET among Ireland's school leavers, their parents/guardians and career guidance professionals (SOLAS, 2014).

With the introduction of SOLAS in 2013 came a drive to join the 'T' of training with the 'FE' of Education. The most significant development initiated by SOLAS has been the FET Strategy 2014–2019 (SOLAS, 2014), though the data derived from our research would suggest that there are still legacy issues delaying the acceptance of this paradigm shift from FE to FET. In the *Education Matters Year Book 2015–2016*, Dr Bryan Field from SOLAS wrote:

> All of the good work that has taken place in 2015 to fully integrate the 'FE' and the 'T' is aimed at improving learner access and outcomes for all who will engage in FET so that they too can fulfil their potential and meet their career employment, personal or developmental aspirations. The FET Strategy points the way forward.
>
> *(NUIG, 2015)*

FET in Ireland has often been seen as the 'poor relation' of HE, with the latter dominating the headlines in the national media. Support for FET tends to come from those championing the 'economic' imperative over its 'social inclusion' agenda. A particular characteristic of the Irish FET system is the promotion of the interdependence of the objectives of economic development and social inclusion. Thus, social forces have always been viewed as key drivers in the promotion of a lifelong learning agenda in Ireland, alongside the economic factors.

England

The FE sector in England caters for over 3 million students annually. Like FE in Ireland, it sits between schools and universities, including all post-compulsory education and training outside of HE. Yet, unlike schools and universities, where there is a common understanding of their remit, purpose and target communities, FE remains an enigma to many politicians and policy-makers, as indeed it does to the majority of the population. This is in part due to the way in which the identities of many FE colleges and providers have morphed and become more heterogeneous over the last three decades as a result of the marketisation of the sector. Another key factor is the lack of a coherent national policy for FE and the ongoing 'strategic drift' (Green and Lucas,

1999) that has characterised successive government interventions in the sector since the early 1990s. Underpinning this strategic incoherence are fundamental questions concerning who FE is for and what its primary purpose is.

While there are similarities in the curriculum offered in FE and schools, with both providing education for teenagers, there are noticeable differences between the two. For example, FE offers a wide range of vocational subjects, work-based learning and community provision. In contrast to schools, FE also caters for a large population of adult returners to learning, often looking to improve their qualifications and/or gain new skills later in life. With a diverse populace of students from all parts of the community and comprising all social groups, FE providers are typically inclusive institutions and have an important role to play in enhancing social integration and social mobility in England as indeed they do in Ireland. The 'diversity' and 'complexity' commonly associated with the English FE sector (Huddleston and Unwin, 2013) also extends to the scale of its organisations with some large colleges catering for over 15,000 full-time and part-time students, compared to small private training providers with less than 50 students.

In England, the FE sector's links to the economy and the position it has traditionally been perceived to occupy between education and the workplace has featured repeatedly in education policy in recent decades. Much of this policy has attributed a largely instrumentalist role to FE, linking it to economic well-being and positioning it as a sector that is readily disposed to meet the perceived skills' needs of the country's workforce (e.g. Foster, 2005; Leitch, 2006). This has resulted in recurring policy interventions. As Keep (2014) argues, investment in education and training in the sector has been a mainstay of successive government policy over the last quarter of a century, largely driven by labour market demands and social inclusion considerations. Broadly speaking, the rationale for this policy focus has been fuelled by the need to improve workers' skills to enable them to compete on the global stage, as evidenced by influential studies such as the Leitch Review of Skills (2006). By upskilling the workforce, it is assumed that not only would this improve its international skills standing, but it would also have a positive impact on increasing levels of productivity and boost the economy (Keep *et al.*, 2006). Yet evidence to date suggests that not only has this failed to happen in England but that it has also slipped further down the international skills' league tables (e.g. Keep, 2014).

Individual/group task

- What do you know about the FE sector in your country?
- What is the role of FE?
- What are some of the key differences between studying at school and in a FE college/provider?
- Who studies in the FE sector and what kind of courses do they study?

Policy perspectives on austerity in FE

England

Shortly after the Conservative-Liberal Democrat coalition government entered office in 2010, George Osborne, the chancellor at the time, unveiled the biggest public spending cuts the country had seen for decades. Buoyed by widespread support in sections of the media and the public, Osborne introduced a sustained period of austerity, using a 'common sense' argument that blamed the previous labour government for spending beyond its means while in power (Spours, 2015). Osborne announced that drastic cuts needed to be made to public spending in order to tackle the country's burgeoning deficit.

Since 2010, FE has experienced a sustained programme of cuts, impacting directly on providers and the infrastructure of the sector as a whole. As a House of Commons Committee of Public Accounts remarked towards the end of 2016, FE has 'experienced a real-terms funding cut of 27 per cent in the last five years' (HC414, 2015:8, para 8).

The practical impact of these cuts has been an extensive catalogue of savings measures in 16–18 education in FE colleges (AoC, 2014), made all the more challenging given that FE has historically been 'funded less generously than 11–16 schooling' (Wolf, 2015:15). Wolf goes on to state that 'its shrinking share of total education funding indicates that it is not, in practice, a top priority for governments' (ibid). And the forecast for the coming years offers little hope of improvement, with some predicting that the overall reduction in the Department for Business, Innovation and Skills' (BIS) budget from 2010 to 2018 will total 43% (e.g. Keep, 2014).

Throughout the government's austerity agenda, schools have remained relatively unaffected, with much of their funding ring-fenced. In contrast, FE has experienced year-on-year cuts since 2010 (AoC, 2014). Like secondary schools, FE colleges in England cater predominantly for teenage students, which inevitably raises the question as to why the sector has been repeatedly targeted and schools have escaped such treatment. Has the government's austerity programme in FE been solely driven by financial factors or are there are other interests at play? The government maintains that its rationale for targeting FE has been based on a model of financial reasoning designed to make efficiency savings, although there are some researchers who question this.

Spours (2015:13), for example, suggests that austerity is an 'ideologically driven agenda rather than economically necessary measures' and argues that the burden of austerity has been spread unevenly across the population in order to protect the Conservatives' core voters and to 'push policies they (the Conservatives) always desired but did not think were possible in normal circumstances' (Jones, 2015:xix). Other researchers in the field have suggested that no one in Whitehall actually cares about FE (e.g. Coffield, 2015). This is an argument that appears to be rooted in class divisions and/or interests and the perceived invisibility of FE in some circles. In other words, FE is a sector that has traditionally catered to the needs of working-class communities and remains largely invisible to others, especially politicians and policy-makers, though it has to be said that this is not a new argument. Almost 20 years ago, in her seminal report on FE, Helena Kennedy wrote that:

> Further education suffers because of prevailing British attitudes … there is an appalling ignorance among decision makers and opinion formers about what goes on in further education. It is so alien to their experience.
>
> *(Kennedy, 1997:1)*

Twenty years later, little appears to have changed. Such ignorance, or what some might even regard as contempt for FE, is not unusual among the establishment. In drawing on the work of King and Crewe (2013) to exemplify their notion of 'cultural disconnect', a term used to describe politicians and civil servants dealing with 'values, attitudes and whole ways of life that are not remotely like their own' (p. 244), Coffield (2015) provides a pertinent example of 'cultural disconnect' in citing an occasion when Boris Johnson – then shadow HE minister – delivered a speech to a group of FE principals and senior managers at a conference in Cambridge. Unsure of who his audience was, he stopped halfway through his speech to ask who it was he was addressing. Once enlightened by one of the principals present, he paused for a moment and replied, 'Ah, I know who you all are. You used to be called Secondary Moderns'. In a similar vein, Vince Cable recounted that in the early days of the 2010 coalition government, civil servants in his department wanted to axe FE completely in order to save money, arguing that 'nobody will really notice' (Wheeler, 2014).

Another factor that has ostensibly contributed to FE bearing the burden of the government's austerity programme is that traditionally it has not had the lobbying presence in parliament afforded to that of schools and the HE sector. As such, it is arguably easier for politicians and policy-makers to dismiss it as a budgetary burden, as Wolf (2015) has suggested.

Ireland

Ireland was significantly impacted by one of the most severe economic and social shrinkages in the international and European financial crisis. As Hearne (2015:4) comments:

> The banking crash was one of the largest in modern history and the costs of the crisis were being imposed by both Irish governments and the IMF/EU/ECB 'Troika' on to the majority of the population-low and middle income households.

A series of austerity budgets were implemented in Ireland from 2008 to 2014, along with an accompanying set of conditions imposed as part of the international bailout from 2010 to 2013. Most of these included cuts to public spending and social welfare, along with a number of tax increases (some of these in the form of stealth taxes), predominantly on middle-and low-income households, of over €30 billion (Hearne, 2015).

Mercille and Murphy (2015:4) maintain that:

> Ireland has been a poster child for the implementation of fiscal consolidation. Whereas a number of countries initially responded to the 2008–9 financial crisis through Keynesian measures, Ireland immediately started to implement austerity on its own.

The austerity reforms happened in the context of a €67.5 billion EU-IMF bailout, which conditionally required 'structural reforms', in particular, within the public sector and education. Though Ireland has since left the bailout programme, it is still subject to regular monitoring from the EMF (European Monetary Fund) and the IMF, and austerity continues to be implemented (ibid). The scale of this change should not be understated. Between 2008 and 2015, it has amounted to approximately 20% of the Irish GDP, almost €32 billion, of which 30% has been accounted for by spending cuts and tax increases.

Austerity measures have purportedly had a considerable impact on attracting new teachers into the profession. The Teachers' Union of Ireland (TUI) warned that it would be forced to consider industrial action unless progress was made on restoring pay allowances for teachers new to the profession. Qualification allowances were removed from teachers entering the profession after February 2012. The union claims this amounted to a pay cut of approximately 20% for some. Since July 2016, however, there have been significant developments. Officials from the Department of Education and Skills (DES), the Department of Public Expenditure and Reform and union representatives had a series of meetings to discuss the issues relating to pay arrangements for newly qualified teachers recruited since 1 February 2012. These discussions took place within the provisions of the Lansdowne Road Agreement and the TUI/DES Agreement of May 2016. Following these meetings, the government agreed in principle to implement a new incremental salary scale for new entrants, designed to address the current difference in pay for teachers recruited since 1 February 2012 (DES, 2016:1). This new arrangement was to apply to members of the teachers' unions that had signed up to the Lansdowne Road Agreement.

Individual/group task

- What are the key factors that have influenced the austerity agenda in England and Ireland?

Research on workforce perspectives on the impact of austerity in FE

Nineteen individual semi-structured interviews were conducted in person and over the telephone with a range of staff working at all levels in the FE sector. The interview sample included college principals, senior and middle managers, lecturers, tutors, learning support staff as well as guidance counsellors and Youth Reach coordinators from a broad sample of providers across England and Ireland. In capturing the voices of differing members of the FE workforce, this section seeks to illuminate some of their lived experiences and reflects on how, individually and collectively, they have dealt with a period of tumultuous change. It also seeks to draw attention to some of the difficulties and concerns facing those working in FE in the light of a sustained period of austerity and how this has impacted on the work they do.

Fear, resentment and uncertainty

As a result of having to manage significantly reduced budgets, many FE colleges in England have found themselves with little choice but to make savings in fixed costs such as salaries. One of the ways in which some colleges have responded to this is by introducing term-time only contracts, as Michael, a learning support assistant describes:

> Another way they're saving money is paying people only in term time. Previously some staff would be on a full-time, permanent contract with paid holiday entitlement. So instead of having a year-long contract they've introduced these new contracts, which some people have had to sign or risk losing their job completely … the new style contracts mean that staff only get paid for working term time.

This trend is reflected in a recent report released by one of the main teaching unions for the sector, the University and College Union (UCU) entitled *Precarious Work in Further Education* (UCU, 2015), which claims that over a third of teaching staff in the sector are employed on what the report refers to as 'precarious contracts', i.e. hourly paid, variable hours or term-time only contracts.

Gurnam, a business studies lecturer, described a climate of continuous uncertainty and instability in his workplace, with all departments going through an internal review in order to rationalise provision and from which there seemed to be two discernible outcomes: The first being redundancy and the second a revised job role with an increase in workload and responsibilities, yet often together with a salary freeze, or even a cut in salary in some cases.

> There's definitely a degree of fear. The principal warned everyone that the area reviews were coming and that we would try and predict the outcomes by exploring a merger with another local college but at the same time he said that there were going to be job losses as a result of the reviews. Ever since then there's been a continuous period of uncertainty as everyone's thinking, 'I wonder who'll be next or which department will be next' … We're also seeing a significant increase in peoples' additional duties.

Job uncertainty and the fear of being made redundant are conditions that have increasingly come to be associated with working in FE in England since the days of incorporation but appear to have become more accentuated during the period of austerity (e.g. Lucas and Crowther, 2016; O'Leary and Smith, 2012).

In Ireland, the research revealed a perception among FET staff that the value of their work was not fully appreciated by the government and this had led to a general erosion of motivation among some working in the sector:

> There is great resentment among people at what they perceive (rightly in my view) as the great undervaluing of FET teachers in comparison with mainline teachers. Salaries and conditions of employment in the FE sector are greatly inferior to those of mainstream teachers.
>
> *(Deputy Principal of a Second Level FE School)*

> People are doing their job. From people I have spoken to, the sense of unfairness in our treatment in relation to teachers in our own sector has led many people to take a step back from the job. Whereas before, we would have, as a matter of course, put in extra hours and effort, now we do what we have to and no more. Many people in Youthreach would have put in extra hours even before the Croke Park and Landsdowne Road Agreements [The Croke Park and Landsdowne Road Agreements were negotiated public sector agreements which dealt with public sector reform related to areas such pay scales, and performance management, not all of the Teaching Unions signed up to the agreements.] For many, it is now less of a vocation and more of a job.
>
> *(Youthreach Coordinator)*

Doing more with less and the consequences for staff and students

Gina, a faculty director from a college in the north of England, talked of the need 'to do whatever it takes to get through a difficult time' and was acutely aware of how 'that doesn't seem fair on staff because it means a lot more work for them' but when faced with reduced resources, there was a need 'to tighten your belt and all pull together'.

The notion of 'do[ing] whatever it takes' manifested itself in a number of different ways for teaching and support staff, many of which seemed to result in increased workloads and extra responsibilities. As Sally, a programme manager for health and social care, succinctly remarked, 'it's about doing more with less'. Teaching staff were often timetabled up to and beyond their contracted hours. Traditionally, 24 contact hours per week have been interpreted as the maximum for teaching staff across the sector. However, in many cases, 24 hours was now being interpreted as the minimum, and, in some cases, it was considered 'not unreasonable to teach up to 28 hours a week' (Bev, art and design lecturer). Participants also spoke of how class sizes had been doubled or even tripled, regardless of whether classrooms could accommodate the students.

Students also experienced the direct impact of austerity. Reduced budgets resulted in many departments demanding increased contributions from students towards the cost of resources. Invariably, these are students who come from low-income families that struggle to pay their weekly household bills let alone cover any extra expenditure. According to Fazia, a hair and beauty lecturer in England, reduced budgets have resulted in departments like her own demanding increased contributions from students towards the cost of resources/equipment. Until recently, such students did at least have the educational maintenance allowance to rely on to cover these costs but this financial support was abolished by the coalition government in 2010.

Michael talked about how at his college some of the most vulnerable learners suffered directly from the cuts as specialist support was either reduced or withdrawn completely. He cited two examples of this: The first, where a specialist member of staff with a cross-college role in supporting learners with severe behaviour difficulties on a one-to-one basis had their role removed. And the second, of a learner with significant disability issues whose support was affected as a result of the budget cutbacks in the college. In both cases, staff were informed that the college was 'no longer able to offer that service' and that such specialist work would now become the responsibility of main grade lecturers.

Similarly, in Ireland, staff expressed their concerns about the impact of sector reform under the auspices of austerity on the students themselves. The introduction of a government levy on students and the reduction in BTEA (Back to Education Allowance) were specific austerity measures that were identified as having a particularly negative impact on students:

> The introduction of the 200 euro levy has affected the number of FE students in our college as we are located in an underprivileged area of north Dublin. The decrease in the BTEA allowance has had the same effects. The moratorium on the replacement of administration staff has had an effect on the service we can provide to students.
>
> *(Senior FET Manager)*

> [The] cap on PLC places means that schools cannot run extra courses, even if there is demand, as they will not get a teaching allocation to run them. Also students with disabilities have to wait several months for supports as the funding from the HEA [Higher Education Authority] only comes through in November/December.
>
> *(FET College Principal and Teacher)*

Policy rhetoric and the remit of FE

One of the recurring themes to emerge across all participants in England was the perception that there was a lack of understanding by central government and policy-makers about what FE is, its underlying purpose and who the students are studying in it. For example, the failure to understand the needs of the local communities FE serves through the imposition of centrally driven policies, regardless of what those local needs might be. This is captured poignantly in the following comment by Richard, a principal with over 30 years' experience in the sector:

> FE colleges are part of the very fabric of local communities. I don't think the government understand that at all. They don't realise the role the sector plays in helping to create rounded individuals. They just see the purpose of FE as a factory for producing skills.

Two examples of this failure to understand the sector and the disconnect between policy rhetoric and reality were prevalent in the data in relation to the funding for apprenticeships and the advanced learner loans. Senior managers expressed their frustrations of how government ministers would talk publicly about responding to the demands of the market and local economic needs, yet the reality of centralised funding diktat meant that they were unable to use funding flexibly to meet the specific needs of students and their local communities. Contrary to the claims that 'the apprenticeship levy and advanced learner loans allowed colleges to develop sustainable business models with less reliance on government funding' (Ratcliffe, 2016), many senior managers commented on their reluctance to want to commit to significant investment in areas where future funding remained uncertain and lacked assurances from the government.

This lack of understanding about the sector, along with it playing second fiddle to schools, was not only peculiar to England but also seemed to be the case in Ireland as the following comment from a college principal reinforces:

> … reform is not complete because FET colleges still operate under second level procedures and the DES has a poor understanding of FET colleges and it is preoccupied with traditional schooling. Most civil servants are products of traditional secondary schools. The fragmented nature of the sector makes it difficult to get decisions and agreements related to FET. Often the decisions taken are for secondary schools and FET colleges are an afterthought.
>
> *(FET College Principal)*

Michael Moriarty, general secretary of Education and Training Boards Ireland (ETBI) and president of the European Federation of Education Employers has argued that:

> The attractiveness and capacity of the further education and training (FET) sector need to be improved … We've been arguing for five years for a capital budget for the sector, not just to build or renovate colleges, but to fit them out with equipment to train people for jobs of today and the future.
>
> *(Murray, 2016)*

Moriarty went on to criticise the government-imposed limits on PLC places, claiming that they restrict the ability of FET providers to cater for more students who are seeking to complete second-level education.

Individual/group task

- What has the impact of austerity been on FE staff from front line to senior managers?
- What is the impact of austerity on students in the sector?
- How might practitioners in the FE sector in England and Ireland best go about influencing government policy?

Conclusion

The impact of austerity and the systemic reforms implemented across FE in both countries have been significant and far-reaching. In Ireland, austerity measures have arguably been a catalyst for wider reform to a sector that has historically been underpinned by an *ad hoc* structure lacking in strategic vision, and one that aspires to develop a greater coherence between the values of social and cultural capital with the need for a strong economy. The creation of the new national strategy for FET 2014–2019 (SOLAS, 2014) is designed to play a key role in meeting the needs of individual students and equally the government's economic policy. It is still early days and whether it succeeds in fulfilling both aims remains to be seen.

In England, the current situation in FE seems less optimistic. In a recent House of Commons report, the public accounts committee report concluded that 'the declining financial health of many further education colleges has potentially serious consequences for learners and local economies' (HC414, 2015:3). As some senior leaders in the sector have commented, current policy is disadvantaging the most disadvantaged students. Far from enhancing the life chances of these students, it is exacerbating the cycle of depravation that is prevalent in so many of the communities that FE caters for. So, what's to be done to protect a sector that faces the most challenging period in its history?

Keep (2014:6) warns that 'it would be unwise to formulate plans for the future of post-compulsory skills policy that are reliant upon a reversal of the existing cuts'. In essence, what this means then is that any new investment would need to be funded by further cuts to existing budgets. Keep's analysis carries with it a deterministic view of funding and resigned compliance. But why should it be this way? Why should the education of one part of the population be guaranteed (i.e. schools) and others discretionary, or at best, proportionate and conditional?

Since the days of incorporation, colleges in England have had to adapt to becoming more entrepreneurial and dealing with the challenges that ongoing changes and cuts to funding have presented. While many have worked hard to generate alternative sources of income, the reality is that colleges are dependent on government funding for their existence. At a time of unprecedented budget cuts in the sector, it is clear that the arrangements for planning and funding for FE need to allow greater flexibility to respond to local needs and less emphasis on nationally set targets. There is a level of complexity to the funding methodology for FE that seems unnecessarily complex and is in desperate need of a major overhaul. But this needs to form part of a wider review of funding for the sector as a whole. This is an issue that the current government needs to address sooner rather than later.

Individual/group task

- What is the relationship between education and employment?
- Do you think that it is the responsibility of FE to prepare students for the workplace?

Recommended reading

Books

Daley, M., Orr, K.and Petrie, J. (Eds.) 2015 *Further Education and the Twelve Dancing Princesses*. London: IoE Press.

Hodgson, A. (Ed.) 2015 *The Coming of Age for FE? Reflections on the Past and Future Role of Further Education Colleges in the UK*. London: Institute of Education.

Murray, M., Grummell, B. and Ryan, A. (2014) *Further Education and Training: History, Politics and Practice*. Maynooth: MACE.

Journals

Research in Post-compulsory Education.

The Adult Learner – The Irish Journal of Adult and Community Education.

References

AoC (2014) *College Funding and Finance – May 2014*. Available at: www.aoc.co.uk/sites/default/files/ College%20Funding%20and%20Finance%201%20May%202014%20FINAL_0_0.pdf. (Accessed 14th May 2016).

Coffield, F. (2015) Resistance is fertile: the demands the FE sector must make of the next government. Keynote speech at *Newbubbles Conference*, 26th March 2015, Thistle Hotel, London, UK.

Condon, N., McNaboe, J. and Burke, N. (2014) *Monitoring Ireland's Skills Supply: Trends in Education and Training*. Expert Group on Future Skills Needs, Skills and Labour Market Research Unit (SLMRU), SOLAS, Dublin.

DES (2016) *New Entrant Pay Issue and Related Commitments*. Available at: www.education.ie/en/ Education-Staff/Information/Public-Service-Stability-Agreement-Haddington-Road/New-Entrant-Pay-Issue-and-Related-Commitments.pdf. (Accessed 3rd November 2016).

ESRI (2014) *Further Education and Training in Ireland: Past, Present and Future*. Research Series Number 35. Dublin: ESRI and SOLAS.

Foster, A. (2005) *Realising the Potential: A Review of the Future Role of Further Education Colleges*. Nottingham: DfES Publications.

Green, A. and Lucas, N. (1999) From obscurity to crisis: the FE sector in context. In A. Green and N. Lucas (Eds.) *FE and Lifelong Learning: Realigning the Sector for the 21st Century*. London: Bedford Way Publications.

HC414 (2015) *Overseeing Financial Sustainability in the Further Education Sector: Thirteenth Report of Session 2015–16*. Published on 16 December 2015 by authority of the House of Commons. London: The Stationery Office.

Hearne, R. (2015) *The Irish Water War, Austerity and the 'Risen People': An Analysis of Participant Opinions, Social and Political Impacts and Transformative Potential of the Irish Anti Water-Charges Movement*.

Department of Geography, Maynooth University. Available at: www.maynoothuniversity.ie/sites/default/files/assets/document/TheIrishWaterwar_0.pdf. (Accessed 20th September 2016).

Huddlestone, P. and Unwin, L. (2013) *Teaching and Learning in Further Education: Diversity and Change* (4th Edition). London: Routledge.

Jones, O. (2015) *The Establishment. And How They Get Away with It*. London: Penguin.

Keep, E. (2014) *What Does Skills Policy Look Like When the Money Has Run Out?* SKOPE. London: Association of Colleges.

Keep, E., Mayhew, K. and Payne, J. (2006) From skills revolution to productivity miracle: not as easy as it sounds? *Oxford Review of Economic Policy*, 22(4), 539–559.

Kennedy, H. (1997) *Learning Works: Widening Participation in Further Education*. Coventry: FEFC.

King, A. and Crewe, I. (2013) *The Blunders of Our Governments*. London: Oneworld.

Leitch, S. (2006) *The Leitch Review of Skills. Prosperity for All in the Global Economy – World Class Skills. Final Report*. London: HMSO. Available at: www.gov.uk/government/uploads/system/uploads/attachment_data/file/354161/Prosperity_for_all_in_the_global_economy_-_summary.pdf. (Accessed 9th May 2016).

Lucas, N. and Crowther, N. (2016) The logic of the Incorporation of further education colleges in England 1993–2015: towards an understanding of marketisation, change and instability. *Journal of Education Policy*, 31(5), 583–597.

Mercille, J. and Murphy, E. (2015) The neoliberalization of Irish higher education under austerity. *Critical Sociology*, 8th October, 2015, 1–17. Available at: www.ifut.ie/sites/default/files/publications/public/report/2016//mercilleandmurphy2015.pdf. (Accessed 30th October 2016).

Murray, N. (2016) *Extra Investment May Cut High College Drop-Out Rate*. Available at: www.etbi.ie/extra-investment-may-cut-high-college-drop-out-rate/. (Accessed 30th October 2016).

NUIG (2015) *Education Matters Yearbook 2015–2016*. Galway: National University of Ireland, NUIG.

O'Leary, M. and Smith, R. (2012) Earthquakes, cancer and cultures of fear: qualifying as a skills for life teacher in an uncertain economic climate. *Oxford Review of Education*, 38(4), 437–454.

Ratcliffe, R. (2016) Sean Bean's battle cry: 'I despair at the state of further education'. *The Observer*, 16th January 2016. Available at: www.theguardian.com/education/2016/jan/16/further-education-colleges-cuts-sean-bean-ainsley-harriott?CMP=share_btn_tw. (Accessed 3rd May 2016).

SOLAS (2014) *Further Education and Training Strategy (2014–2019)*. Available at: www.education.ie/en/Publications/Policy-Reports/Further-Education-and-Training-Strategy-2014-2019.pdf. (Accessed 29th September 2016).

Spours, K. (2015) *The Osborne Supremacy. Why Progressives Have to Develop a Hegemonic Politics for the 21st Century*. Compass: 21st Century Hegemony Project. Available at: www.compassonline.org.uk/wp-content/uploads/2015/10/The-Osborne-Supremacy-Compass.pdf. (Accessed 12th May 2016).

UCU (2015) *'Non-lecturer' Roles in Further Education Teaching and Assessing Teams. A UCU Bargaining and Support Pack for Branches – September 2015*. Available at: www.ucu.org.uk/media/3886/Campaigning-for-associate-teachers-branch-support-pack-May-10/pdf/ucu_associateteachers_branchguidance_oct15.pdf. (Accessed 4th May 2016).

Wheeler, B. (2014) Officials wanted to axe FE colleges – Vince Cable, *BBC News*, 6th October 2014. Available at: www.bbc.co.uk/news/uk-politics-29496475. (Accessed 12th May 2016).

Wolf, A. (2015) *Heading for the Precipice: Can Further and Higher Education Funding Policies be Sustained?* London: Policy Institute, King's College London. Available at: www.kcl.ac.uk/sspp/policy-institute/publications/Issuesandideas-alison-wolf-digital.pdf. (Accessed 4th May 2016).

8 Academic, vocational and pre-vocational education – origins and developments

Patrick Ainley

Introduction

Academic in English education is associated with the brain and vocational with the hand. Institutionally, this was played out in traditional class terms with academic higher education (HE) for the professions endorsed by universities over non-academic trade training for manual crafts in colleges of further education (FE). Most of the rest of the world makes no such distinction but talks about 'tertiary education', whether at college or university following a pre-vocational general education at primary and secondary school usually up to 18, the age of majority in the USA. Now that England has adopted an Americanised mass tertiary system and FE has been decanted into HE, the traditional divisions have eroded but the old terms are still widely used. This causes confusion, which this chapter clarifies through an historical approach leading to considering the changed contemporary meaning of the words as they are used in today's very different circumstances.

> **Individual/group task**
>
> - That condensed paragraph has introduced a number of key terms that are underlined. As a preliminary individual or group exercise, note your own understanding of these words before going on to read the following.

Informal learning and the development of formal education

Elementary schools attended by the mass of the population only developed in industrialising countries in the last 200 years and it is still a world development goal to have all children in primary, let alone secondary, schooling. Now, nearly half or more of young people in many countries progress to tertiary level (see below), but perhaps 10,000 years ago, in the first city states, only a very few were formally educated. Prior to that, during the over 1 million years of human emergence as a species, institutions of formal education did not exist, so all learning was informal and acquired throughout people's lifetimes (as arguably, much of it still is).

The few divisions of labour and knowledge that existed in tribal societies organised by kinship were based upon age and gender. Mental work in handing down the traditions of the tribe and the technical expertise acquired during a lifetime was the specialised function of the old whose wisdom was universally revered. From infancy, the young participated in all activities, inducted by their elders into the work of the group. Through ritual initiation into successive age grades, an individual acquired in turn all the skills shared by their gender in the collectivity as a whole. It was only with the development of technology allowing for the production of a surplus sufficient to feed some members of society who did not have to work to produce it that the mental work of organising the efforts of others became concentrated upon hereditary rulers. They usually took over command from a council of elders only in emergency situations, as in the native American institution of war chiefs, but eventually came to safeguard their privileged position with an armed bodyguard of their relatives. (This paragraph is loosely based on Engels, 1970, first published 1884.)

During the course of this development, it can be supposed that the division of knowledge and labour between the sexes, which at first favoured women, had been reversed. Evidence of a seemingly pan-Neolithic cult of mother worship reflected the importance of childbearing for survival of the group and several feminist studies (for example, Morgan, 1973) have also asserted the social importance of what were in all likelihood the originally exclusively female crafts of midwifery, pottery, basket and cloth weaving, etc. By contrast, male activities like hunting were socially undervalued. Today, such divisions are sustained in developed econ-omies only in remoter pockets of rural life and should not be confused with contemporary gender stereotypes, which, Coleman points out, are 'essentially urban, as are the reactions against them' (1988:38).

In ancient Greek democracy, only adult male slave owners were regarded as full citizens who could vote in the directly elected council running the affairs of city states. This required educa-tion to a late age, especially in rhetorical speech-making to persuade your peers to follow your leadership. There were several schools of rhetoric, including Plato's academy, meaning a grove of trees where it met. Here, young men learnt what Aristotle (Plato's pupil) called 'the knowl-edge necessary to rule'. This was not knowledge about everything but of the rules necessary to order existing knowledge. Plato dismissed inarticulate knowledge like that of those who knew useful crafts, like how to make pots, but could not explain how they did it. Only knowledge that could be expressed in precise and logical mathematical form was recognised. (See further in Thomson, 1972.)

In advanced agrarian societies, the divisions of labour and knowledge became fixed into castes. While these divisions were simple in terms of the numbers of different occupations as compared with today, they were complicated by these few roles being mutually exclusive and at the same time interdependent. Although the peasant majority in medieval societies was inter-changeable with regard to the all-round skills of self-sufficient agricultural labour, a minority of specialists was mutually dependent upon them and upon each other for their means of life, which they could only obtain by exchange for their products. The art of making such goods – be they tools or ornaments – was learnt by apprenticeship within guilds of tradesmen (usually). It was passed down the generations so that lifetimes of concentrated practice developed particular crafts to levels that modern society can still not surpass, even with all the technical aids at our disposal. Even the mysteries of the written word were reserved for a special caste, for in Europe, as in India, priests learned a sacred language that nobody else knew (Latin and Sanskrit). Latin was what was taught in the first English grammar schools preparing boys for the priesthood if they had a calling/vocation for it in the first monastic universities and colleges. Noone else needed to be literate because the priests were, and for a long time, even most kings in early medieval Europe were illiterate.

Comparing the division of labour in such a society with that existing in an industrial society, Ernest Gellner noted,

> .... a subtle but profound and important qualitative difference in the division of labour... [that] the major part of training in industrial society is generic [ie. pre-vocational] training, not specifically connected with the highly specialised professional activity of the person in question, and preceding it. Industrial society may by most criteria be the most highly specialised society ever; but its educational system is unquestionably the least specialised, the most universally standardized that has ever existed... The assumption is that anyone who has completed the generic training common to the entire population can be re-trained for most other jobs without too much difficulty... There is also a minority of genuine specialists, people whose effective occupancy of their posts really depends on very prolonged additional [vocational] training, and who are not easily or at all replaceable by anyone not sharing their own particular educational background.
>
> *(1983:27)*

Schooling after the industrial revolution

On a £20 note is a portrait of the eighteenth-century economist, Adam Smith beside a machine for making pins. In his book *The Wealth of Nations*, Smith described the way pins were previously made by hand:

> One man draws out the wire, another straightens it, a third cuts it, a fourth points it, a fifth grinds it at the top for receiving the head; to make the head requires two or three distinct operations; to put it on is a peculiar business, to whiten the pins is another; it is even a trade by itself to put them into the paper; and the important business of making a pin is, in this manner, divided into about eighteen distinct operations, which, in some manufactories, are all performed by distinct hands...

He compared this with the pin-making machine operated by one person 'making four thousand eight hundred pins a day'. Despite the productive advantages, Smith appreciated the harm done to the workers:

> The man whose life is spent in performing a few simple operations [which were all it took to mind (*sic*) the machine]... has no occasion to exert his understanding... He naturally loses, therefore, the habit of such exertion, and generally becomes as stupid and ignorant as it is possible for a human creature to become.
>
> *(1904:6–7, 267)*

Being a Scot, committed to his nation's tradition of parish schooling, Smith thought the machine minders needed education to give them something to think about – religion mostly, though he probably did not believe in it himself!

The same concern for industrial workers' mental well-being was shown a century later, when industrial production had developed into the huge assembly lines that reversed the process of disassembling cattle in Chicago meat-packing plants to assemble cars in Henry Ford's Detroit factory. 'Scientific management' was applied using Frederick Taylor's work-study of a Dutchman named Schmidt trained to carry 47 instead of 12½ tons of pig iron a day in a barrow. Schmidt, Taylor considered, was an ideal candidate for work-study because he was 'so stupid and so phlegmatic that he more nearly resembles in his mental make-up the ox than any other type' (Taylor, 1947:59). The same methods could also be applied to the burgeoning offices where Taylor also demanded all control in the hands of management.

As it was more or less reluctantly provided in industrially developing countries during the nineteenth century for children no longer working down mines and in factories, mass elementary schooling became, as the socialist President of Germany after the First World War, Friedrich Ebert, described it, 'the vocational education of the working class' (quoted in Institute of Public Policy Research, 1990:1). It was 'designed to control rather than emancipate' (Whitty, 1983:105). Meanwhile, the academic curriculum of the now private but originally English 'public schools' was based upon the classics for about 7% of children (the same percentage as today). It provided the knowledge necessary to rule for a class whose sons governed empire at home and abroad. Grammar schools provided a watered-down version of the same but without additional character training. They enabled limited upward social mobility for a minority of working-class children who passed an 'intelligence test' at 11+ to join the growing middle class of non-manually working managers and professionals that an expanding economy and welfare state required after the Second World War. The grammar (20%) and secondary-modern (80%) state school system established in England and Wales by the 1944 Education Act corresponded with the divisions of labour and knowledge in industrial employment and was completed by technical schools for skilled workers. But these were too expensive to provide for more than around 4%, so trade training developed from surviving industrial apprenticeships (specialized learning on the job at a reduced wage for three or more years leading to legally guaranteed employment in skilled work on completion). Its formal elements became relegated, until recently, to evening classes and day release in FE colleges.

By the 1960s, as many as a quarter of all boys were leaving school at 15 for apprenticeships (FECRDU, 1978:34–35) but after the 1973 economic crisis, British industry collapsed and apprenticeships along with it. With rising unemployment, employers no longer took on young people – let alone trained them – so government's first reaction was to raise the school leaving age to 16 and later to follow this with a series of Youth Training Schemes. The idea was to have everybody trained, ready to hit the ground running when employment recovered; only, this never happened. Instead, after 1979, successive Thatcher governments abandoned control of the national economy and opened it to the new global economy that was developing as mass production grew in low-wage industrializing countries like China. Rather than youth training, most young people preferred to remain in school or go to college and try for the remaining secure professional and managerial jobs requiring academic, A-level qualifications, or apply for the new jobs open to women as much as to men working with computers in what was fast becoming a post-industrial, service economy. They hoped to avoid relegation to a growing precarious class of insecure, interchangeable and often part-time unskilled labour. The universities and polytechnics (technical universities) that had expanded to take around 7% of school leavers after 1965, including a larger proportion of young women, grew rapidly as did school sixth forms and FE colleges as the school leaving age rose incrementally to 18 by 2015.

Comprehensive schools, introduced from 1965 by the 'old' Labour government, were blamed by the Conservatives for rising youth unemployment, but this was really caused by a lack of the 'youth jobs' that heavy industry had previously provided. However, the idea was that if the 'quality' of supply could be raised by providing more young people with academic qualifications then jobs would be found for them, or be created in what was coming to be called the new 'knowledge economy'. Independently run but state-funded schools joined the competition with remaining local authority schools to raise exam standards in the academic National Curriculum introduced in 1988. For those who could not hack all the academic cramming involved, there have been repeated attempts to reinvent 'a vocational route' with modernized apprenticeships. University and college courses also became more 'vocational' beyond the academic profession and those other professional vocations they endorsed. Or, if not for specific employment, they attempted to prepare undergraduates for pre-vocational 'employability' across a range of occupations. Tony Blair's three priorities of 'education, education and education' lasted longer for more and more young people but the suspicion was many were 'studying harder but learning less' (Ainley, 2016:2).

Group discussion

In your view, how much of the pattern of English schooling established after the last World War remains and would it be possible to return to it? For example, the May government's proposal to bring back secondary modern schools – only they talk about bringing back grammar schools – why don't they put it the other way round?

Before the 2010 general election, David Cameron promised, 'Three million apprenticeships', adding, 'that means three million more engineers, accountants and project managers'. Aside from the fact, it didn't happen – why is this what is called a *non-sequitur* (it doesn't follow)?

Employment in *the second machine age*

Transformation of the occupational structure is not directly determined by technology but in free market/capitalist societies, shareholders seeking profit will always have the last word over how to use new technologies to maximise output. As a result, for Brynjolfsson and McAfee (2014), the digital technologies of what they call *the second machine age* are likely to have serious implications for employment and inequality. To begin with, they facilitate the production of infinitely more goods and services than Adam Smith's pin-making machine. In addition, whereas the increases in production associated with the first machine age of industrial production resulted in the creation of a 'mass' workforce, the new digital corporations require only a tiny fraction of employees. Facebook, for example, as Brynjolfsson and McAfee relate, although having almost a billion average daily users, an annual turnover approaching US$13 billion and a net income of nearly US$3 billion, employs only 9,199 people. This strengthens the trend towards the super rich who social geographer Danny Dorling calls 'the top 0.1%'. So, there is growing social polarisation, pulling those at the very top away from those further down.

How far non-routine work can be automated is part of a wider debate about the potential of robotic technology. Mass media advertising endlessly unveils the latest personalised gizmos, pushing technological boundaries to undertake both domestic and workplace tasks. Brynjolfsson and McAfee accept that there will always be activities that even the most intelligent machines find difficult, from walking up stairs to picking up a paper clip and that, unlike machines, humans have the imagination to innovate. It is still the case, however, that 'digital machines have escaped their narrow confines and started to demonstrate broad abilities in pattern recognition, complex communication and other domains that used to be exclusively human' (Brynjolfsson and McAfee, 2014:91).

It is not just manual labouring jobs that have been deskilled and replaced by machines in a 'post-industrial' service economy. The deregulation of employment with erosion of trades union enforced 'restrictive practices' to allow flexible working across formerly specialized crafts has been going on for a long time (see Braverman, 1974). Now these processes are working their way up the employment hierarchy to affect the professions that had associated themselves with HE. Susskind and Susskind (2015) see this as changing what they call 'the Grand Bargain' in a print-based society between the professional gatekeepers of privileged knowledge distributing their expertise to ignorant clients. This solution to the uneven distribution of knowledge in society – since we have seen even Greek philosophers could not know everything that was then known, let alone share it all with everybody else – is increasingly breaking down under the impact of 'a technology-based Internet society'. Nowadays, the Susskinds argue, 'the liberation of expertise' in 'a post-professional society' empowers consumers to bypass the gatekeepers and directly access the information, if not the knowledge, they require. As they conclude: 'in the end, the traditional professions will be dismantled, leaving most (but not all) professionals to be replaced by less expert people and high performing systems… new roles will arise but… these too, in due course, may be taken on by machines' (303).

This potentiality of machinery to replicate professional judgement and diagnosis is being enabled not by artificial intelligence but by massive computer power churning instantaneously through vast quantities of digitized data. The Susskinds provide many examples of the stages of 'disintermediation' that professionals go through as new technology is applied to them, starting with lawyers whose resort to case law has long been captured by searchable databases, likewise medical diagnosis, while accountancy has been packaged into phone apps that customers use to manage their own tax and other affairs. Whole industries have abandoned print to go online, like journalism, or online banking. Face-to-face consultations are replaced by long-distance Skypes. Even new professions, like management consultancy, are embedding themselves into corporate systems to automatically and continuously monitor risk. Consequently, 'before too long, we will need to revisit our ideas about full-time employment, the purpose of work, and the balance between work and leisure' (295). This joins those who see capitalism dissolving itself by somehow transcending human labour, perhaps by transhumanly integrating people with machines.

What does this imply for the more than 200 million post-secondary students worldwide whose numbers, along with their more than 6 million teachers, are expected to more than double by 2030 (Altbach, 2016)? What Altbach says of India is echoed across his survey of global HE, 'Mass higher education plays as much a political and social role as it does an educational one' (215). Large numbers are excluded as well as included; even in the pioneering USA, which enrols more than 90%, many do not complete as the community colleges do not fulfil their potential of integrating mass participation to university. Rather, they often function as holding pens, cooling kids out before they make it through to university. Nevertheless, the social role of a US college degree is to give hope of achieving the American dream by attaining at least semi-professional secure employment. Failure to gain a degree is confirmation of precarious status (Silva, 2015). Indeed, it appears there is something of a double movement going on – two things happening simultaneously but without mutually determining one another: at one end, the consolidation of an elite and at the other end, massification with heightened differentiation in between. Overall, the result is, 'The average quality of students entering postsecondary education declines at the same time that competition for places in the top universities increases' (Altbach, *o.c.*:52). This is 'The Logic of Mass Higher Education', Altbach spells out (29 *et seq.*).

This logic can also be seen in England, where Alison Wolf has said FE has been 'decanted' into mass HE and the Susskind's anticipate that 'people will tend to be trained on a task-basis rather than for undertaking jobs' (2015:263). This turns more or less academic vocational preparation at tertiary level into pre-vocational training of the type that Altbach assumes to have been completed in schools. At secondary level, the Susskinds favour 'personalised intelligent tutoring technology' for more effective cramming, while for tertiary, they endorse 'the one-to-one tutorial system that has worked so effectively at universities like Oxford' (56). This would seem like special pleading for their own prestigious institution, but they have a point that this type of apprentice mentoring can develop genuine vocations, whether academic or not, but often closely related to employment, including the academic vocation for teaching and research. Such a labour-intensive approach is hardly possible in the increasingly managed 'student experience' of mass tertiary education, however. So what is to be done?

Group discussion

Like Brynjolfsson and McAfee visiting a new town, look around to see how much of the work going on around you could be automated – from self-driving buses to vending machines for automatically cooked fast food (McDonalds is already piloting this) and the intelligent supermarket trollies that TESCO (Britain's biggest private sector employer) is experimenting with so that checkout operators are not required, just security guards, since stock replenishment can also be automated. Be imaginative – use apps and drones! Maybe electronic bitcoins, and then who needs banks? Skype/Zoomor virtual reality for working at a distance (some surgeons do this). But, remember, that in order for a robot to take over a human job, the human first has to behave in a robot-like way. Nevertheless, what advantages could be taken of labour-saving machinery in a rationally ordered society?

If you are still reading this chapter and have not despaired by being reminded once again of uncertain graduate prospects, save for the certainty of debt for England's highest undergraduate student fees in the world, discuss why so many people still sign on for what are often not very satisfactory undergraduate experiences. Do most students nurture vocational aspirations, or is anyone actually interested in what they are studying for its own sake as their teachers often urge them to be? How much can be learnt online, or what is lacking from such distance provision? Can a computerised professional provide one-to-one support and expertise? Does it matter if the expert is actually a program and you couldn't tell the difference? If any specialized information required by anybody at any time is readily accessible, what is lacking for society as a whole to make sense of that information?

A good general pre-vocational education for everyone

In the USA, a general secondary school graduation diploma at 18 is linked to the assumption of citizenship and provides entitlement to tertiary-level college or university for those who qualify and can afford to pay for the latter. This has become the general pattern of global tertiary education described by Altbach. Eichlorst *et al.* (2014) list a variety of earlier pathways through vocational and technical schools, training centres across industries or firm-specific formal and informal apprenticeships. They include Germany's dual system that combines apprenticeship with continued schooling. Importantly, this is not regarded as a relegation route as it is in England but is considered an entitlement to learn to work in Germany's productive industries. In the German model, shared with variations across Eastern Europe and Scandinavia plus Holland, such trade training can lead on to technical universities alongside academic ones that follow on from grammar schooling. In a highly regulated system, completion of apprentice training guarantees employment, but in recent years, the same pressures of automation have led more young Germans to opt for the general academic high-school route. So, the German dual system is running into similar problems to trade training elsewhere, even though it is surprisingly resilient (see Busemeyer *et al.*, 2012), relying upon central and regional government regulation supported by both employers and trades unions. It has also been sustained in this way for the 70 years, since it was set up as part of the reconstruction of German industry after the war and so is very difficult to replicate in the deregulated and more post-industrial UK economy. (See the section on 'Why we can't do it like the Germans' in Martin Allen's downloadable booklet in the recommended reading below.)

Perhaps, though, we do not have to look so far for an alternative approach. Scotland's Labour Market Strategy (Scottish Government, 2016) seeks to strengthen its economy following recession and faced with declining North Sea oil revenues. The government is in any case committed to sustainable and renewable energy, so job creation or replacement has to be linked to innovation. In addition, the country that voted against 'Brexit' has to prepare for the uncertainties that may result as a consequence of it, including possible independence in or out of the European Union. This multifaceted strategy also aims to reduce the income inequalities that have widened as they have elsewhere in the UK and thus to make work fairer. The strategy is therefore informed by a Fair Work Framework supported by an independent convention bringing together employers with trades unions in the German style but covering those without formal contracts of employment (including zero-hours, etc.) to provide them also with security. It is thus a matter of better jobs, not just more jobs. Whether such an ambitious programme can succeed remains to be seen, especially as it is perhaps out of synch with the approach being taken in Scottish schools, where the overassessment of a Curriculum for Excellence seems to have borrowed from the English approach to raising standards and has driven Scottish teachers into taking industrial action over their excessive workload.

Ideally, the foundation of general pre-vocational provision by schools would not be so academic, as it has become following the English National Curriculum but would include high-quality technical education and training with work placements to learn about work, not just to learn to work. Such a common curriculum entitlement would also nurture talents through different types of learning – from discussion and working in groups on creative arts projects to scientific investigations, sports, dance, music and other recreations. Secondary school students would not then specialize too soon, save to nurture particular talents, but especially not to start on vocational preparation for work that may no longer be available after their training for it has been completed. Nor should general schooling be too academic, or it turns into what England has now – 'grammar schools for all'. This is a contradiction in terms since grammar schooling selects a minority, as related above, and therefore for the majority today is a vast sorting machine in which cramming for largely literary examination confirms previously more or less expensively acquired cultural background knowledge through private tutoring if not private schooling.

Instead, completing a general diploma at 18 would entitle access to post-secondary or tertiary FHE for those that wanted it – maybe not straightaway but to return to later in life as their employment might require or as their personal interest might take them. Can we not imagine an online intellectual commons maintained by a National Education Service that anyone could access free of charge to take the courses they needed and were interested in, either online and/or by attending the classes also providing them, or just to obtain expert advice and support available on demand, either at a distance or in person? This could lead to a reduction in numbers of full-time young undergraduates. Indeed, the government has been trying to achieve such a *Great Reversal* since 2010 (Allen and Ainley, 2013) but without providing any more attractive alternative since their commitment to economic austerity means further cuts and savings all round. The 2010 Coalition government thought that tripling fees in 2011 would put people off, at the same time as exam reforms made it harder to qualify. Now the Conservatives are encouraging private colleges to offer cut-price, two-year, business-related 'degrees', as well as allowing 'quality'-rated universities to raise their fees to increase 'differentiation' and encourage 'market failure' by institutions that are driven to close or merge. This will only contribute to the current unequal competition to cram in students between mass universities for the many and elite universities for the few. These divisions should be broken down in regional learning infrastructures linking schools, colleges and universities to give first priority to local applicants, many living at home as in mainland Europe and Scotland. Everyone aged 18 or older should be entitled to grant funding towards living costs financed in the absence of tuition fees, which should be abolished. Since so many current loans for fees and maintenance will never be repaid, this would not incur any additional expense and might even save money.

Of course, not everyone wants to go to university, including many who are already there – even if it is free as it still is in Scotland. As stated above, the competition to get in has the effect of sifting students according to their parental background. One social function of mass higher/further/tertiary education is therefore to maintain a social order with its divisions of labour and knowledge that is being rendered obsolete by ongoing technological change. The various discourses graduates acquire in arts and humanities degrees in turn affect their entry to the hierarchy of 'graduatised' employment, where completion of their more or less general (pre-vocational) courses place them at a greater or lesser remove from chances of the secure and semi-professional employment they seek. Still, they know that a degree distinguishes them from non-graduate entry jobs to which the other *Half our Future* (Newsom, 1963), with inferior vocational or no qualifications, is relegated. This is why so many continue to apply, if they do not do so for purely social reasons (see Cheeseman, 2011), or just because it has become normalized and 'everybody else does it', especially better-qualified young women who may be more motivated to live away from their parents for a few years, even if – like most students who have gone away to study – they then return to the parental home, too indebted to move to their own accommodation and often regretting the whole experience (see the latest of many surveys: Aviva, 2016; but more substantially NUS, 2015).

A new tertiary-level correspondence has replaced the previous correspondence between divided secondary schooling and employment described above. Now, at a later age, hope of remaining professional employment requires a degree with precarious labour for those without one. This division is deepened by separating young people into academic or vocational routes at younger and younger ages – a *panacea* repeatedly suggested by pundits, alongside bringing back grammar schools. Instead, a National Education Service would not make this distinction but recognise the vocational nature of the academic alongside 'non-academic' vocational routes. This would include the most prestigious subjects at the most elite institutions, returning them to their original vocational purposes, which indeed they have never lost as professional preparation, like the 'original vocations' of law and medicine. This includes other more or less specialized academic vocations, for example, in science, building upon their general foundation to learn critically from the past to inform change in the future. All undergraduates should thus be aware that they will be expected to make some contribution to the continuing cultural conversation in their area of developing academic/vocational expertise as the final degree demonstration of their graduation. Such development will widen the still-available critical space afforded by HE in which a defence of the public university can be conducted (Holmwood, 2012). This will bring together staff and students, not antagonise them, which is the effect of putting customers/*students at the heart of the system*, as the 2011 BIS White Paper claimed to do.

For the majority who do not progress to university, the government has offered 'apprenticeships' of variable quality, sometimes delivered at college (see Allen, 2016), and May's government is still committed to David Cameron's promise of 3 million of these by 2020. They are of variable length and, without legal guarantee of continued employment, often semi-skilled and many in services not really requiring prolonged training to GCSE levels of learning that 60% of apprentices have already reached in school. One-in-three apprentices surveyed were unaware they were on an apprenticeship and one-in-five reported receiving no formal training, while 6% of apprenticeships lasted less than the legal minimum 12 months. The majority of apprentices continue to be older (25+) rather than younger (18+) and, contrary to the impression given by lavish advertising, most are also women. While the majority of apprenticeships are in low-paid areas at levels requiring little formal training, such as retail, office administration and care (DfE, 2016), these are not like the three and more year industrial apprenticeships described above since most employers no longer want or need apprenticeships, and if they do, they run them themselves – like the prestigious Rolls Royce apprenticeships at Derby that are harder to get into than engineering degree courses at Oxford.

This is not just because high-tech machinery tends also to be automating and so needs fewer people to operate it, but also mainly because, as briefly indicated above, the UK is now a largely deregulated service economy requiring only low skills for most jobs that can be learnt within a few days by fungible employees. Since they are low paid and insecure (often zero-hours), there is a high turnover with many people working at two or three jobs simultaneously just to make ends meet. Especially after the 2008 Credit Crunch, when many people would take any job, this sort of precarious work made it appear that employment had recovered quickly, unlike after previous recessions when millions were laid off or 'parked' on disability benefits. As a result, what Guy

Standing calls *the precariat* now makes up perhaps 40% of the employed population. Following new recessions and a race to the bottom in employment, their numbers may ratchet up again.

Instead, investment in a labour-intensive economy is required in which local authorities and public/voluntary sector alliances generate employment opportunities. Without this, changes to apprenticeship funding, proposed by Richard in 2012, contributed – as Martin Allen showed (2016:*o.c.*) – to a reduction in the number of apprentices, although quantity if not quality were subsequently boosted. Given the intensification of the 'low-skill equilibrium' first related by Finegold and Soskice in 1988 to the deregulated, post-industrial, largely service-based economy that the UK has become, repeated efforts to cajole and bribe employers into subscribing to training and apprenticeships they do not want or need are wasted. Ever since the collapse of industrial apprenticeships, rebuilding a vocational route with 'parity of esteem' to the traditional academic one has been a lost cause. From the sorry history of youth training (Ainley, 1988) to widening participation to tertiary FHE, this has functioned only to sustain illusions in worthless vocational qualifications (Wolf, 2011).

By contrast, traditionally vocational subjects such as law and medicine have until recently always been oversubscribed by those who qualified for them, but less well-qualified young people sign up in their 1000s for newer areas like business studies, which now attracts 10% of all applications and equals about 20% plus of all HE students. In *The Business Studies University* (Ainley, 2016), students outside of BS also undertake more or less compulsory modules tacked onto their courses of study, supplementing them with various aspects of 'BS proper', such as marketing or business organisation, for example, as well as 'entrepreneurialism', or the 'employ-ability' that is as omnipresent here as elsewhere. A high level of applications for degrees that are perceived to be directly vocational is understandable, given the precarious alternative and despite the increases in student fees that need to be recouped through graduate-level employment. Yet, the definition of a graduate job has become ever more elastic, as this is a key indicator on which funding for universities depends. Ironically, this is not only worse for the supposedly more vocationally inclined post-1992 universities but also includes many students who opt for science and technology subjects at other institutions. They often find that, to avoid relegation to technician-level lab work, they have to proceed to post-graduation. This is further turning still larger parts of HE into FE, and squeezing what remains of FE engineering, for instance, out of FE and into HE, as employers prefer graduates to 'apprentices' for increasingly routinized technical work. At the same time, 'high-flying' graduate employers continue to recruit more from a small number of elite institutions than they do from specific subject disciplines.

Raised and differentiated tuition fees can only increase this commodification of student experience and heighten distinctions between students and between their HE institutions, as well as between 'students' and 'apprentices'. Reductions in – if not abolition of   fees are necessary, but there should also be an emphasis on the contribution to knowledge that students can make in their chosen field of study, as suggested above. In this way, tertiary-level education can recover itself in connection with further training to create a 'thick HE' (Silver, 2004), one that is both theoretically informed and practically competent. If this is to build upon but not repeat the pre-vocational schooling outlined above, it requires thinking through what such a foundational and general secondary education could contribute to 'fully developed individuals, fit for a variety of labours, ready to face any change of production, and to whom the different social functions they perform, are but so many modes of giving free scope to their own natural and acquired powers'

(Marx, 1971:494). This is the ideal of a general intellect that could be fostered in comprehensive state schools and developed throughout a democratic society.

Conclusion

Fundamentally, the perception of 'the problem' needs to shift from fixation on better preparing young people for 'employability' by providing 'vocational' secondary schooling alongside supposedly vocational but often actually continued 'pre-vocational' preparation in tertiary F&HE, or through government-backed pseudo-work placements, bogus apprenticeships and interminable internships. Investment in socially useful employment is urgently needed to give the new generations a sustainable future.

Research task

Look into the current systems in some of the countries mentioned above like Scotland, Germany or Holland. In light of the issues raised in this chapter, to what extent are there potential lessons for England and Wales, and how feasible do you consider these to be?

Recommended reading

Ainley, P. (2016) *Betraying a Generation, How Education is Failing Young People.* Bristol: Policy Press.
Allen, M. (2016) *Another Great Training Robbery or a Real Alternative for Young People? Apprenticeships at the Start of the Twenty-First Century.* London: Radicaled.
Bunn, S. (1999) *The Nomad's Apprentice: Different Kinds of "Apprenticeship" among Kyrgyz Nomads in Central Asia,* chapter in Ainley and Rainbird (see below).

References

Ainley, P. (1988) *From School to YTS, Education and Training in England and Wales 1944–1987.* Milton Keynes: Open University Press.
Ainley, P. (2016) The Business Studies University: turning higher education into further education. *The London Review of Education,* 14(1), 106–115.
Allen, M. and Ainley, P. (2013) *The Great Reversal: Young People, Education and Employment in a Declining Economy.* London: Radicaled.
Altbach, P. (2016) *Global Perspectives on Higher Education.* Baltimore, MD: Johns Hopkins University Press.
Aviva (2016) *UK: Generation Regret: Over a Third of Millennials Who Went to University Regret Doing So As They Struggle with Debts and Squeezed Finances.* Press release 11th August 2016. Available at:www. aviva.com/media/news/item/uk-generation-regret-over-a-third-of-millennials-who-went-to-university-regret-doing-so-as-they-struggle-with-debts-and-squeezed-finances-17653/#.V6t3WwOiPG4.facebook. (Accessed 27th September 2016).
BIS (2011) *Higher Education: Students at the Heart of the System,* London: BIS.
Braverman, H. (1974) *Labor and Monopoly Capital, The Degredation of Work in the Twentieth Century.* New York: Monthly Review Press.
Brynjolfsson, E. and McAfee, A. (2014) *The Second Machine Age: Work, Progress, and Prosperity in a Time of Brilliant Technologies.* New York: Norton.
Busemeyer, M., Neubäumer, R., Pfeifer, H. and Wenzelmann, F. (2012) The transformation of the German vocational training regime: evidence from firms' training behaviour, *Industrial Relations Journal,* 43(6), 572–591.

Cheeseman, M. (2011) *The Pleasures of Being a Student at the University of Sheffield.* Unpublished PhD thesis, Sheffield: University of Sheffield.

Coleman, R. (1988) *The Art of Work, An Epitaph to Skill.* London: Pluto Press.

DfE (2016) www.gov.uk/government/publications/apprenticeship-funding-bands October 2016. (Accessed 16th December 2016).

Eichlorst, W., Rodriquez-Planas, N. and Zimmerman, K. (2014) *A Roadmap to Vocational Education and Training around the World.* Bonn: Literaturverz.

Engels, F. (1970) Origin of the family, private property and the state. In *Marx and Engels Selected Works.* London: Lawrence and Wishart.

Finegold, D. and Soskice, D. (1988) The failure of training in Britain: analysis and prescription. *Oxford Review of Economic Policy*, 4(3), 21–53.

Further Education and Curriculum Review and Development Unit (1978) *Experience, Reflection, Learning: Suggestions for Organisers of Schemes of UVP.* London: FECRDU.

Gellner, E. (1983) *Nations and Nationalism.* Oxford: Blackwell.

Holmwood, J. (Ed.) (2012) *A Manifesto for the Public University.* London: Bloomsbury.

Institute for Public Policy Research (1990) *A British Baccalaureat: Ending the Division between Education and Training*, London: IPPR.

Marx, K. (1971) *Capital*, vol 1. London: Unwin.

Morgan, E. (1973) *The Descent of Woman.* London: Corgi.

National Union of Students (2015) *Debt in the First Degree.* London: NUS.

Newsom, J. (1963) *Half Our Future: Report of the Central Advisory Council for Education* (England). London: HMSO.

Richard, D. (2012) *The Richard Review of Apprenticeships.* London: BIS.

Scottish Government (2016) *Scotland's Labour Market Strategy.* Edinburgh: The Scottish Government.

Silva, J. (2015) *Coming Up Short: Working-Class Adulthood in an Age of Uncertainty.* Oxford: Oxford University Press.

Silver, R. (2004) *14–19 Reform: The Challenge to HE.* Presentation to Higher Education Policy Institute, House of Commons, 29 June.

Smith, A. (1904) *An Inquiry into the Nature and Causes of the Wealth of Nations*, Vol. 1. London: Methuen.

Susskind, R. and Susskind, D. (2015) *The Future of the Professions: How Technology Will Transform the Work of Human Experts.* Oxford: Oxford University Press.

Taylor, F. (1947) *Scientific Management.* New York: Harper and Row.

Thomson, G. (1972) *The First Philosophers.* London: Lawrence and Wishart.

Whitty, G. (1983) Missing: a policy on the curriculum. In A. Wolpe, and J. Donald (Eds.) *Is There Anyone There From Education? Education after Thatcher.* London: Pluto.

Wolf, A. (2011) *Review of Vocational Education (Wolf Report).* London: DfE.

Wolf, A. (2015) *Heading for the Precipice: Can Further and Higher Education Funding Policies be Sustained?* London: Policy Institute, King's College London.

9 Comparative issues and perspectives in adult education and training

John Field

Introduction

Adult education is an extremely broad concept, which is defined and operationalised very differently in different national contexts. Indeed, it seems highly likely that national systems for adult education vary more than any other part of the education and training system. In spite of these national variations, adult education has increasingly moved centre stage in international discussions of policies for education and training, and there is a growing body of evidence on the economic, social, health and cultural benefits of adult learning. Unsurprisingly, it has become a frequent focus for international benchmarking exercises. Yet, at the same time, adult educators in many countries see their field as overloaded with public expectations but hugely underresourced and vulnerable.

This chapter will provide a brief overview of different adult education systems and summarise some of the main types of approach in different countries. I argue that while national differences remain strong, the combined effects of globalisation, technological change and intergovernmental policy developments mean that there is a marked shift towards (a) the weakening of national influences on adult education and (b) increasing heterogeneity of provision reflecting factors other than national differences. This chapter will then discuss the role of international organisations in exchanging knowledge and ideas about the role of adult education; this will focus on three different transnational policy actors (EU, OECD and UNESCO), all of which conduct benchmarking exercises and promote policy transfer, but with very different sets of members; and one international advocacy body (International Council for Adult Education), which has a very different focus and approach, presenting itself as a grassroots and nongovernmental initiative.

Defining adult education and training

The field of adult education and training is a broad one, and it is talked about in a number of different ways. UNESCO, which has a broad international focus, uses the term 'adult learning and education', which it defines as encompassing 'all formal, non-formal and informal or incidental learning and continuing education (both general and vocational, and both theoretical and practical) undertaken by adults' (UNESCO Institute for Lifelong Learning 2016:28–29). This sounds suitably comprehensive, though even the term 'adult' is defined differently in different countries. UNESCO's distinction between formal (i.e. planned programmes in an education or training institution), non-formal (programmes provided through non-educational organisations, groups or individuals) and informal (where learning is a by-product of everyday life) is widely used internationally and is a useful way of categorising different types of adult learning, provided we don't treat the distinctions as fixed and unchanging.

Individual/group task

- How would you try to define adult education and training?
- Is there anything different about adult learners – and if so, what?

The idea of adults as a specific and distinct group of learners goes back a long way, but really came of age in the late nineteenth and early twentieth centuries. In Britain and a number of other European countries, adult education movements emerged partly out of struggles for citizenship and suffrage, partly out of the emerging labour movement and partly as a result of the explosion in scientific and technical knowledge. Mechanics' Institutes and Literary and Philosophical Societies developed in urban areas from the mid-nineteenth century, often sponsored by affluent and well-educated patrons, to bring new ideas and discoveries to a wider audience, including many working-class men and women whose school education had been severely restricted (Walker, 2016). The Workers' Educational Association (WEA), founded in 1903, aimed to bring working men and women with university teachers, partly in order to train the future leaders of a democratic society (Goldman, 2000). R.H. Tawney, a prominent socialist thinker, economic historian and long-standing supporter of the WEA, argued in 1914 that:

> All serious educational movements have in England been also social movements. They have been the expression in one sphere – the training of mind and character – of some distinctive conception of the life proper to man and of the kind of society in which he can best live it.
>
> *(Tawney, 1966:88)*

For Tawney, the 'life proper to man' meant a more equal and just society in which all could contribute and all would make the most of their potential, provided they had been equipped with the skills and knowledge so to do. And this meant bringing together the best teachers and scholars with the great social movements of the day.

Individual/group task

- To what extent can we see social movements in our own time that represent positive ideas of a future society? How can and should adult education respond to these movements?

Britain was far from unique in seeing this close connection between adult education and social movements. Similar alliances helped bring about the study circle tradition in the Scandinavian countries, as well as the residential adult colleges (*folkehøjskolen*) in Denmark and elsewhere; they underlay the popular education tradition in France and Spain and helped foster the development of independent adult education institutions in the German-speaking nations (Steele, 2007). Though the labour movement and suffrage campaigns were commonly involved, the precise nature of the movements varied, including the temperance movement in Scandinavia, and Danish nationalism in the case of the early *folkehøjskolen*. Generally, adult skills training was much less prominent, until the First World War posed governments, industry and the armed services with the need to train rapidly large numbers of men and women for new roles, and in many countries, the methods and expertise of adult retraining were carried over into the field of unemployment during the 1920s and 1930s (Field, 1996).

The challenges of new social movements, dramatic changes in scientific knowledge and the mobilisation of populations in new roles all helped to promote the idea of adult education and training as an important and distinctive field. In the later twentieth century, some came to argue that adults are such a distinct group that they require a specialised approach to teaching and learning. Most obviously, adults can draw on life experience, which may be highly relevant to their learning activities. Unlike children, they are rarely made to attend an educational setting as a result of the law; taking part in many, though not all, types of adult education and training tend to be voluntary, and participants are often free to walk away if the programme does not meet their needs; they often combine learning with other commitments, such as paid work or caring for family and so on. Some writers have argued that these characteristics, along with the social psychology of adult cognitive development, mean that teaching and learning strategies that work with children must be at least adapted, and in some cases, completely changed, when supporting adult learners.

Individual/group task

- Identify examples of adult education provision that is voluntary, and examples of provision where participation is compulsory. What are the implications for teachers of these differences?

The best-known writer to take this approach is Malcolm Knowles, who developed the word 'andragogy' to articulate his ideas. For Knowles, the word 'pedagogy' was appropriate for children, taking as it did the classical Greek word for child (*paid*) as its core; he took up andragogy as an alternative, drawing from the Greek word *Andros*, or adult. Knowles identified five basic principles of andragogy (Knowles, 1984:12):

- *self-concept*: as a person matures, they move from dependency on others to being a self-directed human being;
- *experience*: as a person matures, they accumulate experience, which is a resource for their learning;
- *readiness to learn*: as a person matures, their readiness to learn is increasingly related to the developmental tasks of their various social roles;
- *orientation to learning*: as a person matures, their time perspective shifts from one of postponed applications of knowledge to immediacy of application and from subject-centredness to problem-centredness;
- *motivation to learn*: as a person matures, their motivation to learn is internal rather than imposed by the demands of others.

This definition has been much debated by others (see, for example, Jarvis, 2001), but it is still widely cited in the literature, and Knowles is still seen as an authoritative figure.

Individual/group task

- How helpful is Knowles' distinction between pedagogy and andragogy?
- What do you see as the main practical consequences of taking an andragogic perspective?

Even more influential was the Brazilian adult educator, Paulo Freire. His *Pedagogy of the Oppressed* (2000) is one of the most frequently quoted texts in education, particularly in Latin America, India and Africa, and his influence was particularly marked – though certainly not limited to adult literacies teaching. Freire offered first a critique of dominant practice, which he described as the 'banking approach', where facts and skills are transferred from the teacher's mind to the learners' like cash deposits in a bank. For Freire, this was a type of 'domestication', where learners were subtly socialised into the thinking of the status quo and discouraged from asking why they were poor and unschooled in the first place. In place of domestication and the banking approach, Freire emphasised the importance of dialogue between teacher and learner, based on mutual respect and shared humanity, and aiming to liberate rather than domesticate, by focussing on education as a process of 'conscientisation', intertwined with what he called 'praxis' – that is, learning through generating new ways of naming and seeing the world, and thereby making a difference to the world around us.

Freire's insistence that education is never neutral, and must either stand with the poor or be against them, found a ready audience when his work was translated in the early 1970s. In the introduction to *Pedagogy of the Oppressed*, he argued that:

> The radical, committed to human liberation, does not become the prisoner of a 'circle of certainty', within which reality is also imprisoned. On the contrary, the more radical a person is, the more fully he or she enters into reality, so that, knowing it better, he or she can transform it. This individual is not afraid to confront, to listen, to see the world unveiled. This person is not afraid to meet the people or to enter into dialogue with them. This person does not consider himself or herself the proprietor of history or of all people, or the liberator of the oppressed; but he or she does commit himself or herself, within history, to fight at their side.
>
> *(Freire, 2000:39)*

It is little wonder, then, that this book became a foundation text for the critical education movement and has influenced so many leading critical adult educators. Although Freire's influence has waned in recent years, his name is still a familiar one, and his ideas have helped shape approaches to teaching and learning in many areas of adult education.

Individual/group task

- Was Freire more than a product of his time and place? How relevant are his ideas to adult education in the early twenty-first century?

The third set of ideas that I want to discuss is centred on the idea of human capital. Unlike the ideas of Knowles and Freire, the concept of human capital was developed by economists rather than educators, and its aim was primarily to measure the relationship between the costs of education and its benefits. Initially, the concept was introduced in the early 1960s as a way of drawing attention to the contribution of labour to company performance; it recognised that the potential value of labour's contribution could rise, given appropriate investment, for example, in the form of skills training or health promotion. In the hands of the eminent neoclassical economist Gary Becker (1964), human capital thinking became a tool for measuring the effectiveness of different types of investment (such as job-specific training and general education) and calculating the distribution of returns between – say – the employer, the government and individual workers. This idea has obvious attractions for policy-makers and employers, who have to pay for education and training programmes, and therefore want to know whether they produce commensurate results. There are, though, two principal problems with this approach.

 First, a number of educationalists have taken issue with human capital thinking for its neglect of non-economic values. They argue that education is concerned not just with profitable investment in skills and performance but also has a wider human purpose that goes beyond the economic (Coffield, 1999). From this perspective, the very idea of applying a cost-benefit analysis to education is itself a capitulation to a narrow and utilitarian view of what learning is about. The second problem is less concerned with the principle of human capital thinking than its measurement. The standard measures of inputs (or costs) are years of education and qualifications gained, or at enterprise level, the total spending on training activities; the standard measures of the benefits are increases in earning, or at the level of the enterprise, gains in productivity by those trained. Neither of these sets of measures is entirely satisfactory, and the relationship between the costs and benefits is almost impossible to prove as it is affected by so many other factors. Nevertheless, recent research on the wider, non-economic benefits of adult learning – influenced in part by human capital thinking – has helped to provide a firm and robust evidence base on how adult education and training can help change people's lives (Schuller, 2000).

Individual/group task

- How helpful is human capital thinking when it comes to adult learning? How might costs and benefits be best measured?

National adult education systems

Adult education is an extremely broad sector. Very crudely, it encompasses the following:

- basic adult education (literacy, numeracy, second language acquisition);
- popular and/or liberal adult education;
- adult higher education;
- continuing vocational training and continuing professional development;
- family learning;
- much distance and open learning; and
- support services such as educational guidance for adults.

The ways in which these activities are organised can vary widely, even within nations. For exam-ple, basic literacy and numeracy can be provided by public institutions (themselves administered by different state organisations, from local government to national agencies, and encompassing schools, colleges and specialist adult services), prisons, employers (including often the armed forces), trade unions and voluntary organisations. Coordination at national level can be extremely complex, not least because adult learning typically involves several different ministries (educa-tion/higher education, labour, social welfare), as well as the private and voluntary sectors.

Coordination is becoming more complex with the proliferation of providers. In the UK, much public adult education was, until the 1990s, provided by local government through dedicated services; while council adult education services still continue in many areas (especially in Scot-land, where adult education is provided under the rubric of community learning and develop-ment), colleges have played a growing role since the 1990s, and some local council provision, such as short-term residential colleges, has all but disappeared. College provision shrank during the recession as governments, in Scotland and Wales as well as England, opted to focus on full-time courses for young people. University extramural departments are increasingly a rarity, though most higher education institutions (HEIs) are involved in professional updating pro-grammes, and many have specialist part-time programmes for adult learners; two HEIs – the Open University and Birkbeck – provide almost exclusively for adult part-time learners. Voluntary organisations such as the WEA and Women's Institutes are still significant providers, though their importance has declined somewhat in recent decades, while self-help bodies such as the Univer-sities of the Third Age have flourished. At the same time, private providers – commercial and third sector – have expanded rapidly. Although precise numbers are hard to come by, and their scale varies from single person consultancies to multinational training corporations, one survey estimated that there were some 12,300 private training providers in the UK operating above the threshold for value added tax, with the numbers doubling between 2000 and 2008 (Simpson, 2009:9–11). Digitisation and mobile technologies are transforming the prospects for open online learning, with a number of new players developing large numbers of massive open online courses. Finally, of course, employers continue to provide high volumes of education and training at work.

Individual/group task

- Given the range of different types of provider and provision, can we still speak of an 'adult education sector'?

The adult education landscape, of course, looks very different in different countries. In the case of Germany, especially in the former West German states, adult education is still largely provided by the same major public institutions that were active two or three decades ago. The largest and most influential of these are the *Volkshochschulen* (adult education centres, VHS), funded mainly by local government and providing mainly non-credit courses for adults, includ-ing language and citizenship classes for immigrants. The VHS are thought of in Germany as the fourth pillar of the education system, alongside primary, secondary and higher education; each VHS largely sets out its own programme, albeit in consultation with local government and other VHS in the region and most have their own, often rather impressive buildings. Alongside, the VHS are other established providers, including adult education services linked to the main confessional faiths and trade unions as well as *Arbeit und Leben* (Work and Life, broadly comparable to the WEA), and the universities, whose contribution is less through part-time courses for adults than the opening up of lecturers to 'guest listeners', specialist programmes for seniors and a broad range of public engagement activities, which are rarely if ever explicitly conceptualised as adult education. Private providers also play a growing role; one recent survey of continuing and adult education in the *Land* of Hesse, a highly prosperous region whose best-known city is Frankfurt, reported that of the 1,487 institutions who replied, 45% were private commercial bodies, 14%were private not-for-profits and 4% were VHS. That said, the VHS still accounted for the lion's share of learner numbers (Schemmann *et al.*, 2016:11).

Given these broad variations of provision, it is not surprising that participation in adult learning also varies considerably between different countries. Reliable data are most readily available for a rather small number of countries, notably those who are members of the OECD and the EU. Considerably, less information is available for middle- and low-income nations. And within the group of high-income nations, much of the information on participation is collected by international governmental agencies, whose main interest is in workforce development, so that surveys are often designed solely to collect information on those under the formal retirement age. Nevertheless, these surveys give us a broad picture of which countries have high rates of provision and which have lower rates, as well as which people are most likely to participate in adult learning and who is less so.

International survey data for the high-income nations suggests that even within this group there is a range of participation. One analysis of the findings of different surveys identified four main groups of countries. At the peak stand, the small Nordic nations (Denmark, Finland, Iceland, Norway and Sweden), who typically show participation rates of 50% or above; then come the smaller northern European nations plus the 'countries of Anglo-Saxon origin' (Australia, Canada, New Zealand, the United Kingdom and the USA), with participation rates of 35–50%; third is a group of European nations, including Austria, France, Germany and Ireland, with overall rates of 20–35%; finally the Mediterranean nations, along with Chile and some central European states, have participation rates of under 20% (Desjardins *et al.*, 2006).

While rates of participation tell us something about the volume of learning, they do not tell us everything. The amount of time spent learning appears, according to the same overview of survey data, generally to correlate with rates of participation. However, there are exceptions. Switzerland and the UK, for example, are in the second highest group of nations for their participation rates, but they fall below several countries in the third group when looking at the average time spent learning (Desjardins *et al.*, 2006). Measuring and comparing quality is another matter; at present, there are simply no data available, which allow us to say which countries have the highest quality adult learning systems.

One explanation for international variations in participation is the extent to which the state provides a supportive framework. This may seem obvious, if it is taken to mean that direct support to learners will lead to higher rates of participation. One more sophisticated explanation states that participation is shaped less by direct support, and more by the ways in which the state fosters broad conditions that are favourable to participation. This is held to explain the high levels of participation in the Nordic nations, for example, which are said to be particularly effective at reducing both structural and individual barriers to participation (Rubenson and Desjardins, 2009).

Individual/group task

- Can you think of any (other) reasons why the Nordic nations have particularly high rates of participation in adult learning?
- Do you think that these inequalities of participation are probably more or less inevitable? Or are they the result of policies or cultural factors?

Yet while some nations may foster higher participation rates than others, inequalities within nations follow much the same pattern. First, most participation is driven by work. Whether this is a matter of learner motivation, as where workers want to learn new skills, or employer priorities, or state policy (as in training for the unemployed), job-related learning is dominant. It follows that those who are neither in work nor seeking it are less likely to participate. Second, and closely related to the first inequality, participation declines sharply with age. Third, those who are best educated when they are young are far more likely to participate than those who left their early education with low or no qualifications. Fourth, those in routine manual occupations are far less likely to participate than those working in high-skill professional occupations. These are shared international patterns (Desjardins, *et al.*, 2006), though the inequalities tend to be least strongly marked in the high participation Nordic nations. Moreover, inequalities of participation may be mitigated by policies of targeting resources at those who are least likely to take up learning of their own accord.

So, policy can make a difference. At present, a large number of governments say that adult learning is a global priority. National governments and international agencies alike recognise that tackling the challenges and exploiting the opportunities of rising longevity, mass migration, technological and scientific change and sociocultural transformations will require people to develop new skills and knowledge. According to the latest Global Report on Adult Learning and Education, three quarters of the 128 participating countries claim to have made 'significant progress' in their policies for this area since the previous Report in 2009 (UNESCO Institute for Lifelong Learning, 2016:32). Nor is this simply a matter for government: there is growing demand for learning opportunities as people look to make the most of their lives by developing and deploying new capabilities and following up their interests (Field, 2006). Yet, aspirations for a knowledge society are one thing, and educational realities another.

Despite significant change in recent decades, the UNESCO Institute for Statistics estimates that 758 million adults – two-thirds of them women – still lacked basic reading and writing skills in 2014 (UNESCO Institute for Statistics, 2016). And while adult learning may be a public policy priority, it by no means follows that it attracts high levels of public funding. In 2015, out of 97 countries reporting on this issue, 41 reported that they directed less than 0.9% of public education expenditure to adult learning and education, and only 22 spent 4% or more; among those classified by the United Nations as 'low- and middle-income countries', over a quarter spent less than 0.4%. And while most countries (46%) reported that spending had increased since 2009 or had stayed the same (33%), one in eight said that spending had fallen, particularly in Africa and Central/Eastern Europe. Finally, 24 countries said that they had insufficient information to determine what proportion of their education budget was devoted to adult learning (UNESCO Institute for Lifelong Learning, 2016). In all countries, though, the funding of adult learning comes from a mixture of sources: public funding, student fees, employer funding and charitable support.

Individual/group task

- How should adult learning be funded? Should there be different approaches for differ-ent types of provision, depending on such factors as who benefits the most?

The role of international organisations

In recent years, there has been growing interest in adult learning from international organisa-tions. In particular, intergovernmental bodies such as the OECD and EU have adopted policies favouring adult learning as a means of promoting employability, competitiveness and inclusion. For example, the European Commission has argued that:

> Europe has moved towards a knowledge-based society and economy. More than ever before, access to up-to-date information and knowledge, together with the motivation and skills to use these resources intelligently on behalf of oneself and the community as a whole, are becoming the key to strengthening Europe's competitiveness and improving the employ-ability and adaptability of the workforce.

As a result, it recommends that:

> Lifelong learning is no longer just one aspect of education and training; it must become the guiding principle for provision and participation across the full continuum of learning contexts.
>
> *(European Commission, 2000:3–5)*

The Commission set its member states a decade to achieve this goal. Well after this deadline had passed, though, a new strategy for skills pointed out that although most of the European workforce of the next two decades is already in work, only a minority is given the opportunity to learn new skills, and most of those are the already well educated (European Commission, 2016).

It is worth emphasising that this level of international policy interest is relatively recent. Systematic international interest in adult education owes its origins to the period after the First World War, at a time of considerable interest in the role of both international exchanges and adult education in promoting reconciliation and reconstruction (Field *et al.*, 2016). While the early inter-national discussions were very much rooted in practice, and in the belief that practical lessons could be learned from other countries' experiences, they were also geographically limited. The World Association of Adult Education commissioned and published 23 national profiles between 1919 and 1931; most of these covered European countries along with Australia, China, India, Japan and the United States of America. More systematic and comprehensive attempts to study and compare national systems were undertaken after the Second World War, often under the auspices of UNESCO, with more scholarly research-oriented comparative work developing only in the 1960s; and even these more academic studies were undertaken with the aim of influencing policy and developing practice (Field *et al.*, 2016). So the idea that international and comparative adult education should have practical value is certainly not new, but it has been taken to a new level in recent years through the interventions of intergovernmental agencies, and above all the EU and the OECD, both of whom have argued that upskilling is a key strategy for maintaining competitiveness in a context of intensified economic globalisation.

Of course, the OECD and EU are not the only games in town. Historically, UNESCO has tended to position itself on the humanistic end of the policy spectrum. Maren Elfert describes UNESCO's 1972 report on lifelong education, *Learning to Be*, as a deeply humanistic text which embodies a political-philosophical idea of the 'complete man' (*sic*), drawing on contemporary ideas from psychology as well as the countercultural ideas on schooling of Ivan Illich and Paulo Freire (Elfert, 2015:89–90). It sought to connect educational developments in the advanced capitalist 'First World' with those of other global regions, particularly the developing nations of the 'Third World' whose leaders were opening up the political space created by the international conflict between East (the 'Second World') and West. The core argument of the report, which is usually known by the name of its chair Edgar Faure, was that lifelong education should become the 'educational master concept for both developed and developing countries', involving not simply a stronger focus on learning (including informal learning) in adult life but also a rethinking of the purpose and structure of school systems (UNESCO, 1972).

This geopolitical dimension was less marked in the subsequent UNESCO report of 1996, *Learning: The Treasure Within*. As in 1972, the tone was humanist and utopian, though Elfert detects an underlying 'subtle spirit of disenchantment', with the earlier Enlightenment belief in progress giving way to concern over existential threats (Elfert, 2015:91). The Report organised the purposes of learning around four pillars:

- learning to know;
- learning to do;
- learning to live together; and
- learning to be.

While the report argued that pursuing these goals will require 'learning throughout life' (a formulation that is closer to the French 'apprenance pendant tout la vie' than is 'lifelong learning'), it said relatively little about adult learning (UNESCO, 1996).

Individual/group task

- How significant is it that recent policy documents emphasise 'learning' rather than 'education'? Why do you think they do so?

It is difficult to evaluate the direct influence of the two major UNESCO reports. Elfert notes that both were widely discussed at the time of publication and have continued to attract attention from academics; she suggests that the 1972 report had some influence on policy thinking in the developed world, largely as a result of its reception by the OECD, but less so in the developing nations; the 1996 report was widely debated, particularly in Europe and North and Latin America, but had little actual influence (Elfert, 2016).

By comparison, the EU and OECD have had a much more visible impact. During the 1970s, OECD focussed on developing its thinking on recurrent education, which it presented as a strategy for promoting lifelong education. Subsequently, in the early 1990s, in a context of growing concerns over demographic ageing and wakening competitiveness among its member states, the OECD adopted a policy of promoting lifelong learning, with a broad balance between economic and social goals (Schemmann, 2007). As in other areas, OECD has no direct powers over its member states, and it is expected to work by using information (such as large-scale survey data and peer-review reports) to generate discussion across its members. In the field of lifelong learning, OECD is responsible for a large-scale cross-national survey of adult competencies (Programme for the International Assessment of Adult Competencies, PIAAC) and for a series of peer-review reports on education after school in individual member states. PIAAC has been particularly influential, partly because OECD has used it to examine competencies – i.e. what adults can actually do with their knowledge – rather than participation in learning (OECD, 2013). In general, the OECD's influence has helped to raise the visibility and importance attached to adult learning and skills, and its focus on competences has influenced public debate; but OECD lacks direct levers over national governments, and its influence is therefore largely indirect, and in terms of its ability to shape the agenda in ways that its member states regard as valuable.

The European Union is unique among international governmental arrangements in having a large number of legislative and financial powers. The question of whether EU policies were leading to convergence or divergence between the national systems of member states was already being posed in the early 1990s (Siebert, 1994). Unlike UNESCO or the OECD, the EU has direct legislative competences in the field of vocational training, and it has financial responsibility both for a suite of student mobility programmes and development projects, as well as through its financial support for regional economic development (for example, through the European Social Fund) and its research programmes. Furthermore, it has, in recent years, developed ways of influencing policies and practice indirectly, through what it calls 'the open method of coordination'. This includes the publication of data on participation in continuing training and adult education, as well as monitoring and reporting on 'best practice' through seminars, publications and debates (Ioannidou, 2007).

The impact of EU policies varies considerably between different countries. In some of the larger member states with well-developed adult education systems, such as France, Germany or the UK, the impact is relatively limited. Although its policy pronouncements can have some symbolic significance, the EU's influence is mainly felt through the mobility programmes and regional structural funds. Elsewhere, particularly in smaller countries or countries that have historically neglected adult education, the impact has been more significant, and the EU's policies have helped raise both the visibility and status of a previously neglected sector. In terms of the overall direction of EU policies, some authors conclude that at least in the forms that they are implemented their impact has been largely neo-liberal in character, and has promoted a tendency for states to shift provision out of the public sector and into the private and third sectors (Borg and Mayo, 2005; Finnegan, 2008; Fejes and Salling Olesen, 2016; Mikulec and Jelenc Krašovec,

2016). What Brexit means for the place of adult education in the EU's thinking is yet to emerge, but it seems likely that a broad commitment to adult learning as a vehicle of competitiveness and inclusion will continue to shape policy thinking.

Conclusion

While national differences remain strong, the combined effects of globalisation, technological change and intergovernmental policy developments are undoubtedly having some impact on adult education and training. Recent years have seen a general trend towards the weakening of national influences on adult education, though this is probably driven more by factors such as the role of transnational corporations in shaping training and development practices, as well as new forms of digitised open learning become available on a global basis. At the same time, the reduced role of government in many countries and the growing role of private initiative and self-help provision mean that there is also a tendency towards increasing heterogeneity of provision reflecting factors other than national differences. In short, national governments are in many countries withdrawing from their previous roles in providing adult learning at the same time as new actors are becoming more important.

Recommended reading

INFED (infed.org), a website maintained by the YMCA's George Williams College, is an invaluable encyclopae-
 dia of ideas and institutions in adult and community learning.
Avis, J., Fisher, R. and Thompson, R. (2014) *Teaching in Lifelong Learning: A Guide to Theory and Practice.*
 Maidenhead: McGraw-Hill.
Tight, M. (2003) *Key Concepts in Adult Education and Training.* London: Routledge.

References

Becker, G. (1964) *Human Capital: a theoretical and empirical analysis, with special reference to education.*
 Chicago, IL: The University of Chicago Press
Borg, C. and Mayo, P. (2005) The EU memorandum on lifelong learning: old wine in new bottles? *Globalisation,
 Societies and Education,* 3(2), 203–225.
Coffield, F. (1999) Breaking the consensus: lifelong learning as social control, *British Educational Research
 Journal,* 25(4), 479–499.
Desjardins, R., Rubenson, K. and Milana, M. (2006) *Unequal Chances to Participate in Adult Learning: Inter-
 national Perspectives.* Paris: UNESCO Institute for Educational Planning.
Elfert, M. (2015) UNESCO, the Faure report, the Delors report, and the political Utopia of lifelong learning.
 European Journal of Education, 50(1), 88–100.
Elfert, M. (2016) Revisiting the *Faure Report* (1972) and the *Delors Report* (1996): Why was UNESCO's
 utopian vision of lifelong learning an 'unfailure'? Paper presented at the Eighth Triennial Conference of
 the European Society for Research in the Education of Adults, National University of Ireland, Maynooth.
European Commission (2000) *A Memorandum on Lifelong Learning.* Brussels: European Commission.
European Commission (2016) *A New Skills Agenda for Europe: Working Together to Strengthen Human
 Capital, Employability and Competitiveness.* Strasbourg: European Commission.
Fejes, A. and Salling Olesen, H. (2016) Editorial: marketization and commodification of adult education.
 European Journal for Research on the Education and Learning of Adults, 7(2), 146–150.
Field, J. (1996) Learning for work: vocational education and training. In R. Fieldhouse (Ed.) *A History of
 Modern British Adult Education.* Leicester: National Institute of Adult Continuing Education.
Field, J. (2006) *Lifelong Learning and the New Educational Order.* Stoke-on-Trent: Trentham.

Field, J., Schemmann, M. and Künzel, K. (2016) International Comparative Adult Education Research. Reflections on theory, methodology and future developments. *Internationales Jahrbuch der Erwachsenenbildung*, 39, 2016, 109–133.

Finnegan, F. (2008) Neo-liberalism, Irish society, and adult education. *The Adult Learner*, 2008, 54–73.

Freire, P. (2000) *Pedagogy of the Oppressed*. New York: Continuum.

Goldman, L. (2000) Intellectuals and the English working class, 1870–1945: The case of adult education. *History of Education*, 29(4), 281–300.

Ioannidou, A. (2007) A comparative analysis of new governance instruments in the transnational educational space: A shift to knowledge-based instruments? *European Educational Research Journal*, 6(4), 336–347.

Jarvis, P. (2001) Malcolm Knowles. In P. Jarvis (Ed.) *Twentieth Century Thinkers in Adult and Continuing Education*. London: Kogan Page.

Knowles, M. (1984) *Andragogy in Action: Applying Modern Principles of Adult Education*. San Francisco, CA: Jossey Bass.

Mikulec, B. and Jelenc Krašovec, S. (2016) Marketising Slovene adult education policies and practices using mechanisms of the Europeanisation of education. *European Journal for Research on the Education and Learning of Adults*, 7(2), 151–170.

OECD (2013) *OECD Skills Outlook 2013: First Results from the Survey of Adult Skills*. Paris: OECD.

Rubenson, K. and Desjardins, R. (2009) The impact of welfare state regimes on barriers to participation in adult education: a bounded agency model. *Adult Education Quarterly*, 59(3), 187–207.

Schemmann, M. (2007) *Internationale Weiterbildungspolitik und Globalisierung*. Bielefeld: W. Bertelsmann Verlag GmbH & Co. KG.

Schemmann, M. Feld, T. and Seitter, W. (2016) *Weiterbildungsbericht Hessen 2015*. Wiesbaden: Hessisches Kultusministerium.

Schuller, T. (2000) Social and human capital: The search for appropriate technomethodology. *Policy Studies*, 21(1), 25–35.

Siebert, H. (1994) Konvergenzen und Divergenzen in den Erwachsenenbildungssystemen der Europäischen Union. *Internationales Jahrbuch der Erwachsenenbildung*, 22, 40–53.

Simpson, L. (2009) *The Private Training Market in the UK*. Leicester: National Institute of Adult Continuing Education.

Steele, T. (2007) *Knowledge is Power! The Rise and Fall of European Popular Education Movements, 1848–1939*. Bern: Peter Lang Verlag.

Tawney, R.H. (1966) *The Radical Tradition: Twelve Essays on Politics, Education and Literature*. Harmondsworth: Penguin Books.

UNESCO (1972) *Learning to Be: The World of Education Today and Tomorrow*. Paris: UNESCO and Harrap.

UNESCO (1996) *Learning: The Treasure within*. Paris: UNESCO.

UNESCO Institute for Lifelong Learning (2016) *Third Global Report on Adult Learning and Education*. Hamburg: UNESCO Institute for Lifelong Learning.

UNESCO Institute for Statistics (2016) *UIS Fact Sheet 38: 50th Anniversary of International Literacy Day*. Montréal: UNESCO Institute for Statistics.

Walker, M. (2016) *The Development of the Mechanics' Institute Movement in Britain and Beyond: Supporting Further Education for the Adult Working Classes*. London: Routledge.

10 International comparisons in mathematics

Perspectives on teaching and learning

David Burghes

Introduction

There is no doubt that international comparisons in mathematics are feasible to undertake and are useful and informative for the countries involved. The two well-respected international tests, Programme for International Student Assessment (PISA) and Trends in International Mathematics and Science Studies (TIMSS), have had a considerable impact on policy in many countries, including the UK. There is currently great interest in the strategies for teaching and learning mathematics in Shanghai and there has been a focus on the methodology used in Finland (Ofsted, 2010); strategies for teaching and training observed in Japan have had a considerable influence in many Western countries both through their use of 'lesson study' for continuing professional development (CPD) and specifically for mathematics, where their open problem-solving approach is used to develop the mathematical thinking of learners (Tall, 2008; Burghes and Robinson, 2012).

In this chapter, we first summarise the impact that international comparisons have had on education policy in Western countries, with the focus on mathematics. In particular, we consider the success of taking strategies from mathematically high-performing countries and implementing them in the UK and elsewhere. We consider both international comparisons based on rigorous testing of learners at a particular age group and also the importing of strategies from mathematically high-performing countries into other countries and, in particular, into England. We also look at some of the cultural issues that are raised when attempting to implement strategies that have worked well in one country into another country, where the environment and ethos might be rather different. We examine the validity and reliability of some of the tests that have been used for comparisons. Finally, in an age of both increasing international economic competitiveness and enhanced communications, we make suggestions for how countries can work collaboratively for the benefit of teachers and their learners.

Large-scale international comparisons

While international comparisons have been made for centuries, the first rigorous testing of samples of learners in different countries with test questions and subsequent comparing standards between countries has been based on the International Mathematics and Science Studies, particularly TIMSS, the third study, detailed in TIMSS (2005) and the PISA.

We will look in some detail at these programmes and their impact on teaching and learning mathematics in the Western world.

Trends in International Mathematics and Science Studies

The TIMSS study is neatly summarised on the IEA (International Association for the Evaluation of Educational Achievement) website:

> TIMSS 2011 is the fifth in IEA's series of international assessments of student achievement dedicated to improving teaching and learning in mathematics and science. First conducted in 1995, TIMSS reports every four years on the achievement of fourth and eighth grade students. A number of countries participating in TIMSS 2011 will have trend data across assessments from 1995 to 2011.
>
> *(TIMSS, 2011)*

It made a significant impact on policy and practice in part through the associated TIMSS video study, where mathematics lessons for eighth grade learners in America, Germany and Japan were compared. It uncovered many contrasting approaches adopted to mathematics teaching and learning in these three countries: a full account is given by Stigler and Hiebert (1999) in their book *The Teaching Gap*. Even after almost two decades, this book is fundamental in that it is the first rigorous study of teaching strategies across countries, based on the evidence in video clips. We will only reproduce one of the many results of the study that made what was then a breakthrough in our understanding of strategies for the teaching of mathematics: simply that different countries adopt very different strategies.

This is well illustrated in Figure 10.1 (adapted from Stigler and Hiebert, 1999), which gives the average percentage of time spent in three kinds of activities, namely:

- practice procedures;
- apply concepts;
- invent/think.

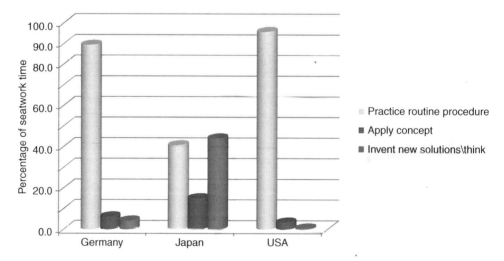

Figure 10.1   Average percentage time spent on mathematical activities.

If nothing else, it illustrated that these three countries had vastly different teaching strategies with America and Germany focussing on practice, while Japan had a strong emphasis on inventing and thinking!

Group discussion task

What style of maths teaching did you experience at school?

Of course, technological advances have contributed greatly to this type of comparison, and the Internet now means that we can so easily compare strategies used in different countries. Strategies used in the Far East have, and still do, fascinated the mathematics education community. A wonderful site for looking at video clips (with lesson notes) of a range of mathematics lessons from countries in the Far East is given by the Asia-Pacific Economic Cooperation project on lesson study (APEC, 2016).

Programme for International Student Assessment

This is the PISA and focusses on the achievements of 15-year-old learners. Developed by the Organisation for Economic Co-operation and Development (OECD), it assesses learners' skills in not just mathematics but also science and reading. It seems to be well respected by governments around the world and a country's current position in the PISA international league table does provoke debate at the highest level of government, even resulting in policies focussed on improving the position of particular countries. The tests in mathematics are taken every three years and are very much based on contextual mathematics rather than basic concepts and skills. An interesting summary of what they mean is given in the NFER publication, *What You Don't Find Out about England's Educational Performance in the Pisa League Table* (2012).

They make four key points:

- It is not always possible to say with certainty from looking at a country's rank position alone whether one country has outperformed another.
- England's position in the international league table is dependent on which countries have participated.
- England has maintained a similar level of performance in maths in the last three rounds of testing (2006, 2009, 2012), although some countries have overtaken England over time.
- PISA alone does not tell us why some countries are higher performing, why some learners perform better than others or which teaching practices result in higher performance.

There are no surprises here and it is important to note that each country's score has a margin of error in it but the reality is the way such ranking is interpreted by governments. If a country does well, the government of the day takes the credit but if it does not do well, either the evidence is buried or it uses the evidence to justify new strategies, intended to improve the performance next time round.

Table 10.1   PISA scores

PISA scores on the maths scale	
2012 PISA results	
Shanghai-China	613
Singapore	573
Hong Kong-China	561
Chinese Taipei	560
South Korea	554
Macao-China	538
Japan	536
Liechtenstein	535
Switzerland	531
Netherlands*	523
Estonia*	521
Finland*	519
Canada	518
Poland*	518
Belgium*	515
Germany*	514
Vietnam	511
Austria*	506
Australia	504
Republic of Ireland*	501
Slovenia*	501
Denmark*	500
New Zealand	500
Czech Republic *	499
Scotland	498
England	495
France*	495
OECD Average	494
Iceland	493
Latvia *	491
Luxembourg*	490
Norway	489
Portugal*	487
Northern Ireland	487
Italy*	485
Spain*	484
Russian Federation	482
Slovak Republic*	482
The United States	481
Lithuania *	479

2012 PISA results

Sweden*	478
Hungary*	477
Croatia*	471
Wales	468
Israel	466
Greece*	453
Serbia	449
Turkey	448
*Romania**	445
Cyprus	440
*Bulgaria**	439
The United Arab Emirates	434
Kazakhstan	432
Chile	423
Mexico	413

Source: Department for Education Achievement of 15-Year-Olds in England, PISA 2012 National Report.
*EU countries, italicised – OECD, non-italicised – non-OECD.

The results for the 2012 round of testing are given here in Table 10.1; these are just the headline figures, giving the average performance for each country. In 2012, the PISA data also evaluated the learners' happiness at school. The overall average showed 80% of the learners as happy with school, and the English sample gave:

- 84% as happy at school;
- 85% as satisfied with their school.

Contrast this with the Pacific Rim countries where a high percentage of learners are happy at school (82–89%) but a surprisingly low level of satisfaction of learners with their school (60–81%).

Table 10.1 summarises the country ranks for the round of testing in 2012. Note that:

- The OECD average is 494.
- Countries between 501 and 487 not significantly different to England.
- Comparing English speaking countries, only Australia is significantly higher than England.
- Shanghai-China is very significantly higher than any other participant.
- Far East countries all perform significantly higher than England.
- Both Russia and USA are significantly lower than England.

It is also important to note that these average scores say nothing about the variation, which it could be argued, is at least if not more important than the average. It is also not too surprising that Finland, with a relatively high average for a Western country, also has a relatively small spread. Their education system ensures that children attend their local school, with intervention widely used to ensure that all learners reach an adequate standard; that is, children are given an education to make sure they are all employable and hence not a drain on public finances as an adult (Sahlberg, 2014).

Individual/group task

- Looking at the research trends in PISA test scores over time, do any of the results surprise you?

The style and form of the questions used in this testing regime are of interest. As noted earlier, the focus is on using maths in context and the questions below, taken from the PISA website, illustrate this.

Question 1

A carpenter has 32 m of timber and wants to make a border around a garden bed. He is considering the following designs for the garden bed (Figure 10.2).

The learners just had to say yes or no to 'Which of the designs could he use?' for each of the options, A, B, C and D. Clearly, there is a context here but not really real world, as the gardener could just buy more timber. On the other hand, it is meaningful for most learners, although there

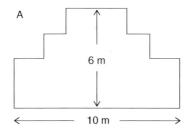
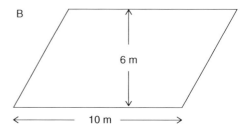
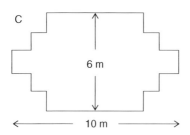
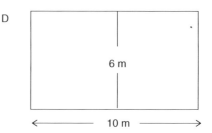

Figure 10.2 Maths question.

may be some countries where the context is not readily understood. So designing questions that are meaningful in a variety of languages and with no change in the level of difficulty is not without hazards. A second more open question is given below.

Question 2: sailing ships

Ninety-five percent of world trade is moved by sea, by roughly 50,000 tankers, bulk carriers and container ships. Engineers are planning to develop wind power support for ships. Their proposal is to attach kite sails to ships and use the wind's power to help reduce diesel consumption and the fuel's impact on the environment.

Due to high diesel fuel costs of 0.42 zeds per litre, the owners of the ship **New Wave** *are thinking about equipping their ship with a kite sail.*

It is estimated that a kite sail like this has the potential to reduce the diesel consumption by about 20% overall. The cost of equipping the New Wave with a kite sail is 2,500,000 zeds.

After how many years would the diesel fuel savings cover the cost of the kite sail? Give calculations to support your answer (Table 10.2).

For a closed book and time-limited exam, this is challenging and also requiring high levels of literacy to read and understand the context. These questions (which are sample questions from PISA) do open up many issues, for example:

- What contexts can be used that are fully understood by learners in all participating countries?
- Do particular contexts give learners from some countries more background understanding and experience and hence an unfair advantage?
- Is it fair to expect learners to have strong language skills?

We will return to some of these points later in the chapter.

Table 10.2   Sailing ships question

Name: New Wave

Type: Freighter
Length: 117 m
Breadth: 18 m
Load capacity: 12,000 tons
Maximum speed: 19 knots
Diesel consumption per year without a kite sail approximately 3,500,000

The relevance of small-scale comparative projects

The two examples given in the previous section belong to the class of large-scale comparative projects, where efforts are made to represent a country fairly by the samples used. To both achieve this and ensure that test questions travel across different countries without bias, considerable time and effort is needed and hence large funding is required (often through contributions from the participating countries and their governments).

Whether such projects are as valuable as some people believe is debatable and given that it is only a snapshot at a particular time, there is some justification in longitudinal studies, even if the samples used are less than perfect. We will describe one here to illustrate the issues and the benefits from such approaches.

The Kassel Project (Burghes, 1999 – set up and coordinated from Exeter University in 1992/5) started as a joint English, Scottish and German project but after the first year of the programme, many other countries joined in, including Hungary, Singapore, Finland and Poland. The aim was to understand what makes for good practice in mathematics teaching and learning. The decision was made to test during what was the last three years of compulsory education (years 9–11) and test the sample of learners with tests in 'Number', 'Algebra' and 'Shape and Space' using similar tests each year in order to measure progress and provide a value-added analysis. A 'Mathematical Potential' test was used as the discriminator between groups of learners. Each country participating had a coordinator (usually from a university with teacher training) and it was their responsibility to organise a representative sample for their country. Sample size varied from country to country but was usually about 500 learners per country. The progress made by the samples from England, Hungary, Scotland and Singapore was carefully monitored over the periods during which each country participated. The data collected was used to produce the average total score on the three tests for learners in each country. The researchers' first shock was the remarkably higher performances by Singapore and Hungary in comparison to England and Scotland. The second shock was the much sharper increase in rate of progress recorded for the two higher countries, and this despite the fact that some learners in Singapore and Hungary were already reaching the ceiling of the test marks available.

It was at least clear that England and Scotland were both performing at a significantly lower level than Singapore and Hungary. The value-added analysis provided the data for indicating where schools and/or classes were progressing either significantly more or less than the average in each country. Coordinators in each country were provided with this analysis and were encouraged to observe classes and note the strategies that the higher performing classes were adopting. This led at the close of the project to a set of recommendations for good practice in mathematics teaching and learning to which all countries signed up. This is repeated below for information; lessons for high-performing classes were normally characterised by the following features:

- lessons well prepared; resources needed at hand;
- lessons had pace and a variety of activities;
- these activities consisted of

   whole class interactive introduction;
   individual or paired or whole class practice;
   whole class interactive review and discussion;

- interaction included learners demonstrating at the board and articulating their solution in front of the class;
- correct notation, logical working and layout and correct mathematical language to be used all the time;
- all pupils actively involved throughout the lesson, with thorough monitoring of individual work and high expectations of what learners can achieve;
- homework set as reinforcement and/or extension after each lesson and reviewed interactively at the start of the next lesson.

The characteristics of effective teachers were also presented:

- they like teaching, mathematics and children;
- they are confident and good communicators;

  mathematically capable;
  understand misconceptions;
  adaptable and flexible;
  patient and good humoured;

- Above all, they provide clear mathematical explanations.

These characteristics were based on a combination of value-added data, observations and the expertise and experience of the country coordinators. Much of the above makes sense even today, some 20 years later!

Individual/group task

- Do you agree with these teaching and learning strategies? Do they reflect your own experience of secondary school mathematics?

Evidence-based practice

Having looked at large-scale testing projects and one example of a longitudinal comparative study, it is relevant to consider the focus over the last decade on evidence-based practice. This has been defined by Cook and Odom (2013:135) as 'practices and programs shown by high quality research to have meaningful effects on student outcome'. This is a more precise definition than, for example, 'good or best practice' or 'research-informed practice' but still not without some ambiguity, as there is no universal agreement on what can be classed as 'high-quality research'.

There are now a number of websites that purport to provide evidence-based practice; these include the following:

- John Hattie's synthesis of meta-analyses at http://visible-learning.org
- What Works Clearinghouse in the USA at http://ies.ed.gov/ncee/wwc/

- Bob Slavin's Best Evidence Encyclopedia at http://www.bestevidence.org
- Teaching and Learning Toolkit in the UK at https://educationendowmentfoundation.org.uk/resources/teaching-learning-toolkit/

These sites contain useful information about successful interventions; for example, the Education Endowment Foundation (EEF) Teaching and Learning Toolkit gives measures on effectiveness with a score of over three regarded as being significant; here are some of the measures:

Feedback	+8
Metacognition	+8
Collaborative learning	+5
Homework (secondary)	+5
Mastery learning	+5
One-to-one tuition	+5
Digital technology	+4
Setting or streaming	−1

While they do provide helpful evidence for good practice, there are two other important, indeed crucial, factors to be considered before interventions are implemented, namely,

- Are the schools able to understand the intervention and do they have the professional wisdom to put this into practice and sustain it over time?
- Is the intervention culturally appropriate to fit with the value, knowledge, skills and experience of teachers as well as parents and carers?

We will consider these issues in the next section in the light of recent developments in mathematics teaching and learning in England.

Recent developments in mathematics teaching and learning

Here, we consider two contrasting and significant developments in government policy for mathematics education in schools and colleges in England, each one based on international evidence.

Core Maths

In 2010, the Nuffield report, *Is the UK an outlier? An international comparison of upper secondary mathematics education* (Nuffield Report, 2010) gathered evidence from 24 different countries to make recommendations for consideration in the formation and implementation of policy. The evidence presented in the report made it very clear that in England we have low participation rates in advanced mathematics post-16, compared to many other countries around the world.

So here is a very different type of comparative study, not in any way comparing standards of attainment but simply the take-up of mathematics in post-16 education.

It does, though, seem to chime with educational opinion from the maths education community and is in line with government policy keen to see a higher take-up of maths in post-16 education, as, for example, the OECD reports suggested a positive correlation between increased participation in mathematics in post-16 education and higher GDP.

There were two major initiatives that occurred at this time, one directly from this report. The first was the announcement (see DfE, 2013) that any students not achieving Grade C or above in General Certificate of Secondary Education (GCSE) Maths would have to continue with some sort of mathematics provision in post-16 education until Grade C was achieved. Students could alternatively take Level 2 Functional Maths courses but the reality has been that about 100,000 extra candidates have taken GCSE Maths, with the expected outcome that most (in fact at least two-thirds) did not achieve Grade C.

As well as the obvious problem of having rather disaffected students with low motivation and morale for resisting GCSE Maths, there was also the problem of finding teachers and tutors for these extra classes, particularly in further education colleges, at a time of severe shortage of qualified secondary maths teachers. This situation has continued to this day but nearly everyone is agreed that this is not helpful to all but to a handful of students and that there has to be a more effective policy that takes into account the aims and aspirations of these students and the now dire situation in terms of supply of teachers.

The second major initiative was the development of what is called 'Core Maths' courses for post-16 education. The government produced in July 2014, what is termed 'Technical Guidance' for the Awarding Bodies to use in the development of their Core Maths courses. The objectives were as follows:

Objective 1: *Deepen competence in the selection and use of mathematical methods and techniques.*
Objective 2: *Develop confidence in representing and analysing authentic situations mathematically and in applying mathematics to address related questions and issues.*
Objective 3: *Build skills in mathematical thinking, reasoning and communication.*

Again, this was influenced by practice in other countries with the aim of producing a Level 3 qualification, equivalent to an AS Level, that would bridge the gap between GCSE Mathematics and A and AS Level Mathematics courses. It is aimed at students who have achieved a Grade C or better at GCSE Mathematics but who do not take AS or A Level Mathematics.

Individual/group task

- Do you think it is a good idea for all post-16 students to have mathematical instruction? Justify your position on this.

The syllabuses on offer include topics such as

- Financial Maths
- Risk and Probability
- Linear Programming and Critical Path Analysis
- Regression and Correlation
- Hypothesis Testing

All based on practical problem solving and aiming to help prepare students either for further statistical work in higher education or for the world of work. The Core Maths Support Programme (2014–2017) was set up to help schools and colleges implement these courses, using two strategies based on international evidence, namely,

- open problem-solving approach, based on countries such as Japan and New Zealand, where the problem motivates the mathematics needed to analyse the situation;
- lesson study, now used in many countries, to innovate and sustain this development in the classroom.

Table 10.3 shows a typical problem, based on an event at the close of 2016, namely tennis rankings.

We are only at the end of the first pilot and it is probably not wise to make predictions but all the evidence points to the success of this initiative in terms of teachers enjoying the freedom to teach in a much less structured way and students motivated to engage in activities and appreciate the role of mathematics (and statistics) in real problem solving. It has also met the targets set by the government in terms of take-up and, despite the lack of suitably qualified teachers, has proved a real catalyst for supporting teachers and potentially increasing their retention in the classroom.

Table 10.3   Ranking in tennis

Ranking in tennis

ATP Rankings are based on points scored in competitions:

Grand Slams, Barclays ATP World Tour Finals
ATP World Tour Masters 1000, ATP 500 and ATP 250

It is calculated every Monday, based on performances in the previous 52 weeks and based on:

4 Grand Slams
8 ATP World Tour Masters 1000
Barclays ATP World Tour Finals
6 best performances from other events

The points scored are summarised in the table below:

	W	*F*	*SF*	*QF*	*R16*	*R32*	*R64*	*R128*
GS	2000	1200	720	360	180	90	45	10
Barclays	1500*							
ATP 1000	1000	600	360	180	90	45	10	
ATP 500	500	300	180	90	45	20		
ATP 200	250	150	90	45	20			

*ATP World Tour Finals 1,500 for undefeated Champion (200 for each round robin match win, plus 400 for a semifinal win, plus 500 for the final win)

Questions: *What are the key points that underpin this ranking model?*

Is it fit for purpose?
Can you suggest an alternative fairer model?

Mastery learning

This is another example of importing a strategy from other countries with the expectation that it will be successful in the UK context. There have been government-funded exchange visits with Shanghai, having noted its very high performance on PISA tests (see above) and these have brought mastery learning to the forefront in the teaching of mathematics, particularly in the primary sector. Mastery teaching is seen as one of the most important facets that underpins the great success of Shanghai and other Pacific Rim countries in mathematics education. It is, though, far from a new strategy!

In the late 1960s, Bloom observed that teachers displayed little variation in their teaching strategies although their students' achievement showed great variation. To counter this variation in outcome, he developed what he termed methods of mastery learning, in which the curriculum was divided into units of work with specific concepts and skills to be mastered. Initially, there would be a formative assessment (this could take the form of a test or more informal verbal questions) so that the teacher would be sure that all the learners were starting with the appropriate skills and knowledge. Some of the learners might need help in achieving the required starting point and 'corrective' instruction would be given, for example, intervention guidance, additional practice or collaborative working, while those who were ready would be engaged in extension work or other motivating activities. In this way, *all* class members would be ready to start the new work. He called this 'just-in-time' learning that prevents minor learning problems or misconceptions from accumulating and becoming a major issue.

This method is clearly relevant to the linear nature of mathematics, where topics and concepts build on earlier work. Bloom suggested that the learners should take the formative assessment again to ensure that they were all ready to move on to the new topic or concept (see Bloom, 1968). He believed using this method would provide learners with more appropriate instruction than is possible with traditional approaches to teaching where learners' usual relationship between aptitude and achievement fits a normal distribution, as illustrated below in Figure 10.3.

With learning for mastery, aptitude now transforms to a very positively skewed distribution for achievement.

Despite early positive results, the initial enthusiasm for mastery learning was not sustained in Western countries; the many reasons given for this included ineffective implementation of mastery learning methods and the intransigence of teachers to change! It should be noted that the EEF notes in their 'Teaching and Learning Toolkit' that the global evidence for mastery learning appears to lead to an impressive additional five months' progress over the course of a year, BUT that in the evaluation of their recently funded Mathematics Mastery programme (EEF, 2016), on average only one month's progress was gained. They suggest that some of this programme may

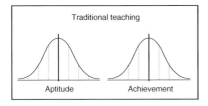

Figure 10.3   Traditional teaching versus mastery teaching.

not have included some key features of mastery learning that were previously associated with higher impacts.

So what are the key elements? The NCTEM website (NCETM, 2016) gives a summary:

- Maths teaching for mastery rejects the idea that a large proportion of people 'just can't do maths'.
- All pupils are encouraged by the belief that by working hard at maths they can succeed.
- Pupils are taught through whole-class interactive teaching, where the focus is on all pupils working together on the same lesson content at the same time, as happens in high-performing education jurisdictions such as Shanghai. All pupils master concepts before moving to the next part of the curriculum sequence, allowing no pupil to be left behind.
- If a pupil fails to grasp a concept or procedure, this is identified quickly and early intervention is put in place so that the pupil is ready to move on with the class in the next lesson.
- Lesson design identifies the new mathematics that is to be taught, the important points, the difficult points and sets out a careful teaching sequence. In a typical lesson, pupils sit facing the teacher and the teacher leads the interaction, which includes questioning, short tasks, explanation, demonstration and discussion.
- Procedural fluency and conceptual understanding are developed in tandem because each supports the development of the other.
- Practice is a vital part of teaching and this is intelligent – both reinforcing fluency with mathematics procedures and developing conceptual understanding in the process.

Readers familiar with primary maths teaching will quickly realise that many of the attributes above fly in the face of the established strategies experienced by most primary teachers when at school themselves and given prominence in their teacher training courses. Recent funding for the now established Maths Hubs around England aims to establish mastery learning over the next three years in half of all state primary schools.

This can be seen as a brave and far-reaching strategy to turn mathematics round in England and, once and for all, establish maths as a subject in which all can reach at least an acceptable level (that is, they will, in the future, be employable). Either this or it is a foolhardy venture bound to fail in the same way that any cascade model has in the past and, while it works well in Shanghai, the context and environment in England is not just different but poles apart.

For example, the context in Shanghai is characterised by certain key differences:

- Primary schools are very large (many with 10 classes in each year group) and they have, for example, dedicated year 1 maths teachers, etc.
- Teachers only teach two or three lessons each day and have time to study, reflect and plan their lessons.
- Most parents have only ONE child and they are dedicated to ensuring their only child succeeds at school.
- Many children have extra lessons after school and/or parents helping.

This is a far cry from England, where there is less emphasis now on education, in part as we are comparatively wealthy and so it feels as if we do not have to strive for educational success. It will be of great interest to see if mastery learning can be effectively incorporated and implemented into primary maths teaching without losing the key elements of the strategy, and will achieve the success predicted by the evidence-based practice websites.

Conclusion

There is a place for international comparative studies in mathematics; the subject itself makes it much simpler to compare attainment and progress but we do need to be wary that strategies that work well in the context and environment of one country will not automatically transfer successfully to another country. This is not to say that we cannot learn much from other countries and other countries from us; we have, for example, introduced probability and statistics as an important component of key stages 3 and 4 Mathematics, when some countries, for example, Japan, have been slow to introduce these topics in their curriculum even though they form an important part of higher education study in many disciplines. The advances in new technology means that we can indeed look in real time at mathematics teaching in classrooms in many parts of the world and both learn from these observations and recognise the limitations of some of the strategies observed. We can also gain information and insight from the curricula employed for mathematics in many countries and it is important to recognise the conditions of service for teachers and learn from continued professional development for teachers, where CPD is both a right and expectation. In summary, comparative studies are a very valuable research and development procedure to enhance teaching and learning of mathematics and, of course, for other subjects, too.

Recommended reading

Burghes, D. (1999) The Kassel Project. In B. Jaworski and D. Phillips (Eds.), *Comparing Standards Internationally*. Oxford: Symposium Books.

Burghes, D. and Robinson, D. (2012) *Lesson Study: Enhancing Mathematics Teaching and Learning*. Available at: http://www.cimt.org.uk/papers/lessonstudy.pdf. (Accessed 16th September 2016).

Crehan, L. (2016) *Cleverlands: The Secrets behind the Success of the World's Education Superpowers*. London: Unbound.

References

Asia-Pacific Economic Cooperation (2016) *A Collaborative Study on Innovations for Teaching and Learning Mathematics in Different Cultures among the APEC Member Economies*. Available at: http://www.criced.tsukuba.ac.jp/math/apec/. (Accessed 10th November 2016).

Bloom, B.S. (1968) Learning for mastery. *Evaluation Comment*, 1(2), 1–12.

Burghes, D. (1999) The Kassel Project. In B. Jaworski and D. Phillips (Eds.), *Comparing Standards Internationally*. Oxford: Symposium Books.

Burghes, D. and Robinson, D. (2012) *Lesson Study: Enhancing Mathematics Teaching and Learning*. Available at: http://www.cimt.org.uk/papers/lessonstudy.pdf. (Accessed 16th September 2016).

Cook, B.G. and Odom, S.L. (2013) Evidence-based practices and implementation science in special education. *Exceptional Children*, 79, 135–144.

Core Maths Support Programme (2016) *It All Adds Up*. Available at: http://www.core-maths.org. (Accessed 1st September 2016).

DfE (2013) *Post-16 Mathematics*. Available at: https://www.gov.uk/government/news/major-reform-will-help-hundreds-of-thousands-of-young-people-get-good-jobs. (Accessed 21st October 2016).

EEF (2016) *Mathematical Mastery Evaluation*. Available at: https://educationendowmentfoundation.org.uk/our-work/projects/mathematics-mastery. (Accessed 20th September 2016).

NCETM (2016) *Mastery Learning*. Available at: https://www.ncetm.org.uk/files/37086535/The+Essence+o f+Maths+Teaching+for+Mastery+june+2016.pdf. (Accessed 10th November 2016).

NFER (2012) *What You Don't Find Out about England's Educational Performance in the PISA League Table*. Available at: https://www.nfer.ac.uk/publications/FFEE04/FFEE04.pdf. (Accessed 1st September 2016).

Nuffield (2010) *Is the UK an Outlier?* Available at: http://www.nuffieldfoundation.org/sites/default/files/files/Is%20the%20UK%20an%20Outlier_Nuffield%20Foundation_v_FINAL.pdf. (Accessed 5th November 2016).

Ofsted (2010) *Finnish Pupils' Success in Mathematics*. Available at: http://dera.ioe.ac.uk/1144/1/Finnish%20pupils%27%20success%20in%20mathematics.pdf. (Accessed 20th November 2016).

Sahlberg, P. (2014) *Finnish Lessons 2.0: What Can the World Learn from Educational Change in Finland?* New York: Teachers College Press.

Stigler J.W. and Heibert, J. (1999) *The Teaching Gap: Best Ideas from the World's Teachers for Improving Education in the Classroom*. New York: Free Press.

Tall, D. (2008) *Using Japanese Lesson Study in Teaching Mathematics*. Available at: https://homepages.warwick.ac.uk/staff/David.Tall/pdfs/dot2008d-lesson-study.pdf. (Accessed 20th November 2016).

TIMSS (2011) *TIMMS and PIRLS*. Available at: http://timss.bc.edu. (Accessed 14th October 2011).

11 Higher education – from global trends to local realities

Richard Budd

Introduction

We live in the age of globalisation. But what does this mean, and what are the implications for universities? As we see accelerations in the movement of people, resources and ideas, universities are both caught up in globalisation and also contribute to the process itself. At one level, it is possible to discern worldwide trends around an increase in the numbers of students and then graduates, how this and research are funded and how universities are managed. Universities and university sectors are becoming more similar in some ways but it would be a mistake to think that they are (or will ever be) identical. 'Below' the global, we have the regional, national and local dimensions, and each of these is crucial in considering what life for – and in – universities might be like.

The structure of this chapter is as follows. First, it will look at globalisation as a phenomenon before considering how it relates to higher education, which involves an outline of global shifts in university policy. Dynamics at the regional level will then be considered before we examine how these trends play out in practice in Germany and England. This will provide the background against which we can delve a little deeper into what it might be like to be a student in each country. The answer is, of course, the same but different.

Globalisation

Globalisation has been neatly summarised as a 'compression of space, time and meaning' (Alexander, 2005:82). In other words, as technology allows people, information and resources to traverse the globe in shorter periods of time, we have become increasingly connected to one another. We can fly halfway round the world in just over 24 hours, send and receive text messages, email instantly and video chat, with people anywhere in the world, something that 20 years ago was in the realms of science fiction. We can also see news unfolding around the world in real time and transfer money in moments. This brings distant people and interactions into what can be an immediate proximity with one another, and the reduction in distance has a number of important effects.

First, we come to share more information, ideas and even values – this constitutes the compression of meaning. As Simon Marginson (2011) describes, we are coming to 'synchronise' globally because we are aware of globalisation and have developed a sense of being connected to other people, places and phenomena. This comes about through a greater awareness of other people's lives on social and other media, enabling us to feel connected to them, and issues such as global warming or armed conflicts that lead to refugees or even imported terrorism in our communities. We are also, according to Marginson, 'desevering' or feeling distant places to be closer than before. Over time, as we travel virtually and in person, meeting diverse people and sharing ideas, we develop better understandings of one another. Overall, this generates a sense of being less isolated, more interconnected and moving to a shared global rhythm.

A second important effect of globalisation is that countries and organisations are more interdependent. We should not, though, fall prey to 'methodological nationalism' (Dale, 2005), the assumption that countries are ideationally and legislatively discrete. People and ideas have always traveled, and significant events in one place are affected by, and in turn affect, events elsewhere. What has changed is that the connections are faster, more frequent – and constant. Local and national policy must therefore be created with an eye on the broader picture, sometimes in rapid reaction to developments elsewhere in the world and often in consultation with others outside their national jurisdictions. Policy-makers must make allowances around overarching rules and conventions frameworks on international law, human rights and trade or environmental agreements. This brings in the need for collaboration between countries or groups of countries, often through supranational 'global governance institutions' (Buchanan and Keohane, 2011) such as the World Trade Organisation (WTO) or between and within multi-country alliances such as the European Union (EU).

This observation connects to a final, crucial point, which is that globalisation is not simply a phenomenon emerging from technological progress. We must, of course, acknowledge the 'bottom-up' effect of billions of individual interactions and reactions that is changing the way we think of ourselves and act. However, we also need to consider the 'top-down' side of the equation. When we look at this issue in the context of globalisation, it is important to recognise that global governance institutions may not be operating as neutral intermediaries but may themselves be powerful policy actors with political agendas (Robertson, 2012). The influence can be direct, such as the enforced privatisation of state industries or austerity conditions that accompany International Monetary Fund (IMF) development loans (Dreher *et al.*, 2015). A less direct form is through international comparative exercises such as the OECD Programme for International Assessment (PISA). When the results are published, policy-makers in 'weaker' countries feel impelled to divert resources to remedy supposed shortcomings in their national education systems (Meyer and Benavot, 2015). So, while globalisation offers us the chance to share experiences and ideas, it also presents an opportunity for those with less altruistic intentions, particularly at the apex of power, to promote their own interests.

Individual/group task

- To what extent might globalisation be seen as both a social phenomenon and a political project?

Globalisation and the university

Globally connected universities

Universities have always been international, with scholars moving between countries, and research findings and ideas being shared widely. We can see synchronism in action as academics and students are increasingly internationally mobile, electronic communication facilitates contact and collaboration and research has become more accessible in online journal articles and reports. It is far easier to be aware of the latest findings in our fields; in fact, it has become unacceptable not to be. Desevering has also become the norm, as an international – global – orientation is expected of universities and university staff (King, 2011). This, in part, is the cumulative effect of countless international interactions on the psyche of higher education, but the policy level also plays a not insignificant role.

The neoliberal knowledge economy

Much of the analysis of higher education from the 1980s onwards has been associated in some way with the emergence of the 'neoliberal knowledge economy' as the dominant global policy trend. Neoliberalism is a political ideology that adopts an economic logic, primarily (or even solely) considering situations from a financial perspective. It is a reductive approach that can ignore aspects such as social or cultural value in part because they are difficult to measure and can thus be convenient to ignore. Neoliberals view the public sector as inherently inefficient, with free markets as the optimal solution because rivals have to continually up their game to survive. They argue that governments should therefore deregulate, making markets as unencumbered by red tape and legislation as possible and/or creating new markets by privatising public services. The counterarguments to this are largely twofold. First, a lack of regulation opens up the system to abuse, as it offers the opportunity to act in a way that serves personal interests regardless of the consequences on others. The 2008 economic crisis was partly caused by this, as financial institutions inflated a housing price and loan bubble, which eventually burst but made huge profits in the process (Kotz, 2009). The second criticism is that markets are an inappropriate way of providing products or services that are essential to the functioning of society. We could argue that bananas or holidays are well suited to markets as people can survive without them, but if some people were excluded (i.e. could not afford) services such as the police, healthcare – or education – it would create significant social problems. In such cases, opponents of neoliberalism would argue, these should be provided by the state and funded by taxation, because markets are exclusionary.

The concept of the 'knowledge economy' emerged in the 1960s, when the seeds of globalisation as we know it today were sown. Falling transport costs saw manufacturing move away from wealthy countries, who grew increasingly concerned about their economic health as jobs and profits moved overseas. They envisioned a new future where they were the 'head' of the global order – doing the thinking and inventing – while the poorer countries constituted the 'body', producing the goods (Brown *et al.*, 2011). Central to this was the principle that knowledge has commercial value and should be exploited for profit/competitive advantage. This in itself is not new – patents and copyrights have long existed to allow the founders of new technologies, medicines and so on, a period to recoup their research costs and turn a profit. What was new was that this principle became applied to knowledge more generally and this became embedded in government policy. To follow this logic through, the best knowledge is that which can be used to gain a competitive advantage (i.e. generate profit) for individual organisations and/or national economies. By implication, knowledge that cannot be exploited in this way has less purpose or even none at all.

Universities in the knowledge economy

How universities are positioned within a knowledge economy can be drawn out in three interrelated ways: students, funding and governance. We will now examine each in turn.

Neoliberalism appropriated a concept known as 'human capital theory', which assumes that the countries with the most highly skilled workers outperform their competitors, and furthermore, that those workers earn more because of their value to employers (Brown *et al.*, 2011). It is therefore in the national interest to drive up the number of graduates. The number of people attending university has been growing since the 1950s for several reasons, such as more people completing upper secondary education and a growing demand for graduates on the labour market (Williams and Cochrane, 2010). However, the number of students has skyrocketed since the 1990s, actively encouraged by governments buying into human capital theory. In the 35 OECD countries alone, 22% of 25–64-year-olds had a degree in 1998, and by 2013, it was 34% (OECD, 2000; OECD, 2015). To put this in perspective, it represents an increase of almost 80 million graduates in 15 years.

This rise in student numbers creates a problem for governments that pay their students' study costs, but the presence of the so-called 'earnings premium' from a degree – i.e. graduates' higher salaries – provides a solution, as it justifies the implementation of tuition fees. Universities in countries like the USA have had fees for sometime, particularly at private universities, but the overall trend is that more and more countries are implementing and/or raising them (Tilak, 2015). This in itself creates other problems such as the potential exclusion of poorer groups from university or the disappearance of degrees in less obviously lucrative subjects (such as those in the humanities and social sciences).

If we apply the same financial rationale to research, then STEM (science, technology, engineering, maths) subjects should attract more (or all) funding because they lend themselves more easily to competitive advantage and profit. The social sciences and humanities, in comparison, would merit little or no research support. It is, of course, the (neoliberal) logic of the market that the weakest perish, but weakness here is determined by economic gain, not value to social and/or cultural life (Codd, 2005). The financial argument, though, is held by some to be the persuasive one, particularly in times of global recession and austerity. There are also signs that privately commissioned research in universities is on the rise as governments tighten their belts and encourage universities to seek other sources of funding. This reduces the strain on state budgets but returns us to the problem of favouring research allied with commercial gain at the expense of philanthropy. The picture seems, in the main, to point towards a fall in public funding and an increasing presence of private finance in higher education (OECD, 2015).

The third significant area of change comes in the form of governance. We can divide this into external (i.e. government or other bodies) and internal (i.e. management). We have already seen how the OECD's PISA can trigger changes in school education policy, and it is in the process of conducting a global 'AHELO' (Assessment of Learning Outcomes in Higher Education) project. As with PISA, this has been criticised for developing generic standards that may be inappropriate to some countries but against which they will nevertheless be judged (Ashwin, 2015). These comparative projects also reflect a neoliberal disposition towards measurement as a way of encouraging competition. We can see this in an increase in competitive bidding for research funding (Auranen and Nieminen, 2010), a form of resource allocation that tends to be dominated by a small number of strong universities, leaving the rest out in the cold. A more publicly visible way that competitive market environments are encouraged is through the implementation of rankings, as universities focus on improving their position in relation to their peers (Hazelkorn, 2008). This 'audit culture' is also transferred into universities as working practices are increasingly atomised and quantified (Shore, 2010). The intention is to identify areas of weakness that can be addressed to maximise efficiency, but the measures are often based on 'proxy' measures that approximate what they are intended to capture. Student satisfaction, for example, is often held as a reflection of teaching quality, but there is a broad spectrum of factors that contribute to students' well-being, and many of these are unrelated to teaching.

Individual/group task

- Can you see neoliberal approaches in other areas of education or in other sectors? How appropriate do you feel this approach is there?

Summary

The story so far has used a broad brush to describe the character and influence of the knowledge economy on higher education, and it is apparent that there are some tensions there. These have long existed, but the literature suggests that we are at a particular 'pinch point' now. What seems to be under threat is the university's role as a public institution, as its functions and benefits are privatised and potentially excluded from the public. (See Calhoun, 2006 for a good overview of public 'versus' private.)

There are counter discourses and movements to a competitive, commercially oriented higher education model (see, for example, Neary and Saunders, 2016). However, a broad consensus supports the view that the knowledge economy is the globally dominant one, and we can see neoliberal university policies implemented from Africa (Croché and Charlier, 2012) to Australia (Marginson, 2006). This worldwide view is important because it gives us a real sense that there are globally connected trends playing out, rather than a case of countries operating entirely independent of each other. They are not; they are reacting to one another, in competition, in a knowledge arms race. It is also vital, though, to acknowledge that 'globalisation is local' (Douglass, 2005) because while we can generalise without detail, the implementation and effect of policy is 'on the ground', in the practices and lives of organisations and people. Before we arrive at the national, though, it is necessary to briefly examine an intermediary level: the regional.

The regional (European) dimension

As mentioned earlier, supranational but 'sub' global alliances or blocs are formed to develop shared policies. Germany and England, the countries we will shortly examine in more detail, are both – at least at the time of press – members of the EU and also the European Higher Education Area (EHEA).

The EHEA, created in 2010 through what became known as the 'Bologna Process', describes itself as a space in which 48 countries 'continuously adapt their higher education systems making them more compatible and strengthening their quality assurance mechanisms' (EHEA, 2016). University systems in Europe at the end of the 1990s produced qualifications that followed one of three contrasting degree structures. This made graduating in one country and working in another problematic because university and professional qualifications were not easily transferred to others (Corbett, 2006). The solution was for all countries to adopt the same 'Anglo' (Bachelor-Master-Doctorate) degree system. This involved an enormous undertaking, as most countries' universities, professional bodies and domestic labour markets had to change in order to align across the EHEA. There was also a concern that the standard of degree provision varied considerably, and therefore a common approach to quality assurance was seen as important (Fried *et al.*, 2006).

Outside these issues, what became increasingly apparent was that the establishment of a common European university space was a bold outward-facing move to create a globally competitive zone for knowledge creation (Robertson, 2009). Alongside the Bologna Process, the 'Lisbon Strategy' sought to 'turn the EU into the most competitive knowledge-based society…to increase productivity and [meet the] competitive pressures of a globalised economy' (European Commission, 2014). This would be achieved through, among other things, opening up markets, cutting red tape, investing in human capital and integrating financial markets, with the intention of maintaining Europe's international advantage in knowledge and innovation. Here, we can see the EHEA as a strategic move to construct a global higher education hub to attract students, highly skilled workers and funding. In other words, Europe was seeking to establish itself as a central player in the now familiar global knowledge economy. It is important to mention here that, at the time of publication, the position of the UK in relation to the EU was hanging in the balance. While the EHEA is not an EU-specific space, there are concerns that the movement of other EU countries' students and academic staff into and out of the UK might negatively impact its national university attractiveness and research capacity.

The national

We can now turn our attention to Germany and England; the focus here is primarily on England within the UK because of its particular tuition fee system, although at times the policies and available data make the UK and England indivisible from one another. As we have seen, both Germany and the UK belong to some of the same political (EU) and higher education (EHEA) groups and (now) have similar degree structures. We can also discern in their university sectors those trends of more students, changes to funding and new modes of governance. However, as we examine each of these areas in more depth, contrasts begin to emerge.

Student numbers

While Germany has three main types of tertiary provider, we will chiefly concern ourselves with the 'Universität' as the more research oriented of the three. There were 15 Universitäten in 1945, and now there are now over 150 (Hochschulrektorenkonferenz, 2016). England had 10 universities in 1945 and currently has 108 (HEFCE, 2016). In line with the general trends described earlier, the number of students in both had risen steadily post World War II, resulting in a number of new universities being built in the 1960s and 1970s (Mountford, 1966; Teichler, 2008). While in England, the creation of new universities kept pace with the expansion in university entrants, demand for places in Germany began to fast outstrip their availability in the 1970s. A decision was made to increase the number of universities and also to allow them to admit more students than they had capacity for (Bloch, 2009). Intended as a short-term measure to stop those with lower qualifications being squeezed out of vocational courses altogether, this is essentially still in place as student numbers have continued to increase. The 1990s trend of rapidly escalating student numbers was also repeated in both England and Germany, but it has been far more marked in England. English-specific figures are not available, but the proportion of people with a university education in the UK has risen from 26% to 42%, while in Germany it has risen from 23% to 27% (OECD, 2015). The way in which this has been funded has differed considerably, as we will see.

Funding

The increase – beyond universities' capacity – in the number of students in Germany hugely over-stretched institutional resources (Pritchard, 2006). Tuition fees were not levied, and in 2002, the national government prohibited their imposition by law. This was immediately and successfully contested as overstepping the jurisdictions of the individual federal states (Bundesländer) that constitute Germany. About 7 of the 16 Bundesländer then imposed fees at around €500 a year, but over the next 12 years, their local governments changed and tuition fees were revoked. In England, the story could not have been more different. Fees of up to £1,000, dependent on parental income, were introduced on a UK-wide basis in 1998, and in England, they rose to £3,000 in 2004 and then £9,000 from 2012. Scotland abolished tuition fees for its students in 1999, and Wales and Northern Ireland subsidised their students somewhat. Both Germany and England saw public demonstrations against tuition fees at various points, but the chief difference is that there was political resistance in some political parties in Germany but very little in England.

The federal system in Germany also influences how its research is supported, with all universities being awarded 'primary funding' that covers their main research and teaching activities. Both the Bundesländer and the national government then award further grants for additional projects. The most notable of these is the 'Excellence Initiative', launched in 2002, that provides large grants in particular research areas. Just under a third of the 150 or so of Germany's universities have won funding through this route, although nine of those have received considerably more than the rest (DFG, 2013). Outside the Excellence Initiative, though, the research income for German universities seems to be relatively predictable and stable. Funding for research in the UK, on the other hand, is almost entirely awarded on the basis of external evaluation and competition. Sectoral audits of research quality – currently called the Research Excellent Framework – were phased in from the 1980s and have dictated the share of state funding for research (Auranan and Nieminen, 2010). Other sources include disciplinary research councils, philanthropic bodies and industry, by and large awarding money on the basis of competitive application. In practice, a relatively small number of established universities dominate, particularly the 'golden triangle' of Oxford, Cambridge and London (Harrison, 2009). It is also notable that the proportion of private investment in higher education research in the UK is currently estimated at around 35% (EI, 2015), with 43% of UK university funding (including tuition fees) overall coming from the private sector. In Germany, the total figure is 15% (OECD, 2015).

Governance

In addition to being state funded, almost all German universities are publicly owned and governed, meaning that changes to their management structures and internal policies can be quite slow and bureaucratic. As Krücken and Meier (2006) have identified, the German Universität traditionally had no decision-making capacity in the same way as companies or other organisations. English universities, on the other hand, have an established history of being autonomous. This changed in the 1980s, when state funding was reduced to encourage improvements in efficiency and orient universities more towards the private sector (Walford, 1991). This policy has been continued and extended ever since, accompanied by – as in Germany – major expansions in the size, authority and reach of the management and administrative staff (Blümel *et al.*, 2010; Shattock, 2013).

Both countries have also seen the emergence of external, disciplinary or pan-disciplinary bodies that issue guidelines on the content and/or practices of degree delivery. From the research perspective, Germany's Excellence Initiative and the UK's Research Excellence Framework, in addition to providing a way of allocating research funding, serve as publicly visible markers of quality and, as such, increase the sense of competition for status (and funding). These are bolstered by university rankings, which began to appear in both countries in the 1990s. However, in Germany, they entered a largely unreceptive milieu because the established view was one of institutional parities across the country (Kosmützky, 2012). This is further undermined by the fact that there is no price differential and universities do not compete for students – they are already overstretched and students tend to study locally because there is no perceived variation in quality or status. There has also been resistance to rankings in the academic profession, with some disciplines and universities refusing to submit the requisite data for analysis and publication (Kaube, 2012). This is possible because of the universities' safe status as state organisations and the professoriate's protected employment position as civil servants. The Excellence Initiative was intended to improve Germany's position in international rankings (which it has done), and while it has undermined the sense that all universities are the same, it is more a case of a minority elite with the remainder being more or less equal.

The higher education sector in England/the UK has long been recognised as highly stratified (Teichler, 2008), and league tables have simply reified and reinforced this. The perception that 'older is better' holds true because the longer a university is operational, the more advanced its research culture, expertise in applying for grants and ability to attract seasoned academics and the highest attaining students. This has meant that the league table positions are largely stable because the measured and perceived differences are reproduced year on year (Roberts and Thompston, 2007). All universities charge almost exactly the same amount for undergraduate degrees, but in all other aspects, the sense of differential status is acute.

What all of this means in practice is that universities in Germany and England appear to be autonomous but that this autonomy exists in different forms. German universities, because of heavy regulation, are somewhat protected from change (for better or worse), but the tenured academics at least have considerable freedom. In England, the universities are heavily steered via external agencies and the way that the state-sponsored market distributes funding and students, and the freedom they have to make changes is very much dictated by external forces.

Individual/group task

- Some have described globalisation as leading towards a worldwide convergence. How might you justify or refute this position?

From national to local

What do these differences in German and English higher education mean for students? Data collected by the present author in early 2012, just before tuition fees were raised to £9,000 in England, provided some interesting insights.

The sample

Thirteen undergraduate students – six German, seven English – across a range of ages, backgrounds and disciplines were interviewed about how they saw and experienced their university contexts (Budd, 2014). They were recruited from 'Mill University' in England, 'Feuerbach Universität' in Germany and research-intensive universities in regional towns, with 15–20,000 students and founded in the 1960s–1970s. Both offer subjects across the disciplinary spectrum but lean towards STEM. However, Mill, in common with other English universities of this age and type, is well ranked and operates a highly selective admissions system. Feuerbach, as with other German universities of its type, does not have exclusive entrance standards and is not considered one of the small elites. It should be noted here that the sample size, and the fact that all universities are somewhat unique, means that none of the findings below are generalisable. The point here is illustration, not extrapolation, and we will be looking at three interrelated areas – the broader context, teaching and non-academic activities.

Individual/group task

- What aspects might influence the experience of being at university between university departments, universities and countries?

Broader context

One area of distinction between the groups was in their views, and use, of rankings. None of the German students had considered them – perhaps unsurprising, as Feuerbach was not of high status – but they also knew little about them and viewed them sceptically. One German student had, in fact, begun his studies at one of the elite universities but transferred to Feuerbach at the end of the first year. He was aware of the status difference but saw rankings as 'nothing but hot air...before all the universities were seen as the same and I think they essentially still are'. The English students had all used rankings as a key factor in their choice of Mill – again, unsurprising given its high status – but were knowledgeable about the kinds of metrics used to compile them. They were slightly sceptical of some of those measures, but by and large did not question that rankings represented the reality of variations in quality and did not seem to see that they induced competition.

Tuition fees were another area where contrasts emerged. The English students mostly approved of fees and gave a range of justifications for their imposition, such as the poor economic climate, and there was broad acceptance of a degree as 'an investment' in future earnings. They were mostly aware of the potential barrier to poorer students that fees might pose, but beyond this there were few arguments against them. The German group was almost exactly opposite, claiming that there was no guarantee of a good jobs, and they were all well-versed in arguments against fees while presenting few supporting arguments. An interesting point that emerged in the German accounts was that tuition fees were often seen as inappropriate because they made the university partly responsible for students' academic success. This connected with a key difference in how the groups saw the role of the university.

Learning and teaching

First, while both students cited responsibility for one's own learning as being a fundamental principle underpinning degree studies, this was more marked in the German students. Other than an introduction to module choices at the beginning of their degrees, they were very much on their own. Tuition fees, they claimed, undermined this independence because the university became obliged to help you rather than leave you to help yourself. For the English students, the responsibility for doing well was still theirs, but the university was expected to facilitate this by providing good quality teaching as well as appropriate academic (and non-academic) facilities. The fact that they paid fees, though, was seen as a way of applying leverage to ensure that provision was suitable. Comparing the two universities, Mill was seen as a partner in actively engaging with students and improving their chances of doing well, while Feuerbach was relatively passive – as one of the students there saw it, 'the university doesn't care if you fail'.

This emerging distinction in the role of the university towards students also featured in the way that degrees were taught. The German group generally referred to two teaching formats, lectures and smaller classes. Most experienced both, and two students mentioned smaller, graduate student-led sessions, but some courses were almost entirely taught in 90-minute lectures. The English students, on the other hand, named a far greater range, with 45-minute lectures, seminars, tutorials and practical workshops. The fact that teaching at Feuerbach was heavily lecture-based, combined with access to academics being limited and very formal, created a clear divide between students and academics. Some of this might be connected to the fact that the university was operating beyond its capacity, something that all of the Feuerbach students mentioned. At Mill, in addition to each student having a named tutor who was responsible for their academic well-being, students were often encouraged to address their teaching staff by their first names, and there was an 'open door policy' where they could approach academics directly. It would have been possible in some subjects at Feuerbach to complete almost the entire degree without having a conversation with an academic, while at Mill this would have been unimaginable.

Non-academic activities

A third area of major difference in the participants' accounts was in the way that the two groups talked about the non-academic aspects of a degree. Mill, in common with other English/UK universities, had an extensive range of sporting and other activities that students were expected to engage with. Many of the English participants referred to the importance of these not only for fun and relaxation but also as a way of improving one's CV. As one of the students explained, 'they drill this into us...work places are asking what activities you do and what interests you have because they don't want people that are just academic'. Employability was a pervasive topic, being connected to other aspects such as mixing with international students 'because we'll be working internationally' and work experience – 'some companies are only accepting people that have been on placements'. This connected with a strong sense across the English group of a need to optimise one's combination of academic and non-academic performance in order to be successful on a highly competitive labour graduate market. The status of the university was also seen to be a contributing factor, while for the Germans it was considered irrelevant, and research has shown that both groups may have been right about their own national contexts (Leuze, 2011). The German students talked about international students being good to have as they brought different perspectives to discussions, but there was no other value associated with these or internships even though all German students do one as part of their degree. Feuerbach had sports facilities and some social groups, but they were far less extensive and prominent, and this contributed to the sense that the university was less central in its students' lives than Mill was. Feuerbach by and large provided learning opportunities that the students could to choose to avail themselves of (or not), while Mill was somewhere that students spent a great deal of their academic as well as non-academic time.

Conclusion

What can we learn from this? Starting from the local and working our way backup, we can see that university can 'feel' quite different in different countries. It is important to note here that the differences have been highlighted, and there were similarities in their descriptions such as good (and bad) lecturers, or that criticality and academic freedom underpinned university activity as a whole. We can see, at the local level, though, how Mill – driven by rising tuition fees and university rankings – aggressively promotes the employability agenda, or that Feuerbach took a much less active role in its students' degrees and lives. This is likely to differ at other universities in each country, but it also connects with the higher education policies and cultures in each country.

At the national, the rise in student numbers featured for both groups, but for the Germans, it came through in their sense that the university was overflowing (although they saw this as a local, not a national issue), while for the English students, the job market for graduates was heavily congested. Tuition fees and rankings came through in different ways, with the Germans being more opposed to the former and sceptical and/or lacking awareness of the latter. It should also be noted that much has been made of the fact that tuition fees frame students as passive and demanding customers (Tight, 2013). The English students did expect more from their university, but this seems due more to the national/local culture of what a university does. Tuition fees may change the way that students see a degree, but it is not the only contributing factor.

Through this, we can begin to identify how global trends become visible not only at the national level but also at the local, and how they might manifest themselves differently between and across those levels. In some senses, we can see that Mill University and the English students have been influenced more by the logic of the knowledge economy, while those at Feuerbach were more insulated from it. Time and space may have come closer for them through globalisation, but the meanings were still quite different.

Recommended reading

Budd, R. (2016) Undergraduate orientations towards higher education in Germany and England: problematizing the notion of 'student as customer'. *Higher Education*. Available at: http://link.springer.com/article/10.1007/s10734-015-9977-4?wt_mc=internal.event.1.SEM.ArticleAuthorOnlineFirst.

References

Alexander, J.C. (2005) "Globalization" as collective representation: the new dream of a cosmopolitan civil sphere. *International Journal of Politics, Culture and Society*, 19, 81–90.
Ashwin, P. (2015) Missionary zeal: some problems with the rhetoric, vision and approach of the AHELO project. *European Journal of Higher Education*, 5(4), 437–444.
Auranen, O. and Nieminen, M. (2010) University research funding and publication performance—an international comparison. *Research Policy*, 39(6), 822–834.
Bloch, R. (2009) *Flexible Studierende? Studienreform und studentische Praxis*. Leipzig: Akademische Verlagsanstalt.
Blümel, A., Kloke, K., Krücken, G. and Netz, N. (2010) Restrukturierung statt Expansion: Entwicklung im Bereich des nichtwissenschaftlichen Personals an Deutschen Hochschulen. *Die Hochschule*, 20(2), 154–172.
Brown, P., Lauder, H. and Ashton, D. (2011) *The Global Auction: The Broken Promises of Education, Jobs, and Incomes*. Oxford: Oxford University Press.
Buchanan, A. and Keohane, R.O. (2011) Precommitment regimes for intervention: supplementing the Security Council. *Ethics & International Affairs*, 25(1), 41–63.
Budd, R. (2014). *Students as Neo-Institutional Actors: A Comparative Case Study of How German and English Undergraduates Understand, Experience and Negotiate Higher Education*. Bristol: University of Bristol.
Calhoun, C. (2006) The university and the public good. *Thesis*, 84, 7–43.
Codd, J. (2005) Academic freedom and the commodification of knowledge in the modern university. *Learning for Democracy*, 1(1), 69–87.
Corbett, A. (2006) *Higher Education as a Form of European Integration: How Novel Is the Bologna process?* ARENA Working Paper No 15. Oslo: University of Oslo.
Croché, S. and Charlier, J.-E. (2012) Normative influence of the Bologna Process on French-speaking African Universities. *Globalisation, Societies and Education*, 10(4), 457–472.
Dale, R. (2005) Globalisation, knowledge economy and comparative education. *Comparative Education*, 41(2), 117–149.
DFG (2013) *Exzellenzinitiative auf eienen Blick. Der Wettbewerb des Bundes und der Länder zur Stärkung der universitären Spitzenforschung*.Bonn: Deutsche Forschungsgemeinschaft.
Douglass, J.A. (2005) All globalization is local : countervailing forces and the influence on higher education markets. CSHE Research and Occasional Paper Series, 1.05. Berkeley, CA: University of California, Berkeley.
Dreher, A., Sturm, J.-E. and Vreeland, J.R. (2015) Politics and IMF conditionality. *Journal of Conflict Resolution*, 59(1), 120–148.
EHEA (2016) The European Higher Education and Bologna Process. *EHEA and Bologna Process Website*. Available at: www.ehea.info/. (Accessed 30th September 2016).
EI (2015) *What Is the Relationship between Public and Private Investment in Science, Research and Innovation?* London: Economic Insight Ltd.

European Commission (2014) The Lisbon Strategy for growth and jobs. *CORDIS-Community Research and Development Information Service*. Available at: http://cordis.europa.eu/programme/rcn/843_en.html. (Accessed 30th September 2016).

Fried, J., Glass, A. and Baumgartl, B. (2006) Summary of an extended comparative analysis on European private higher education. *Higher Education in Europe*, 31(1), 3–9.

Harrison, M. (2009). Does high-quality research require 'critical mass'? In D. Pontikakis, D. Kyriakou and R. van Bavel (Eds.)*The Question of R&D Specialisation: Perspectives and Policy Implications.* Luxembourg: Office for Official Publications of the European Communities.

Hazelkorn, E. (2008) Learning to live with league tables and ranking: the experience of institutional leaders. *Higher Education Policy*, 21, 193–215.

HEFCE (2016) Register of Providers. *Higher Education Funding Council for England*. Available at: www.hefce. ac.uk/reg/register/search/Overview. (Accessed 30th September 2016).

Hochschulrektorenkonferenz (2016). *Hochschulkompass*. Available at: www.hochschulkompass.de/. (Accessed 25th September 2016).

Kaube, J. (2012) Widerstand gegen den Unfug des 'Rankings'. *Frankfurter Allgemeine Zeitung*, p. 5. Available at: www.faz.net/aktuell/feuilleton/forschung-und-lehre/uni-ranglisten-widerstand-gegen-den-unfug-des-rankings-11863221.html. (Accessed 15th May 2016).

King, R. (2011) Globalisation and higher education. In J. Brennan and T. Shah (Eds.) *Higher Education and Society in Changing Times: Looking Back and Looking Forward*. Milton Keynes: CHERI, Open University.

Kosmütsky, A. (2012) Between mission and market position: empirical findings on mission statements of German higher education institutions. *Tertiary Education and Management*, 18(1), 55–77.

Kotz, D.M. (2009) The financial and economic crisis of 2008: a systemic crisis of neoliberal capitalism. *Review of Radical Political Economics*, 41(3), 305–317.

Krücken, G. and Meier, F. (2006). Turning the university into an organizational actor. In G. S. Drori, J. W. Meyer, and H. Hwang (Eds.) *Globalization and Organization: World Society and Organizational Change*. Oxford: Oxford University Press.

Leuze, K. (2011) How structure signals status: institutional stratification and the transition from higher education to work in Germany and Britain. *Journal of Education and Work*, 24(5), 449–475.

Marginson, S. (2006) Investment in the self: the government of student financing in Australia. *Studies in Higher Education*, 22(2), 37–41.

Marginson, S. (2011) Imagining the global. In R. King, S. Marginson and R. Naidoo (Eds.) *Handbook on Globalization and Higher Education*. Cheltenham: Edward Elgar Publishing.

Meyer, H.-D. and Benavot, A. (2015) PISA and globalization of education governance: some puzzles and problems. In H.D. Meyer and A. Benavot (Eds.) *PISA, Power, and Policy: The Emergence of Global Educational Governance*. Oxford: Symposium Books.

Mountford, J.F. (1966). *British Universities*. Oxford: Oxford University Press.

Neary, M. and Saunders, G. (2016) Student as producer and the politics of abolition: making a new form of dissident institution? *Critical Education*, 7(5), 1–23.

OECD (2000) *Education at a Glance 2000: OECD Indicators*. Paris: OECD Publishing.

OECD (2015). *Education at a Glance 2015: OECD Indicators*. Paris: OECD Publishing.

Pritchard, R. (2006) Trends in the restructuring of German universities. *Comparative Education Review*, 50(1), 90–112.

Roberts, D. and Thompson, L. (2007) *University League Tables and the Impact on Student Recruitment, Reputation Management for Universities*. Working Series Paper No. 2. London: The Knowledge Partnership.

Robertson, S.L. (2009) Education, knowledge and innovation in the global economy: challenges and future directions. *Keynote Address to Launch of Research Centres, VIA University College, Aarhus, Denmark, 6th March, 2009*.

Robertson, S.L. (2012) Researching global education policy: angles in/on/out …. In A. Verger, M. Novelli and H. Altinyelken (Eds.) *Global Education Policy and International Development: New Agendas Issues and Practices*. New York: Continuum Books.

Shattock, M. (2013) University governance, leadership and management in a decade of diversification and uncertainty. *Higher Education Quarterly*, 67(3), 1–17.

Shore, C. (2010) Beyond the multiversity: neoliberalism and the rise of the schizophrenic university. *Social Anthropology*, 1, 15–29.

Teichler, U. (2008) Diversification? Trends and explanations of the shape and size of higher education. *Higher Education*, 56, 349–379.

Tight, M. (2013) Students: customers, clients or pawns? *Higher Education Policy*, 26, 291–307.

Tilak, J.B.G. (2015) Global trends in funding higher education. *International Higher Education*, e-prints (Marketization and Economic Themes), pp. 5–6. Available at: https://ejournals.bc.edu/ojs/index.php/ihe/article/download/7882/7033. (Accessed 10th May 2016).

Walford, G. (1991) The changing relationship between government and higher education in Britain. In G. Neave and F. van Vught (Eds.) *Prometheus Bound: The Changing Relationship between Government and Higher Education in Western Europe*. Oxford: Pergamon.

Williams, R. and Cochrane, A. (2010) *The Role of Higher Education in Social and Cultural Transformation*. Centre for Higher Education Research and Information (CHERI). London: The Open University.

12 Some final reflections on educational comparison

Brendan Bartram

Introduction

In some ways, concluding a book like this might at first sight seem something of a challenge. Each contributor has focussed on a specific sector or form of education in particular countries. It might be suggested that the differences between the chapters outweigh any common ground between them. On closer analysis, however, this may not be an entirely accurate assessment. A large number of educational issues in an equally varied set of contexts have admittedly been explored, but it is nonetheless possible to identify a set of common threads throughout the chapters.

Individual/group task

- Review and reflect on each of the chapters and draft a list of common 'background' themes that you have detected.

Educational convergence

That a number of common themes emerge is perhaps less surprising than might initially be thought. For some years now, many commentators have noted the ways in which 'convergence theory' is playing out in the global educational arena. As long ago as 1983, Inkeles and Sirowy (1983) analysed patterns of change across a large number of education systems and concluded that tendencies towards educational similarity were 'pervasive and deep. It is manifested at all levels of the educational system, and affects virtually every major aspect of that system' (p. 326). Since then, these ideas have been the subject of much debate and theoretical analysis. Globalisation – much mentioned throughout the book – has become a perennial fixation for scholars in many fields, not least of all comparative education, where discussions have centred on the nature and processes of globalising influences. (For more insight into theories on this, see Robin Shields, 2013, listed below.)

For some (e.g. Friedman, 2007), globalisation operates predominantly on the basis of competitive pressures on and between nation states – driven by a common quest for competitive advantage, countries increasingly come to adopt policies and practices that are commonly perceived to deliver 'the best results'. This view is challenged, however, by those like

Wallenstein (2000) – who see globalisation as a process of conflict – world system analysts attribute globalising tendencies and trends to the privileged position and influence of powerful 'core' countries. Economically advanced states thus exert their influence on poorer countries at the 'periphery' who are manipulated by the core players into acting and thinking 'their way' about what is important in education and other spheres of life. An alternative view is offered by world culture theorists who see increasing convergence arising as a result of a growing international consensus around common cultural values, such as democratic citizenship, respect for individual rights, autonomy and the importance of technological applications. Entities such as the EU and OECD mentioned throughout the book become important in this respect because they act as mediating structures, setting 'common agendas' increasingly followed by governments around the world.

Individual/group task

- Which of these three different views on globalisation are you most inclined towards? Can you think of educational examples that support how this theory operates in practice?

How does all this relate to the subjects of the chapters in this book? Reexamining them, it can be argued that a number of common educational concerns and themes are noticeable. In no particular order, I would suggest some of these could be as follows:

- The relationship between the world of work and learning;
- Education as an economic agent;
- Increasing participation and engagement in education;
- Responding to economic challenge and austerity;
- Maintaining and improving educational standards and outcomes;
- A focus on assessment, testing and rankings;
- The inculcation of values;
- Tensions between the social and economic functions of education;
- Increasing political scrutiny of education;
- Educational diversity, experimentation and inclusion;
- The varied influences and effects of globalisation.

Individual/group task

- How does this list compare with the one you produced in the first exercise above?
- Focus on each of the above themes and try to establish where you can detect them in the different chapters. Did you identify additional themes?
- Which ones appear to be the most conspicuous, and what does this suggest to you about current educational trends?

Conclusion

Finally, it is hoped that the book has illustrated some of the central tenets and aims of comparative education, referred to in the introduction. The chapters have shown how educational developments are always firmly rooted in sociocultural specifics, and that we need be aware of these contextual factors in order to interpret what is happening and why it is happening. Broader social values, economic conditions and political priorities form complex amalgams that not only shape educational phenomena but also help us understand them. Rozsahegyi and Lambert, for example, show us how differently balanced social values and 'outlooks' have resulted in different approaches to early-years training and pedagogy in Hungary and England.

We have also seen how common global preoccupations and concerns become differently translated in different contexts: we saw, for instance, how growing labour market competition has led to the growth of shadow education in East Asia, the expansion of HE in Germany and England and greater attention to work-based forms of learning in many countries. In addition, the chapters have illustrated a range of educational thinking and alternative modes of operating in relation to an equally varied number of topics. Comparison in this way performs a useful service in encouraging us to reflect on different approaches, helping us maintain a questioning attitude and an open mind – which must surely be our default position as both educationists and educators. As the chapters have shown, however, distilling lessons – let alone specific policies – from comparison remains as ever a challenging undertaking, but a worthwhile intellectual and practical endeavour all the same.

Recommended reading

Shields, R. (2013) *Globalization and International Education*. London: Bloomsbury Academic.

References

Friedman, T. (2007) *The World is Flat: The Globalized World in the Twenty-First Century*. London: Penguin Books.
Inkeles, A. and Sirowy, L. (1983) Convergent and divergent trends in national educational systems. *Social Forces*, 6(2), 303–333.
Shields, R. (2013) *Globalization and International Education*. London: Bloomsbury Academic.
Wallenstein, I. (2000) Globalization or the age of transition? A long-term view of the trajectory of the world system. *International Sociology*, 15(2), 251–267.

Index